PIPE FITTINGS

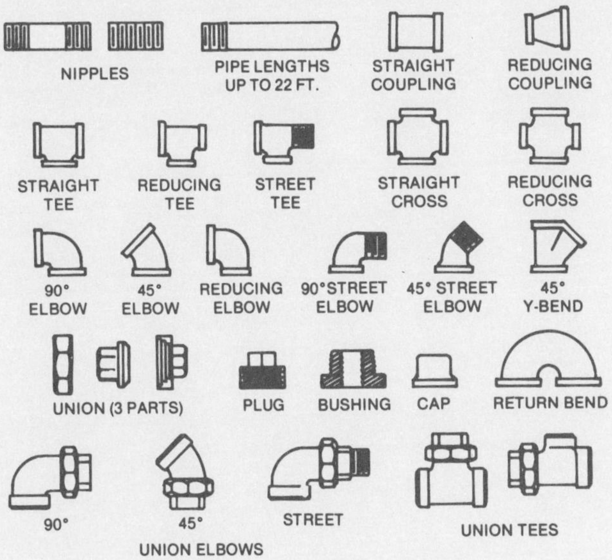

Here are the common steel pipe fittings. Nipples are simply short lengths of pipe threaded on both ends. Reducing fittings join two different sizes of pipe.

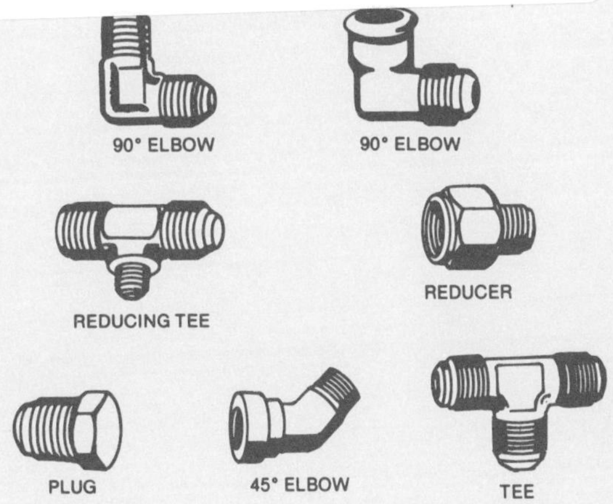

Compression fittings of the flared-tube type are the easiest for the novice to handle when working with copper tubing.

STANDARD STEEL PIPE (All Dimensions in Inches)					
Nominal Size	Outside Diameter	Inside Diameter	Nominal Size	Outside Diameter	Inside Diameter
1/8	0.405	0.269	1	1.315	1.049
1/4	0.540	0.364	1 1/4	1.660	1.380
3/8	0.675	0.493	1 1/2	1.900	1.610
1/2	0.840	0.622	2	2.375	2.067
3/4	1.050	0.824	2 1/2	2.875	2.469

SQUARE MEASURE

144 sq in = 1 sq ft
9 sq ft = 1 sq yd
272.25 sq ft = 1 sq rod
160 sq rods = 1 acre

VOLUME MEASURE

1728 cu in = 1 cu ft
27 cu ft = 1 cu yd

MEASURES OF CAPACITY

1 cup = 8 fl oz
2 cups = 1 pint
2 pints = 1 quart
4 quarts = 1 gallon
2 gallons = 1 peck
4 pecks = 1 bushel

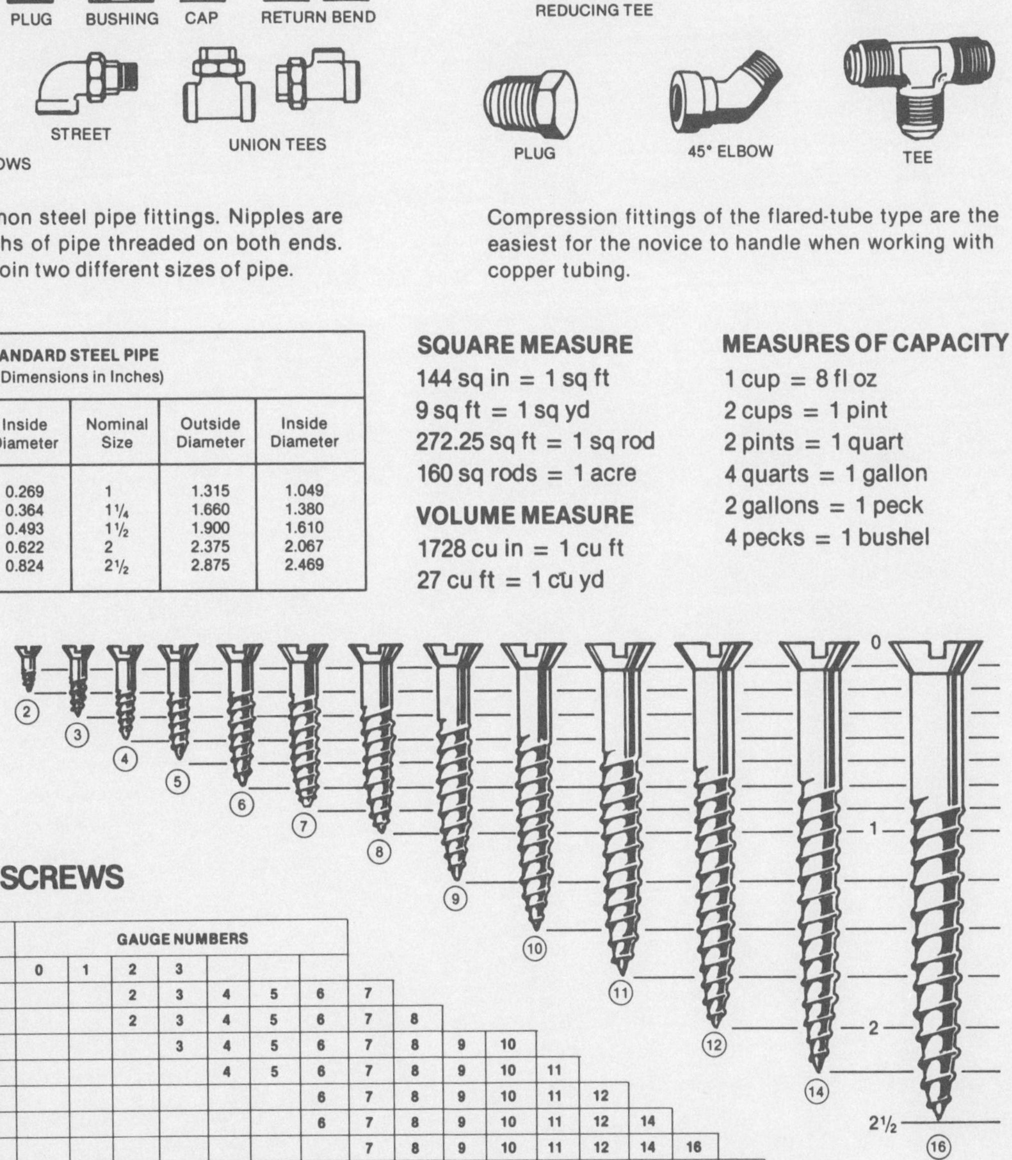

WOOD SCREWS

LENGTH	GAUGE NUMBERS																
1/4 INCH	0	1	2	3													
3/8 INCH			2	3	4	5	6	7									
1/2 INCH			2	3	4	5	6	7	8								
5/8 INCH				3	4	5	6	7	8	9	10						
3/4 INCH					4	5	6	7	8	9	10	11					
7/8 INCH							6	7	8	9	10	11	12				
1 INCH							6	7	8	9	10	11	12	14			
1 1/4 INCH								7	8	9	10	11	12	14	16		
1 1/2 INCH							6	7	8	9	10	11	12	14	16	18	
1 3/4 INCH									8	9	10	11	12	14	16	18	20
2 INCH									8	9	10	11	12	14	16	18	20
2 1/4 INCH										9	10	11	12	14	16	18	20
2 1/2 INCH													12	14	16	18	20
2 3/4 INCH														14	16	18	20
3 INCH															16	18	20
3 1/2 INCH																18	20	24
4 INCH																18	20	24

WHEN YOU BUY SCREWS, SPECIFY (1) LENGTH, (2) GAUGE NUMBER, (3) TYPE OF HEAD—FLAT, ROUND, OR OVAL, (4) MATERIAL—STEEL, BRASS, BRONZE, ETC., (5) FINISH—BRIGHT, STEEL BLUED, CADMIUM, NICKEL, OR CHROMIUM PLATED.

Popular Mechanics

do-it-yourself yearbook

The best illustrated home reference guide from the world's most authoritative source for today's how-to-do-it information.

1995

HEARST DIRECT BOOKS

This book is published with the consent and cooperation of POPULAR MECHANICS Magazine

POPULAR MECHANICS Staff:
Editor-in-Chief: Joe Oldham
Managing Editor: Deborah Frank
Graphics Director: Bryan Canniff
Home Improvement Editor: Steven Willson
Electronics/Photography Editor: Frank Vizard
Boating/Outdoors Editor: Joe Skorupa
Science/Technology Editor: Gregory T. Pope
Automotive Editor: Don Chaikin
Art Editor: John Bostonian Jr.
Copy Editors: Peter Burns, Nancy Coggins

POPULAR MECHANICS
1995 YEARBOOK
Editor:
C. Edward Cavert
Managing Editor:
Beth Helfont
Book Design and Production:
The Bookmaker
Fairfax, Virginia
Editorial Assistance:
Wilma Cavert
Cover Photo:
Cy DeCosse, Inc.
Cover Design:
Harold Perry

ISBN 0-87851-122-9
Library of Congress Catalog Card Number: 85-81760
GST Hearst Registration No. R105218291

10 9 8 7 6 5 4 3 2 1
Printed in the United States of America.

CONTENTS

Refinisher's toolkit

The really interesting thing about refinishing tools is that many of them are unlike any other tools in the workshop. Instead of being mechanical, they're chemical. Although they're relatively inexpensive and easy to use, these chemical tools are the result of some very high-tech research and development. Like any other collection of tools, the list of things you need to meet every contingency can get a little out of hand. At the same time, what you need for one specific project might only require a few minutes in the hardware store and a $10 or $20 investment. The refinisher's toolkit shown here includes most of the things you need to complete a variety of refinishing jobs, and it is designed to serve as a guide for getting started.

Strippers—Most refinishing jobs start with a chemical stripper. Up until a few years ago, that meant a product that might be as hazardous to you as the finish it dissolves. These days we have another option—water-base strippers that are less caustic and more environmentally friendly. If you run across a finish that standard strippers won't touch, you've probably stumbled onto an old milk-base coating. The solution here is to use a lye-base stripper. Strippers commonly range in price from $6 to $8 per quart.

Solvents—This chemical tool both thins finishes before application, and cleans tools and surfaces throughout the refinishing process. After stripping, you'll also use a solvent to clean away the stripper and the dissolved paint. The universal solvent for handling oil-base finishes is mineral spirits (about $1.50 per quart). If you're using shellac, keep an alcohol shellac solvent on hand for cleanup and thinning, and lacquer thinner is appropriate for some strippers. Always check the manufacturer's recommendations for the appropriate solvent.

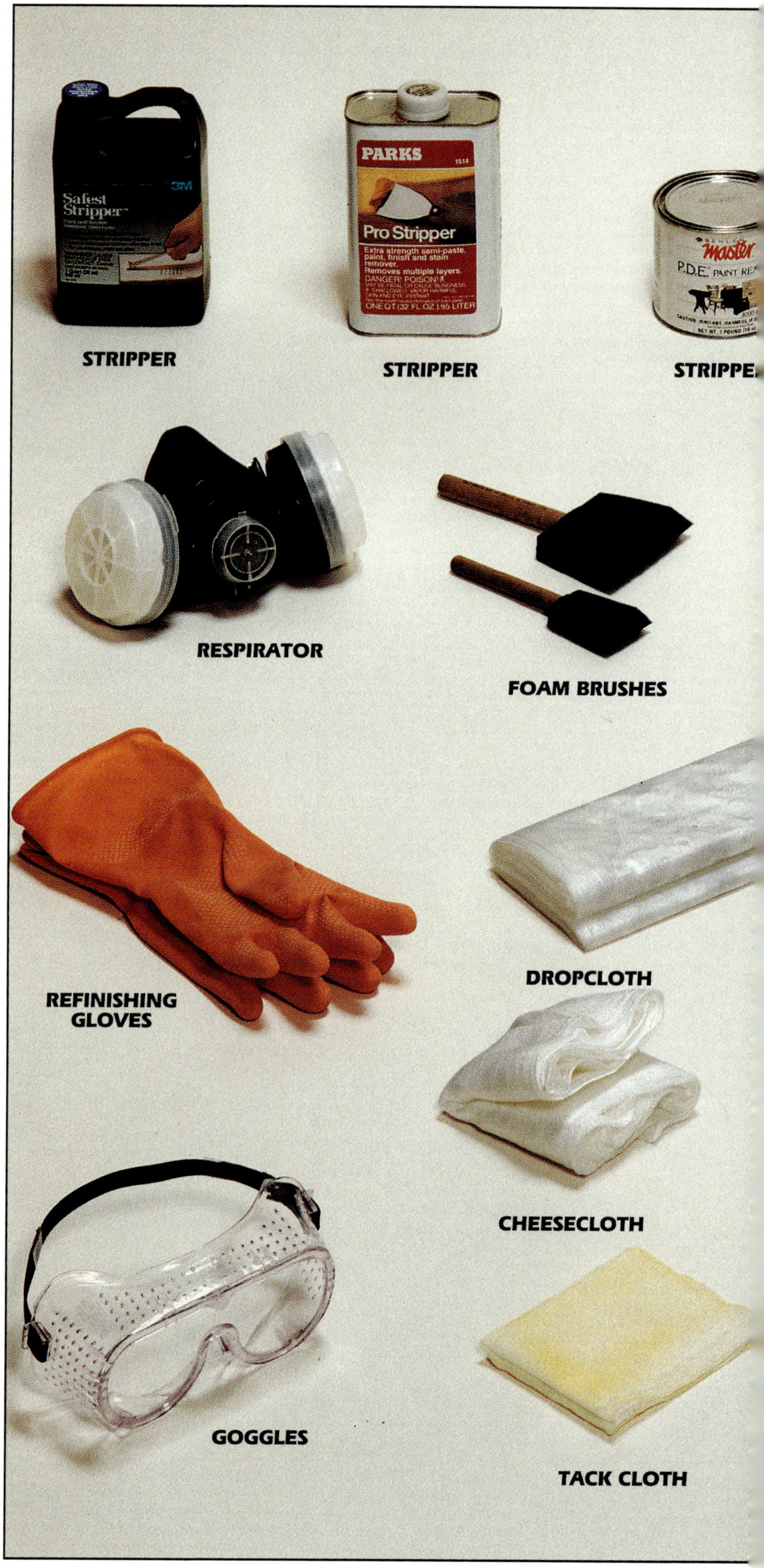

PARKS
Paint Thinner
SOLVENT
Lacquer Thinner
SOLVENT
BEHLEN
PASTE WOOD FILLER
PASTE WOOD FILLER
SANDING WOOD SEALER
MANTROSE-HAEUSER
SEALER
SCRAPER
PLASTIC WOOD
WOOD FILLER
BRUSHES
PUTTY KNIVES
PLASTIC SCRAPER
ORBITAL SANDER
MITCHELL'S ABRASIVE CORDS & TAPES
SANDING CORD
SHAVEHOOK
SANDPAPER
STEEL WOOL
PLASTIC-BRISTLE BRUSHES
BRASS-BRISTLE BRUSH
SANDING BLOCK
ABRASIVE PADS

Scraping and Abrading Tools—After your stripper has softened the finish, it's time to scrape it away. A putty knife ($2 to $8) is a good tool for this, and special plastic knife-type scrapers are less likely to mar the wood. A paint scraper will also come in handy if it's kept sharp and used with care. For tight inside corners and moldings, contoured scrapers called *shavehooks* (about $12 to $24) do a good job.

For carved wood or intricate moldings, it's best to opt for a stiff plastic-bristle brush, available at hardware stores for about $3. Another useful tool for cleaning up and smoothing is a brass-bristle brush. These small brushes, often called *oven-cleaning brushes*, cost about $2.

Steel wool has long been a favorite for cleaning and smoothing. This abrasive tool comes in a range of grades and costs about $1.50 for a package of eight pads. It is less than ideal when used with water-base products because embedded particles will rust. One solution is a synthetic variation. These abrasive pads also come in a range of coarseness grades and can be washed out and reused (about $3 for a package of six pads).

Sanding Tools—Sandpaper types differ in grit material and the size of the grit, or grade. Flint paper is the cheapest, but wears quickly. A better choice is garnet paper—a red-colored paper that holds up longer (about 50¢ per sheet). Aluminum-oxide paper will stand up better than garnet paper and is the choice for power sanders. Aluminum-oxide paper is also available as wet/dry paper for wet-sanding finishes between coats. Emery paper comes in extremely fine grades for producing the smoothest possible surface.

For flat surfaces, you need a sanding block ($2 to $9) to hold the sandpaper. Where there's a lot of sanding to be done, a small orbital sander (about $35 to $100) will speed up the work. (Be sure that each successively finer grade removes the sanding marks left by the previous sanding.) Ornately turned legs pose a sanding problem that sandpaper doesn't handle well. Here, sanding cord is often the solution. This abrasive cord can be wrapped around turnings for cleaning out tight details. Sanding cord costs about $10.

Cloths—Hardware stores sell cheesecloth (about 60¢) for wiping on stains, oils and other refinishing products, although soft, lint-free rags also work. If you're planning to use a grain filler in the finishing process, have burlap rags on hand to wipe away the excess filler.

Another important type of rag is called a *tack cloth* (about 65¢). This is a cloth that's impregnated with a resin that holds dust. Use a tack cloth after sanding and just before finishing to clean surfaces. In addition to an assortment of rags, have a dropcloth on hand to protect both your work surface and the floor.

Safety Equipment—Rubber gloves (about $2 to $4) are a must for stripping. They not only protect your hands, but they make cleaning up quicker and more agreeable. Eye protection is also a requirement—choose goggles that completely protect your eyes from the sides, bottom and top, as well as from the front.

When sanding, a dust mask provides protection against the larger airborne particles. For better protection from both dust and toxic fumes, choose a respirator (about $35 to $50). These masks use filters for the dust and cartridges to absorb vapors. Different cartridges handle different vapors, so be sure to get the right cartridge for your job.

Finish Applicators—The simplest tool for applying oil finishes and many stains is a soft, lint-free cloth. Varnishes are usually applied with a brush. In general, use a natural-bristle brush for the traditional oil-base varnishes and synthetic brushes for water-base finishes. Natural brushes range from about $5 to $35, and synthetic brushes range from about $1.50 to $10. Another tool that works well with polyurethane varnishes and other modern formulations is a foam applicator. These lay down a smooth uniform coating, and their low cost (35¢ to 75¢) makes them a good disposable option.

Fillers and Sealers—To fill the pores and create a smooth surface on woods such as oak, mahogany and walnut, use a paste wood filler before finishing. Paste wood fillers are applied to the surface, and then wiped to leave filler in the pores. They cost about $12 for a 1-quart can. Another prefinish component is a sanding sealer. This is applied to the wood to reduce finish absorption and provide a good base for the next coat.

Keep a can of wood filler on hand for filling nail holes or other small defects. Used sparingly and colored with a refinisher's felt marking pen, filled nail holes can be made nearly invisible.

Stains—Stains come in two basic types: pigment stains and aniline stains, often called dyes. Pigment stains are what you generally find at your local hardware store or home center (about $4.50 per quart). These are made up of a pigment that's suspended in a solvent base. They're applied with a rag or brush, and then wiped to leave a colored film on the surface. Many professional woodworkers prefer to work with aniline dyes. These penetrate the surface of the wood and produce a more uniform coloration. Besides these two types, stains are also available in an easy-to-apply gel form or in combination with a polyurethane finish.

Finishes—You can choose an oil finish, varnish, shellac or lacquer. Oil finishes ($7 to $12 per quart) are penetrating finishes that generally produce a thin, low-luster protective coating. With penetrating oil products (actually thin varnishes), one popular option is tung oil.

Varnishes include traditional oil-based formulas, polyurethane and new water-base variations. Where durability is a concern, opt for polyurethane (about $9 per quart). If you intend to rub out a quality furniture finish to a high, smooth gloss, however, choose a traditional rubbing varnish. Paste wax (about $6) is useful for adding the final glow. It can be used on bare wood, but permits water stains to form on the surface.

Refinisher's Toolkit was written by Thomas Klenck. Photos by Rosario Capotosto.

Strippers and finishes

Finishing products are being regulated on two fronts: VOCs (volatile organic compounds)—substances suspected of reducing the Earth's ozone layer—and direct-exposure hazards. While it's hard to say just where things are headed, the VOC issue is the one most likely to result in regulated limits nationwide within the next few years.

The direct exposure issues are more likely to result in comparative-risk statements and warning labels, mostly because safety precautions can reduce risk. In other words, intensive consumer education can be expected regarding relative hazards and acceptable safeguards.

While it's not possible to attribute a definite risk rating to every product, keep in mind that the latex or water-base alternatives are generally safer and less volatile.

Strippers

Chemical strippers contain solvents that are aggressive enough to break down the protective surface films formed by paints, oils, varnishes, lacquers, polyurethanes, epoxy coatings and polyesters.

They're available in several consistencies to suit the application. If the piece you are stripping has detailed carvings and can be held horizontally, then a liquid stripper will do a better job reaching into the crevices. If you're working with vertical surfaces or overhead woodwork, then a semi-paste or paste does a better job.

Strippers also differ in terms of flammability. About 40 years ago, Klean-Strip offered the industry's first nonflammable stripper, which made stripping indoors a good deal safer. Today, nearly every manufacturer offers both flammable and nonflammable products. As a rule, flammables are less potent than nonflammables.

The workhorse ingredient in the most popular strippers is methylene chloride. This aggressive solvent is quick and thorough, often requiring only one application. It's also effective on the widest range of finishes.

Methylene chloride strippers are available in several strengths. The weakest and least expensive is diluted with acetone and toluene (flammables). This type may require several applications on the newer finishes or on multiple coatings.

Typical Finish Strippers

	METHYLENE CHLORIDE	ATM (acetone, toluene, methanol)	NMP (N-methyl pyrrolidone)	DBE (dibasic-ester)
BEST FOR	All finishes except some epoxies, polyesters, milk-base paint	Varnish, lacquer, shellac, latex paints, some oil-base paints	Most paints and varnishes	Lacquer, varnish, shellac, some latex paints
CLEANUP	Water, lacquer thinner, mineral spirits	Lacquer thinner, mineral spirits	Water	Water
PROS	Available in liquid and semi-paste, fast-acting, medium price, nonflammable	Available in liquid and semi-paste, fast-acting, inexpensive	Available in gel, medium fast-acting	Safe to use with little ventilation, nonflammable, protective clothing not required, semi-paste
CONS	Suspected carcinogen, heart and lung hazard	Flammable, hazardous to user and offspring, may be absorbed through skin	Not effective on epoxies, relatively expensive, suspected reproductive hazard	Not effective on epoxies and polyesters, relatively expensive, slow-acting
SAFETY MEASURES	Good ventilation, eye protection and solvent-resistant gloves*	Good ventilation, avoid sparking devices (switches, tools) keep skin protected, use respirator and goggles	Good ventilation, use goggles and respirator, wear long sleeves and gloves	No long-term data on DBEs. Use goggles, gloves may be necessary but not required

Chart includes commonly available stippers that handle modern finishes. Milk-base paint requires lye stripper. Respirator cartridges do not filter methylene chloride.

The most popular type is a mid-strength formulation, which is usually a blend of methylene chloride and methanol. This nonflammable stripper works well on most finishes with the exception of the newer solvent-resistant epoxies and polyesters.

The strongest formulations contain acids (oxalic) and alkalies (ammonia). Those with acid additives are pretty much limited to commercial use, while the alkali blends are often sold as marine strippers because they work on epoxies, polyesters and baked-on finishes. Alkali-fortified strippers should not be used on hardwoods that won't be painted, however, as they tend to darken the wood.

Methylene chloride evaporates fairly quickly—and when it evaporates, the stripper stops working. One solution is to add paraffin wax to the formula. When applied, the wax separates from the solvents and forms a seal over them, retarding evaporation. Some of the wax is invariably left behind, so a final rinse with denatured alcohol or lacquer thinner is a good idea. Other sources suggest covering the applied stripper with fabric or plastic. One company provides a laminated fabric cover with some of its strippers. When you lift up the fabric, the dissolved coating comes up with it.

While methylene chloride is effective, it's a suspected carcinogen and may trigger heart failure in those with existing heart conditions. While the debate is far from over, manufacturers opted years ago to develop alternative strippers.

One of the departures is a blend of acetone, tolune and methanol (ATM). The ATM class of strippers works reasonably well on a variety of finishes, and is still relatively fast-acting. In fact, it shares many characteristics of methylene chloride strippers, including volatility, but is thought to be less toxic.

It too is available in liquid and semi-paste consistencies. Lacking a wax evaporation retardant, however, liquids are less effective on paints, varnishes and polyurethanes. The semi-paste ATM strippers work best in these cases. Liquids do work well on lacquers and shellacs, however. The primary advantage of the ATM class is lower cost. Its primary disadvantage is flammability.

While the ATM class is inexpensive, its next rival is not. Strippers containing N-methyl pyrrolidone (NMP) are roughly twice as expensive and would not have found a niche in the market if not for a more health-conscious consumer. NMP strippers evaporate very slowly, have a low flammability rating and are less toxic. In most respects, they work well (if a little slower) on traditional finishes. They are not as effective on the newer synthetic finishes.

Like the NMP class of stripper, the newer dibasic-esters (DBE) class does away with both methylene chloride and flammable solvents. These water-base strippers are safer than methylene chloride and the ATMs and cheaper than the NMPs—but at a cost. Although lab tests indicate shorter stripping times, some pros complain of slow and erratic performance. Some finishes will strip away in less than an hour, but multiple coatings and the tougher finishes may need to be left overnight and given additional coats.

As DBEs are water-base strippers, many complaints are often water related. When water is left in contact with wood for a prolonged period, it can warp the thinner solid-wood components and delaminate veneers. It also will raise the grain, which then requires sanding. As the water is slow to evaporate from wood, you may need to wait a week to apply a finish.

One type of finish that all modern strippers have a problem with is milk-base paint—a relatively common coating on old furniture. The traditional solution to this problem is lye. The problem with straight lye is that it's enormously dangerous (caustic) to use. A drop on your skin will cause serious burns, while a drop in your eye could cause blindness. Moreover, lye reacts with tannic acids in some hardwoods and causes staining. While today's lye-base strippers are safer than mixing your own, caution still must be maintained.

When checking out the price tag on strippers, keep in mind that the key is projected coverage. While some strippers will cover 125 sq. ft. or more per gallon, a few specialty strippers will cover as little as 16 sq. ft. Read the labels carefully for both content and capacity.

Finishes

When most of us think of finishing, we think of varnish. At one time, the term *varnish* was used for any coating applied as a liquid that dried to a hard, solid film. Today, varnish is still a catchall term, but it is usually confined to finishes that contain oil and natural or synthetic resins, or, lately, latex and hardeners like polyurethane. The new, user-friendly water-base latex varnishes go on white and dry clear, in contrast to the yellowing tendencies of older formulations.

While polyurethane resins are found in just about everything these days, they also deserve a category of their own. These plastic coatings are hard and resistant to scratches, abrasions, heat and moisture, and almost nothing sticks to them.

Unfortunately, polyurethane has trouble holding its grip on raw wood, and spot repairs are difficult because an old coat won't accept a new coat. Polyurethane is so good at repelling things that it even repels additional coats of polyurethane once it has cured. Still, for high-traffic surfaces, such as tabletops and floors, it's hard to beat its durability.

Oil finishes come next on the list of popular coatings. Originally, furniture was finished with linseed oil. But linseed oil never really dries hard. For that reason, most woodworkers prefer tung oil, Danish oils or other so-called penetrating oils. Several coats of tung oil, which usually comes thinned and fortified with drying agents, provide a low-luster satin finish that remains flexible and resists moisture and impact. Because tung oil dulls fairly quickly and is not terribly resistant to scratches, it's not the best finish for dining tables and other high-use surfaces.

Penetrating oils may contain tung oil or linseed oil, but they go beyond these oils by incorporating resins that harden in the wood. As such, these finishes are actually thin varnishes. They offer the subtle appearance of an oil finish, but are generally harder and more resistant to scuffs, abrasions and scratches.

Shellac is an old-world standby that has found new favor, though it's far from perfect. Although available in dry form, most woodworkers today buy shellac premixed with alcohol. It has a limited shelf life and does not cure well on damp days. It brushes on easily and dries with great speed. Shellac forms a poor barrier for standing liquids and can be redissolved with alcohol. While not tougher than polyurethane, it does provide a hard finish that often clings to wood better than synthetic resins.

Lacquer is probably the most popular finishing product with professionals because it yields a durable protective coating that dries fast. Lacquer is usually applied with a spray gun, and it's highly flammable. This means that you need a controlled environment with explosion-proof ventilation and switches. Brushing lacquers are available to get you around the spray equipment problem, but they're still volatile. New, water-base substitutes are available for spray application.

With wax polishes in spray cans these days, it's hard to remember that wax was originally a finish and not a finish dressing. The wax we're referring to here is paste wax, which is a blend of bee's wax and carnauba wax. While paste wax can be applied over raw wood, its poor resistance to water makes a preliminary finish a requirement. Periodic touchup coats are necessary to maintain luster. Some pros recommend removing the wax with turpentine every few years, and reapplying it.

Stains

By far, the most popular stains are comprised of a pigment suspended in an alkyd (solvent) or latex base. You apply this type with a brush, roller or cloth, and then wipe the excess until the coverage is uniform. If these products have a down side, it's that they're messy. They also can leave lap marks if they are not applied properly.

To simplify application, manufacturers have developed wipe-on gel stains. These products are made with a low-volatility base and thickeners. Because the pigment suspended in the gel is absorbed more slowly, you have more control.

Though not technically stains, aniline dyes are another coloring option, especially if you're partial to primary colors and pronounced grain. Comprised of coal-tar derivatives that dissolve in water or alcohol, these dyes penetrate deeper into the wood, yet do less to soften the grain than pigmented stains. Aniline dyes are the usual choice of professionals.

Finally, several manufacturers offer one-step stain and finishes by blending synthetic resin hardeners, such as polyurethane, with thick wiping gels. The primary disadvantage of these products is that gels make finishing more time-consuming, and are therefore better suited to small projects.

Strippers and Finishes was written by Merle Henkenius.

Typical Surface Coatings

	POLY-URETHANE VARNISH	SYNTHETIC, NATURAL RESIN VARNISH	WATER-BORNE LATEX VARNISH	PENETRATING OIL (THIN VARNISH)	TUNG OIL	SHELLAC	LACQUER	WAX
SOLVENT	Mineral spirits	Mineral spirits	Water	Mineral spirits	Mineral spirits	Alcohol	Lacquer thinner	Mineral spirits
TYPICAL APPLICATOR*	Brush	Brush	Brush	Cloth	Cloth	Brush	Spray	Cloth
BEST FOR	High wear areas, floors, worktables, kitchens, baths	Medium wear areas, furniture	High and medium wear areas, furniture	Medium to low wear areas, furniture	Medium to low wear areas, furniture	High wear areas, furniture	High wear areas, furniture	Low wear areas, adding luster
FINISH QUALITY	Gloss, satin, matte	Gloss, satin, matte	Gloss, satin, matte	Satin, matte	Satin, matte	Gloss	Gloss	Gloss, satin
DRYING TIME	8 to 10 hours	8 to 10 hours	2 hours	8 to 10 hours	24 hours	10 to 20 min.	20 min.	10 min.
PROS	Good moisture, wear and scratch resistance	Good adherence to wood and previous coats	Non-yellowing, easy cleanup dries fast, no odor	Easy to apply and repair, thin natural appearance	Easy to apply and repair, thin natural appearance	Quick application, easy to repair and touch up	Easy to repair, easy application for experienced sprayer	Easy to apply
CONS	Ambers over time, thick consistency	Ambers over time, not as tough as polyurethane	Low resistance to liquids	Slightly less durable than polyurethane	Less durable than urethane, needs periodic application to maintain luster	Poor water resistance, dissolved by alcohol	Spray application although brushing lacquer is available, brittle	Poor water resistance, needs periodic applications

Chart shows the most common finishes available for furniture. VOC regulations currently affect formulation and availability of traditional mineral-spirit solvent finishes. Application methods may vary depending on technique and requirements.

Spraying finishes

After hours of stripping, sanding and repairing, all that remains is to choose your finishing product. Well, perhaps, if you're locked into the two basic application methods: cloth and brush. There is, however, another way to go. A way that the pros embrace with almost unanimous support, and that more and more home refinishers are turning to—spray finishing.

The reasons are compelling. First, spraying is fast—less of a concern if you're finishing a coffee table, but a big deal if you're taking on a dining room suite. The second advantage of spraying is the quality of the finish. With a little practice, you can lay down coats of remarkable uniformity. Brush and lap marks are a thing of the past and, if it's a fast-drying finish, dust is less of a problem.

Text and photos for *Spraying Finishes* by Rosario Capotosto. Sidebar on *Choosing Spray Tools* by Thomas Klenck.

On the down side, traditional high-pressure spray finishing is wasteful—a large percentage of the finish never reaches your work at all. The usual finishes are highly flammable, making an expensive spray booth equipped with explosion-proof electrical components and impressive ventilation a necessity.

Fortunately, two modern developments have changed the picture. High volume, low pressure (HVLP) spray equipment reduces the overspray waste problem, and new water-base finishes eliminate the need for a dedicated spray booth with special wiring and ventilation.

Whichever system you choose, the application techniques are the same. In all cases, be sure to work in a well-ventilated area, wear a respirator and adhere to manufacturer's precautions and instructions.

Adjusting the Gun

There are two adjustments on the spay gun: one that controls the spray pattern and another than controls the material flow. To adjust the spray pattern, turn the ears on the spray cap to form either a round or a fan shape (Fig. 1). Use the round pattern—ears set diagonally—for spraying small areas. For large areas, set the ears either vertically or horizontally for a fan-shaped pattern. Use the vertical position for making horizontal passes, and the horizontal position for vertical passes.

To adjust the material flow, turn the knob at the rear of the handle (Fig. 2). Each job and finish necessitates minor adjustments to material flow. For example, if you change the size of the spray pattern by moving closer or farther away from the work, you have to adjust the flow accordingly. Generally, the working distance should be around 8 in., but may be between 1 in. and 12 in. depending on the job at hand. The best way to learn how to adjust the flow is experimentation with your equipment.

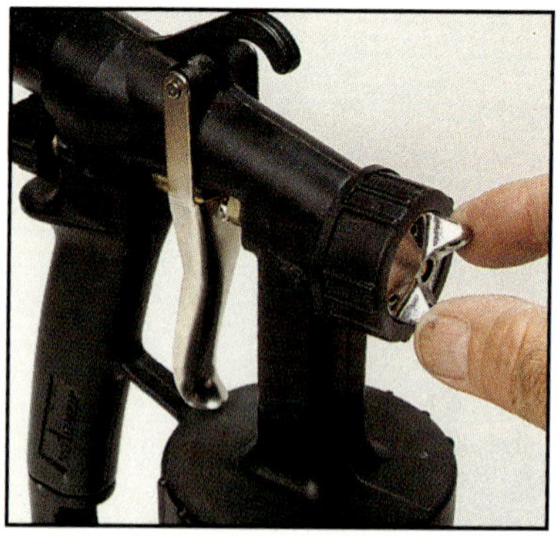

1 Adjust cap diagonally for a round spray pattern. Vertical and horizontal spray-cap positions produce elongated fan patterns.

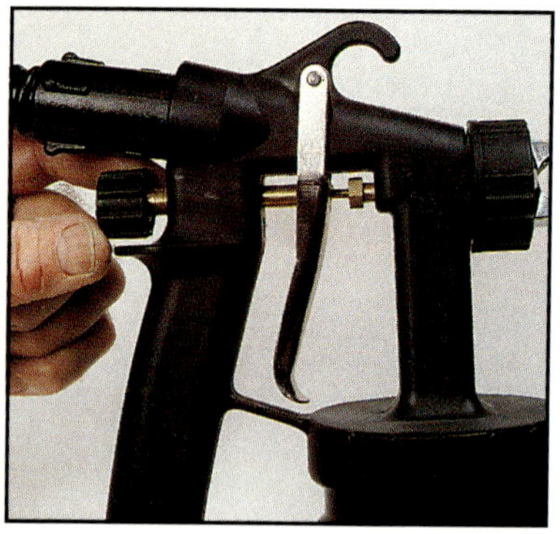

2 Control the amount being sprayed by adjusting knob at the back of handle to suit spray pattern and distance from work.

Preparing the Finish

Your spray equipment is designed to work best when handling a fluid in a specific viscosity range. Therefore, the first thing to do is to check your finish for proper viscosity, and thin it if necessary. Both the spray gun manufacturer and finish manufacturer offer directions for achieving the right viscosity for spraying and using the appropriate solvent for thinning. Be sure to check the spray gun manual and the instructions for your finish.

3 To determine proper finish consistency, measure the time it takes material to flow through viscosity cup. Thin if necessary.

4 After checking viscosity, pour finish in spray gun cup through a strainer. This removes lumps that may clog the spray gun.

Most spray guns come with a viscosity cup to measure the consistency of the material to be sprayed. To use the cup, pour the finish into it and measure the time it takes for the finish to empty through the small hole in the bottom of the cup (Fig. 3). Then, compare this time with the recommended time stated in the manufacturer's timing chart.

After checking the viscosity and thinning if necessary, pour the mixture through a strainer into the spray cup of the gun (Fig. 4). The strainer removes any lumps that may clog the gun.

Spray Technique

Like most other techniques, skill with a spray gun comes with practice. While it's easy to make a few mistakes at first, it's equally easy to learn to apply the uniform thin coats necessary for a good finish.

Begin practicing on cardboard or sheets of newspaper. Use opaque paint for your practice sessions because it's easier to see the results. Experiment to get the feel of triggering the gun to start and stop the paint flow. Practice making uniform strokes and experiment with the paint-flow adjustment knob.

5 Always move spray gun parallel to the work surface. Practice moving gun in a straight line to uniformly cover flat surfaces.

6 For even coverage, overlap each pass about 50%. Start each pass so pattern is centered on bottom edge of last pass.

7 To achieve a uniform spraying rate, start and end each pass outside the work area. Press trigger only over the work area.

8 Spray corners from an angle so adjacent faces are covered simultaneously. Set the spray gun air cap for a round spray pattern.

9 After the corners are finished, spray the surfaces with a fan pattern. Set the cap vertically for horizontal application.

CHOOSING SPRAY TOOLS

If you decide to set up for spray finishing, you have a few choices to make—not only in terms of the system you buy, but in terms of price and flexibility.

An HVLP system is recommended because of its minimal overspray qualities. One system that's well suited to home-shop uses is the Wagner FineCoat system (about $180). This kit comes complete with gun, viscosity cup and turbine. Because HVLP systems use large volumes of air at low pressure, standard air compressors are unsuitable.

Standard high-pressure spraying does have a few pluses, however. First, the air compressor you use to drive the gun is useful for other jobs as well—like pumping tires and running pneumatic equipment. Keep in mind that air compressors are rated by the amount of air they move at a specific pressure. When choosing one, make sure it handles the range of tools you use.

Compressors without tanks run continuously to maintain airflow. For spray painting, team up this type with a bleeder-type spray gun that allows the airstream to continue even when the trigger is released. With tank compressors, such as the Sears model No. 15292 (about $300), you can use a nonbleeder gun.

In terms of guns, you'll find a wide range available in bleeder, nonbleeder, pressure feed and siphon feed. Choose pressure feed for thicker finishes that need to be moved faster, and siphon feed for extra-fine work. Many guns can be converted from one type to the other. Although you can pay more than $150 for a professional model, small-shop models are available in the $30 to $50 range.

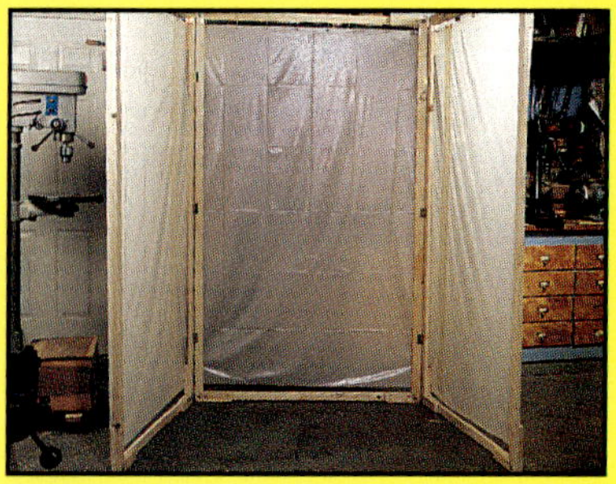

This spray booth helps confine overspray in small shops. It's designed for HVLP systems and nonflammable finishes.

After cutting 1x2 stock to length, secure cleats to the ends of each long member. Set cleats back 1½ in. from ends.

Assemble frames with carriage bolts and wingnuts. Then attach frames with loose-pin hinges for easy disassembly.

With the shower curtain removed and the frames disassembled, the spray booth can be packed away for easy storage.

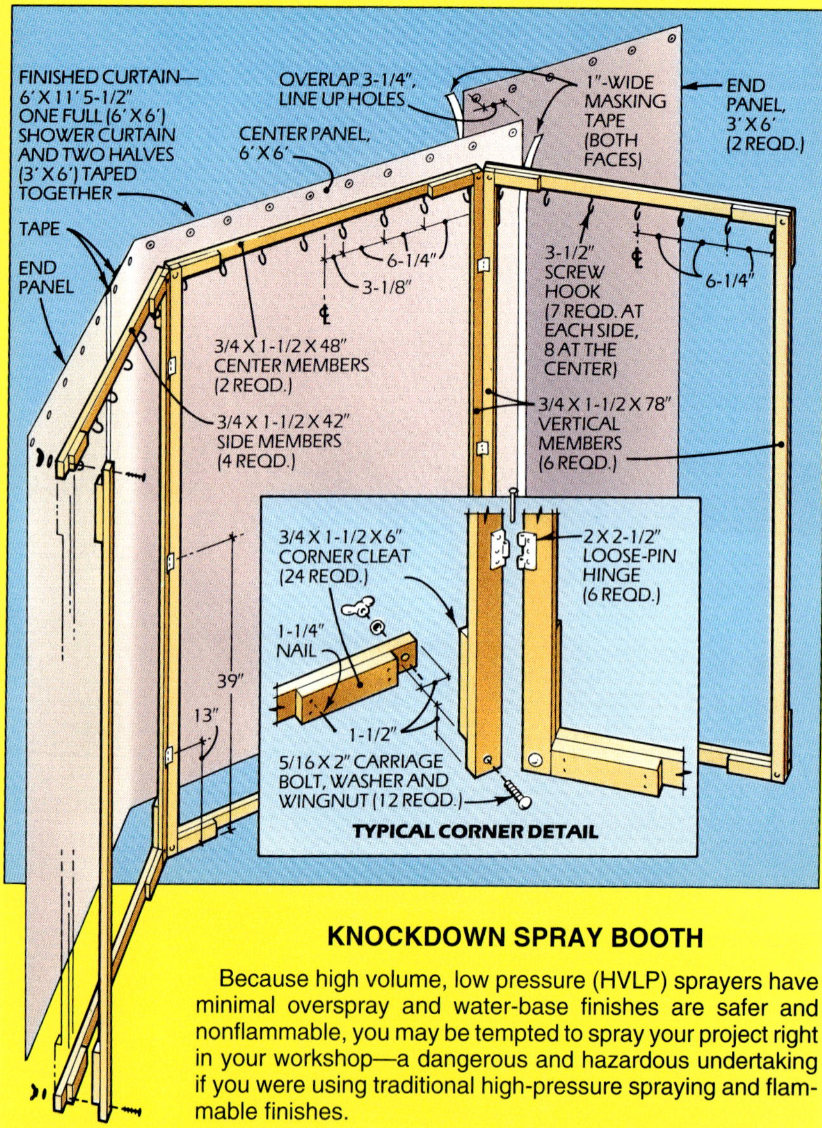

KNOCKDOWN SPRAY BOOTH

Because high volume, low pressure (HVLP) sprayers have minimal overspray and water-base finishes are safer and nonflammable, you may be tempted to spray your project right in your workshop—a dangerous and hazardous undertaking if you were using traditional high-pressure spraying and flammable finishes.

You will have some overspray to contend with, however, and one solution to the problem is to build this 3-sided, knock-down spray booth. Made of 1×2 pine stock, a couple of shower curtains and easy-to-find hardware, this booth will keep the overspray away from the rest of the shop and then fold up quickly for easy storage.

To build the unit, first cut 1×2 pine to length to make the six vertical, two center and four side members as shown in the drawing. Then cut the 24 1½ × 6-in. cleats. Secure a cleat to each end of the vertical, center and side members with nails and glue, so that each cleat is set back 1½ in. as shown. Next, bolt the components together with carriage bolts and wingnuts to make three separate frames. Drill pilot holes and attach the screwhooks to the top member of each frame at the specified centers. Then, link the frames together with loose-pin hinges.

Cut one of the shower curtains in half, and tape each piece to an edge of the uncut curtain with a 3¼-in. overlap. Make sure the curtain holes line up. Finally, hang the curtain on the frames. To disassemble, simply remove and fold up the curtain, and separate the frame members by removing the carriage bolts.

Remember, all spraying has some degree of overspray and no finish is truly safe for human consumption. Always provide adequate ventilation and wear a respirator. This spray booth is not designed for high-pressure spray equipment or flammable finishes such as standard lacquer.

Hold the gun about 8 in. from the surface, pull the trigger and observe the spray pattern as you move the gun parallel to the surface. If the pattern is weak and dusty, the gun is moving too fast, too little paint is flowing, or both. If the paint piles up causing runs or sags, you're either moving the gun too slowly or too much paint is flowing.

Next, work on operating the trigger and maintaining a proper stroke. Set up a 4-ft.-wide test panel, and adjust the air cap for a vertical fan pattern. Practice moving the gun in a straight, horizontal line across the panel and parallel to it. Be sure to move your entire arm from the shoulder to avoid a natural tendency to move the gun in an arc (Fig. 5). A parallel stroke will deposit a uniform coating across the board.

10 When spraying horizontal surfaces, start at the edge nearest you and work toward the far edge to control overspray.

11 Use a round spray pattern with a vertical motion for turned legs. Do all edges and corner first. Then spray broad areas.

For uniform coverage of a flat surface, move the gun at a constant speed and overlap each stroke by about 50%. Aim the center of each stroke at the bottom edge of the preceding stroke (Fig. 6).

To avoid excess paint at the edges of the object, start the stroke outside the area and press the trigger as soon as the stroke reaches the area. Then, release the trigger at the end of the area, but continue moving the gun a short distance beyond (Fig. 7).

When spraying corners, avoid spraying each adjacent face separately. Instead, spray diagonally into or at the corner so that both adjacent faces are covered simultaneously (Fig. 8). After the corners have been painted, fill in the faces with a fan-shaped spray pattern (Fig. 9).

It's always better to orient the work so that the gun is held relatively level. In some cases, however, such as finishing a tabletop, you'll have to tilt the gun down. When painting the top of a horizontal surface, start spraying at the edge nearest you and work toward the back so that the overspray doesn't settle on a wet area (Fig. 10). This is especially important when spraying fast-drying finishes.

Remember to adapt the spray pattern to suit the object and spray motion. Use a round spray pattern for corners and for turned furniture legs (Fig. 11). When spraying pieces with many edges, do the edges first with a small round pattern, followed by vertical or horizontal fan patterns as required.

Refinishing a painted cupboard

Refinishing a Painted Cupboard was written and photographed by Rosario Capotosto.

Although this old country cupboard boasts sensitive detailing, the green paint needs to go and repairs need to be made.

After stripping, repairing and refinishing, the cupboard features a warm amber glow and a durable satin clear finish.

The question most folks ask when they stumble on a nicely proportioned and detailed cupboard is "Why ever did they cover that beautiful piece with paint?"

This cupboard was found in a local antique shop. Like everything else on display, this cupboard had charm. From the beaded back panels to the stately molding details, this example of country furniture had all the elements for a challenging refinishing project.

The first job was to remove the old paint. In doing so, it was discovered that the work went beyond a simple strip and finish.

A few corners were badly worn, and although they might have been left alone, they could call for careful repair. Also, several discolored areas demanded careful touchup to create a uniform base for the finish.

One fascination with stripping painted furniture is discovering the wood that the builder used. Although most pieces of this type are pine, this cupboard was made of fir. After stripping, a stain was applied to impart a mellow antique look, and the job was completed with a satin wipe-on finish.

Preparation

To prepare for stripping a cabinet, first remove all hardware (Fig. 1). It's best to remove the components that are easy to take off before stripping.

If you already know the type of finish on the piece, choose a stripper that's appropriate. If you're not sure, make spot tests with several striper types (Fig. 2). If none of the usual strippers work, the finish is probably a milk-base paint, in which case you need a lye stripper.

1 Begin the job by removing all hardware, doors and drawers. Check the condition of the hardware screw pilot holes.

2 If you're unsure of the old finish, spot test with several strippers to determine the best. A water-base stripper was used here.

3 Lightly sand the old finish with 150-grit paper before stripping. The scuffed surface makes the stripper more effective.

4 Apply the stripper with a soft brush. Avoid overbrushing water-base stripper. Let stand until paint is soft.

5 Use a scraper to remove the softened paint. Although gloves aren't required for a water-based stripper, they're a good idea.

6 Where a large flat scraper can't reach, use a synthetic abrasive pad. Avoid steel wool with water-base products.

The stripper used here was a water-cleanup formula that's nonflammable and doesn't give off harmful fumes. These considerations are important when you're working indoors. Before applying the stripper, lightly sand the surface with 150-grit paper, scuffing the surface to help the stripper penetrate the finish (Fig. 3).

Stripping

After the hardware, doors and drawers are removed and the old finish is scuff sanded, pour the stripper into a can and use a large, soft-bristle brush to apply a thick coating (Fig. 4).

Each stripper formula will have specific instructions for application, so be sure to check the instructions on the container. Also, be sure to follow all safety precautions. When using the stripper, avoid overbrushing the thick semi-paste coating. This is important because the stripper skins over the surface to contain the solvents in the layer that dissolve the paint. Back-and-forth brushing breaks down this crust, allowing the solvents to escape.

Next, allow the stripper to dissolve the finish. Don't rush the job, but check occasionally to see if the paint is sufficiently softened for removal. When the old finish is ready to come off, use a plastic scraper to remove it (Fig. 5). Where the plastic scraper can't reach, use abrasive pads moistened with stripper to remove the remaining traces of paint. If the paint coating was very thick and some paint remains, you may have to repeat the stripping process.

7 Clean small beading on tongue-and-groove back panels with stripper-dampened abrasive pad and small scrapers.

When using a water-base stripper, avoid using steel wool, as small particles can remain on the surface and will rust. A better choice is a synthetic abrasive pad made with plastic fibers. Use the pads with a shavehook or profiled scraper to remove the softened paint in the moldings and crevices (Fig. 6).

The beaded tongue-and-groove paneling in the back of this cupboard was particularly difficult to strip completely. Use a combination of abrasive pads and small profiled scrapers to get the job done (Fig. 7).

After all the surfaces have been scraped, rinse away the stripper residue with clean pads and fresh water.

8 Fixing splintered and worn wood means finding matching stock. Use small pieces cut from a hidden area like the cabinet top.

9 To repair this worn area on the case side, first use a sharp utility knife to define a uniform area to be cut away.

10 Use a sharp chisel to remove the worn section. Pare the sides of the notch smooth and flat so the patch seats well.

11 Cut each patch slightly oversize to fit the trimmed area. Glue and hold in place with masking tape until dry. Then trim flush.

12 Fill nail holes and small cracks with wood filler. Apply the filler with a small putty knife and sand it flush when dry.

13 Where iron in nails has discolored wood, bleach the area with oxalic acid. Wash off residue when bleach has dried.

Repair

Once the paint has been removed, you may find numerous dents, gouges, cracks, scratches and wear areas that were concealed by the paint. While you might choose to leave these imperfections to impart an antique or country character to the piece, most can be easily repaired before refinishing.

This cabinet had torn-out areas at the bottoms of the side panels and some deep wear areas. While replacing missing wood with a patch cut from new stock rarely makes a good match, you can find closely matched stock by cutting small portions from a hidden component of the piece. Ample material was cut for these repairs from the top surface of the top panel (Fig. 8). If you can't find an area from which to cut repair stock, select new wood carefully for both color and grain pattern.

To repair a worn area, first make straight cuts around the section with a sharp utility knife (Fig. 9). Then, use these cuts as guides and remove the waste area with a chisel (Fig. 10). Once the work area has been cut away and the surfaces of the notch are smooth and flat, cut a patch so the grain direction matches the surrounding wood as closely as possible. Cut the patch slightly oversize to allow for flush trimming and sanding after it's secured.

Repair torn sections in the same way. After trimming the edges of the area and leveling the bottom to make a firm base for the patch, cut an appropriate patch and glue it in place. Use masking tape to hold it until the glue dries (Fig. 11).

Dents and shallow scratches also can be repaired. For dents, press a hot clothes iron over a damp cloth placed on the dent. The steam produced will swell the compressed wood of the dent and raise the wood to the original level. For shallow scratches, lightly sand with fine paper. Avoid excessive sanding in one small area—it's better to sand the surrounding area as well to keep the surface as flat as possible.

Repair gouges, cracks and nail holes with wood filler. Apply the wood filler with a small putty knife, and sand it flush when it's completely dry (Fig. 12). Although most fillers are available in a range of colors, you may find it hard to match the wood you're filling exactly. You might have better luck with scratch remover markers applied over the filled areas. These markers are available in 12 wood colors.

To remove dark stains caused by a reaction between the iron in the nails and the wood, spot bleach the areas with oxalic acid. Oxalic acid is available in powder form at paint and hardware stores. Make a solution by dissolving $1\frac{1}{2}$ ounces of the powder in 1 pint of water. Always add the acid to the water, never the other way around.

Then apply the bleach solution to the stain with a small brush (Fig. 13). If the stain persists, try a more concentrated solution. When the wood dries, rinse away the residue with water.

14 Use an orbital sander to speed smoothing of broad areas. Finish by hand sanding with the grain to remove any swirl marks.

15 Hand sand tight crevices with folded sandpaper. Use a sanding block on narrow flat surfaces to avoid rounding corners.

Sanding

After the repairs are done, sand with 120-grit paper and move to 220-grit paper in preparation for finishing. To smooth broad areas quickly, use an orbital sander (Fig. 14). When you're done power sanding, lightly sand by hand with the grain to remove any swirl marks left by the sander. Moldings, narrow edges and other details must be hand sanded. Use a sanding block on small flat surfaces to avoid rounding over the corners. Fold over sandpaper to reach inside beaded details and the inside corners of moldings (Fig. 15).

16 To match brass hardware with the original black iron bin pulls, spray with black paint formulated for metal.

17 Use dowels to plug worn screw pilot holes. A doweling jig will yield the most accurate holes for dowels.

Hardware

The porcelain doorknobs were to be replaced with catches that match the original black iron bin pulls. Because suitable catches were only available in brass, these were painted with black spray paint for metal (Fig. 16). Then give the original bin pulls a fresh coat of paint as well. Before finishing, it's a good idea to check that either new or original hardware can be secured properly. To fix worn hinge screwholes, use a doweling jig to bore oversize holes. Then glue dowels in place, and bore new screw pilot holes (Fig. 17).

Finishing

It was decided to finish this piece in keeping with the idea of how a country cupboard might look today if it had never been painted—deep amber in color with a satin texture. The amber color simulates the look of wood that has darkened over the years, and the medium-gloss finish reflects just enough light to accent the moldings and details.

To do this job, an easy-to-apply gel stain and a gel clearcoat was chosen. Staining softwoods, however, often results in a blotchy appearance due to variations in the absorbency of different areas of the wood surface. To solve the problem, first apply a coat of wood conditioner to ensure even staining. Apply the conditioner with a brush and wipe it off with a cloth after about 10 minutes (Fig. 18). Then let the surface dry completely.

To tone the wood to the desired color, you can use a gel stain. This is a mixture of pigment and dye stains that blends easily with each stroke, leaving no lap marks. Simply wipe on the stain with a soft, lint-free cloth, and allow it to dry (Fig. 19). If the application looks a little light, reapply the stain after about 4 hours to intensify the color. If it looks too dark, wipe the wood with a cloth dampened in mineral spirits.

After the stain is dry, apply two coats of gel clear finish. Use a cloth for the main application (Fig. 20). In tight crevices such as the beaded tongue-and-groove back panels, however, switch to a brush for adequate coverage, and wipe away the excess with a cloth. Besides being easy to apply, an advantage of a wipe-on gel finish is that dust, brush marks, runs and sags are never a problem.

18 Apply wood conditioner before staining to prevent blotchy, uneven coloration. Wipe off excess after 10 minutes.

19 Use a cloth to apply gel stain. If the application is too light, apply a second coat. If too dark, wipe with mineral spirits.

20 Apply two coats of gel clear finish with a cloth. Wipe-on finishes eliminate dust problems and visible brush strokes.

Restoring a veneered table

Restoring a Veneered Table was written and photographed by Rosario Capotosto.

Showing signs of age and abuse, this table is an ideal candidate for a new finish that recreates the original luster and color.

After stripping, refinishing and polishing, this table is ready to grace the decades ahead with timeless elegance from the past.

When you're dealing with a few coats of old paint, it's not difficult to start stripping. After all, once down to bare wood, things can only get better. Some pieces, however, require a slightly different strategy. More sophisticated pieces were often made out of particularly attractive woods, finished clear and perhaps stained to highlight the grain and color. Because these pieces were valued for their natural look, they're still likely to have the finish they had when they left the maker's shop. In this case, you have the opportunity to recreate a finish that matches the original.

This small mahogany drop-leaf table is a prime example. It features intricate carving and reeding and has a veneered top. It also has an assortment of water stains, and the finish has literally worn away on some areas of the top and legs.

Of course, the first step is stripping. Then, to reproduce an authentic-looking finish and bring out the beauty of the mahogany veneer, you want to use the coloring agent many pros use—aniline dye. The large pores of mahogany necessitate a grain filler to smooth the surface before anything goes on. Lastly, you want to sand between each coat of varnish to achieve the flattest surface possible in preparation for the final rubbing.

1 First, disassemble the piece and remove all hardware and metal components. Separate pieces are easier to strip and finish.

2 Use paper to plug holes left after removing hardware. This prevents stripper and finish products from dripping through holes.

Preparation

Begin by disassembling the piece, removing all hardware and any components that are screwed together (Fig. 1). Check that all the hardware is in good condition. If some components need to be replaced, order them before refinishing the table in case screw pilot holes need to be moved or plugged.

After removing drawer or door pulls, plug the holes with paper so the stripper, stain and finish won't drip through (Fig. 2). Inspect the surface for broken veneer or other problems, and make repairs.

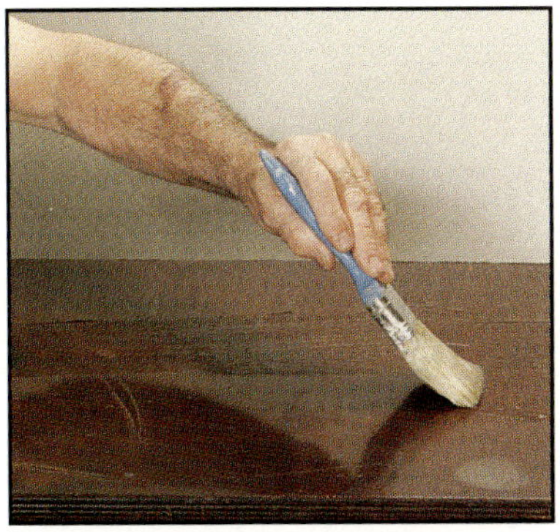

3 Use a brush to apply stripper. Non-water-base stripper is best for veneered work where water may delaminate veneer.

4 After the finish has softened, remove the old finish on flat surfaces with a plastic scraper or a wide putty knife.

5 For small carvings and details, use an old toothbrush or small plastic-bristle brush to remove the stripper and finish.

6 On larger carved areas, remove the stripper waste with a large plastic-bristle brush. Be sure to reach all the crevices.

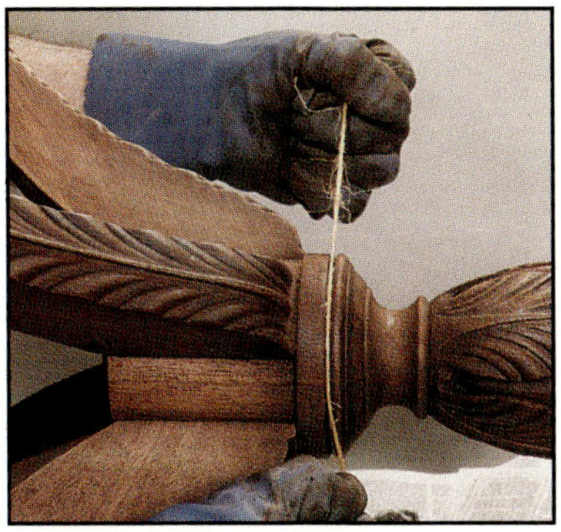

7 For detailed turnings, use coarse twine to remove the waste. Wrap twine around the turning, and pull back and forth.

8 After the stripper has been removed, rinse away residue with recommended solvent. Don't use water on veneered work.

Stripping

The first job is to select the best type of stripper. For veneered furniture, it's best to stay away from water-base strippers because the water used in cleanup can lift the veneer. When the intricate carving is involved and there's a heavy buildup of finish in the crevices, you want a fast-acting, strong formula. Finally, if you're doing the job indoors, use a product that's nonflammable.

Based on these requirements, a methylene chloride stripper was chosen. Keep in mind that methylene chloride is toxic. A conventional respirator won't help, although expensive ventilated respirator systems exist. So simple, good ventilation is a necessity. You also need neoprene gloves, and wear goggles for the entire stripping operation.

Begin by spreading newspaper or a dropcloth under the work, and pour a small amount of stripper into a wide-mouth can. Use an inexpensive bristle brush to lay on a heavy coat, working one section at a time (Fig. 3). Load the brush fully after each stroke, and be sure to avoid brushing back and forth. Allow the finish adequate time to work, and wait until the old finish bubbles and lifts off.

Use a plastic scraper to remove the loosened finish from flat surfaces (Fig. 4). When it comes to removing the sludge from crevices, a variety of tools come in handy. For small areas, use a small brush or old toothbrush (Fig. 5). For larger carved areas, use a plastic scrub brush (Fig. 6). Fine turnings are best handled with a piece of coarse twine (Fig. 7), and abrasive pads work well on molded areas. After removing as much old finish as you can, wash away the residue with lacquer thinner or denatured alcohol. These materials are flammable, so work on small areas to minimize vapor buildup (Fig. 8).

Staining and Sealing

Before applying the stain, use fine sandpaper to smooth the wood. Don't use a power sander on veneer—the veneer may be only 1/40 in. thick, and it doesn't take much to accidentally sand through to the substrate underneath. Use a soft-bristle brass brush to smooth out coarse spots in the carvings and an extra-fine abrasive pad to smooth the curved surfaces and moldings.

When the work is sanded, clean and dry, it's time to apply the stain. To recreate the rich, deep-red mahogany color of the original finish and enhance the grain, use Behlen's Solar Lux NGR Medium Red Mahogany aniline stain. Unlike typical water-based aniline formulas that raise the grain and create a fuzzy surface, this product is non-grain raising (NGR). It is a fast drying stain, however, intended for spray application, and doing the job by hand easily causes ruinous lap marks. To solve the problem, use a special Behlen's retarder to extend drying time. Mix the retarder and stain 1-part retarder to 10-parts stain.

9 To color wood with aniline dye, first mix with retarder to eliminate lap marks. Apply with a soft cloth in grain direction.

10 Use a small brush to reach crevices when staining detailed carvings and moldings. Blot up any excess with a cloth.

11 After the staining is done, apply a thin coat of shellac to act as a sealer and form a good base for the paste wood filler.

Apply the stain mixture to the flat surfaces with a soft cloth, and wipe parallel to the grain direction (Fig. 9). Use a small brush to stain the irregular surfaces (Fig. 10), and follow with a rag to blot up any accumulation in the carving crevices.

Allow the stain to dry thoroughly, and then apply a 1-pound-cut shellac wash coat to facilitate wiping on the grain filler—the next step in the finishing operation. To make the 1-pound-cut shellac sealer, mix 3 parts of 3-pound-cut shellac to 4-parts alcohol. Use a soft cloth to apply a uniform coat of the thinned shellac sealer to the entire stained surface (Fig. 11).

Grain Filling

Like oak and walnut, mahogany has large open pores that remain apparent if the raw wood is simply varnished. To obtain a smooth, flat surface for the final finish, the open pores must be filled after staining.

To do the job, you need a paste wood-grain filler. Paste wood fillers (not to be confused with wood fillers used to plug nail holes or cracks) come in a variety of stain colors and either in a heavy paste, which must be thinned before use, or a ready-to-use formulation. When you buy paste wood filler, be sure to check its compatibility with topcoats and choose your final finish accordingly.

Apply the filler with a stiff brush, working small areas at a time. First, brush it on with the grain, and then across the grain to fill the pores (Fig. 12). When the filler loses its wet look, wipe across the grain with a coarse cloth, such as burlap or a deep-pile towel (Fig. 13). The object is to remove the excess so that the filler remains packed only in the pores. Then, gently wipe with the grain using a soft, clean cloth. Use a plastic-bristle brush to remove most of the excess filler from the carved areas (Fig. 14).

After the filler is thoroughly dried, use fine sandpaper to remove any filler that remains on the flat surfaces. Use a gentle touch and be careful to avoid sanding through the stain. Then, use an abrasive pad to clean up the dry residue on the curved areas, and clean up the carving details with a soft brass-bristle brush.

Varnishing

Finish the table with four coats of rubbing varnish. Rubbing varnishes are designed for a fine abrasive polish after the last coat. If you intend to rub out the last coat, make sure that your varnish is suitable for this technique.

Thin the first coat of varnish with an equal part of mineral spirits to serve as a sealer. After this coat has dried overnight, lightly dry-sand with 320-grit wet/dry silicon-carbide paper.

12 Apply appropriate color paste wood-grain filler with a brush. Work first with the grain, then across to fill the pores.

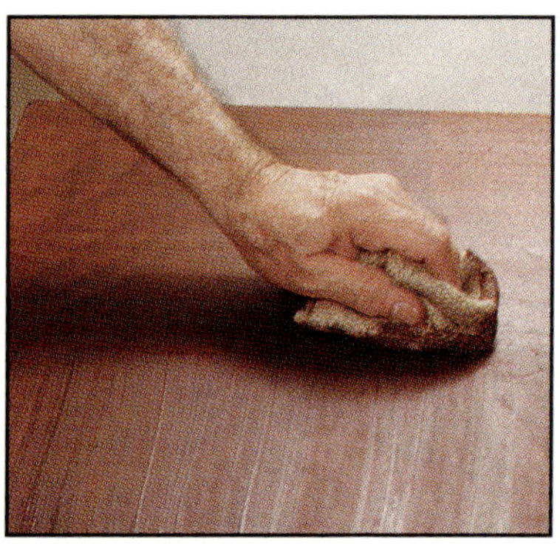

13 After the wet look of the filler is gone, wipe away the excess with a burlap cloth. This leaves filler packed in pores.

14 To remove the excess paste wood filler from crevices in carved details, use a stiff plastic-bristle brush.

Next, prepare a can to hold the varnish with a strike wire—a piece of wire stretched across the open end of the can. You'll use the strike wire to wipe the excess varnish gently from the brush after each dip.

Pour some varnish into the can and dip about one-half the bristle length into the varnish. Then, gently strike off the excess on the wire. Flow the varnish onto the surface slowly to avoid bubbling. Work across the grain first, then with the grain to smooth the coat (Fig. 15). Next, wipe the brush over the strike wire to remove the excess. Then, brush lightly with the grain, allowing only the tips of the bristles to touch the surface to level out lap marks, runs and sags (Fig. 16).

On the carved areas, first spread the varnish over the surface. Then dab in the brush tips to reach the crevices. Pass the brush over the strike wire, dab again and gently lift out the brush to soak up any puddles.

After the second coat is dry, use a firm rubber sanding block and 320-grit paper to dry-sand the surface and level high spots (Fig. 17). Then apply a third coat of varnish. When it's dry, wet-sand with 400-grit wet/dry paper moistened with water. Dip the paper frequently and rub with care—especially at the corners. After the final fourth coat, wet-sand with 600-grit paper (Fig. 18).

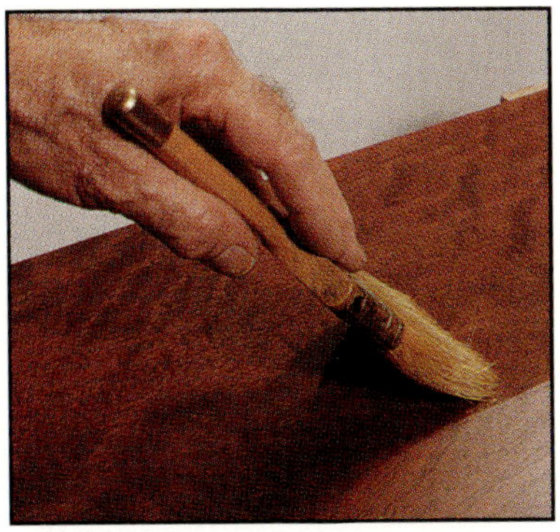
15 Fill half the bristle length with varnish and wipe excess on wire affixed to can. Flow on across grain, and then with grain.

16 Then, remove all excess varnish from brush and gently wipe the wet coat with the bristle tips in the direction of the grain.

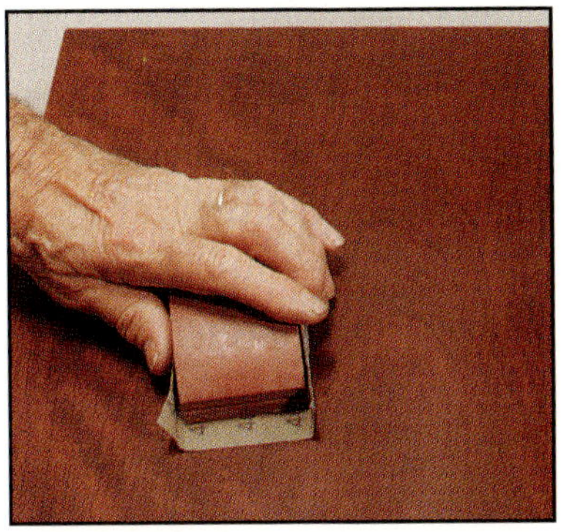
17 After the first two coats, dry-sand with 320-grit paper. Use a rubber sanding block to maintain a flat uniform surface.

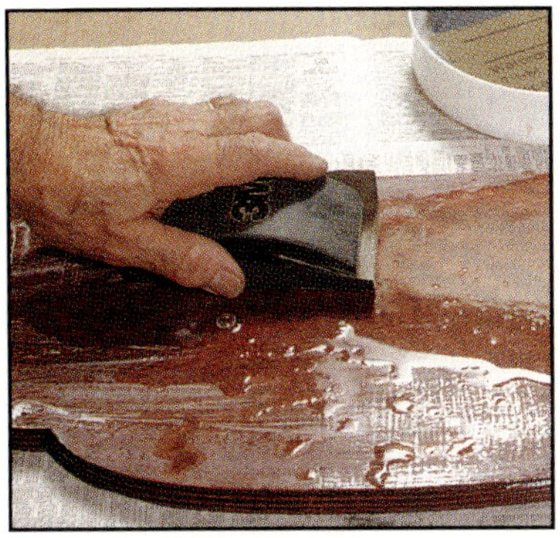
18 After the third coat, wet-sand with 400-grit paper and water. Move to 600-grit paper to wet-sand the final fourth coat.

Finishing the Finish

Two final procedures impart a pleasing gloss without the harsh glare of raw varnish. The first step is to rub the finish with rottenstone. This is a fine abrasive powder available in hardware stores and furniture finish dealers.

Sprinkle water and rottenstone powder on the surface, and then rub gently but thoroughly using a felt pad or a wood block surfaced with short-nap carpeting (Fig. 19) Use a brush on the carved areas (Fig. 20). Periodically, wipe off the slurry to check your progress. When you're satisfied with the uniformity and level of the gloss, thoroughly clean the surface with a damp cloth.

When the finish is clean and dry, apply a coat of paste wax according to the directions on the can. Apply a thin layer with a clean cloth or cheese-cloth, and then allow the wax to dry for about 15 minutes. After the wax is thoroughly dry, use a clean cloth to buff the surface (Fig. 21).

19 Begin the final rubbing with rottenstone and water. Use a soft cloth to smooth the surface, checking progress frequently.

20 Use a small plastic-bristle brush to apply rottenstone to carved details. Then, clean the entire piece and let dry.

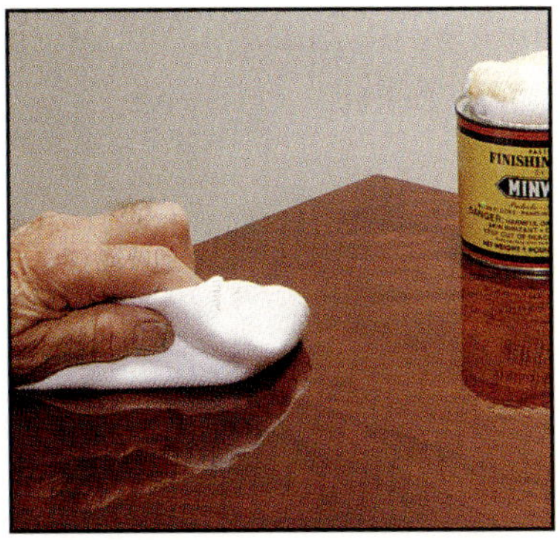
21 Finally, apply a thin coat of paste wax. Let the wax dry thoroughly. Then buff with a soft cloth to achieve desired luster.

Cleaning up an old chair

Pictures and text for *Cleaning Up An Old Chair* by Rosario Capotosto.

Wear areas and changes in color gave this old rocking chair a character that was too good to lose by refinishing it.

Three-step rejuvenation process of cleaning, buffing and finishing retains original look while adding new life.

There's one important fact you have to face about refinishing an old piece. When the job is done, you no longer own an original chunk of history, you own a hybrid—a piece with materials and design from the past, combined with a high-tech finish of the present. While refinishing may be the only solution for many examples, there are times when the original finish is best left in place.

Take this Windsor-style chair as an example. When it was found in an antique shop, it stood out—not only because of its sensitive design, but because the original finish enhanced the chair's character. Areas of wear on the armrests and back had lightened the dark stain, producing gentle transitions in tone that no refinishing job could duplicate. The chair did need some help, however. The finish was dull and dirty and some spindles had come loose. The strategy, therefore, was to first restore the chair's structural integrity and then rejuvenate the finish cosmetically.

There are no hard-and-fast rules for deciding when to refinish or when simply to clean up the old finish. Bear in mind, however, that an old piece of furniture is more than just a design in wood, it's a complete example of the techniques and styles of the past. More than that, it tells a story. Sometimes, that story is just too interesting to rewrite.

Structural Repairs

It's not uncommon for the joints in old furniture to have loosened. Of all furniture types, chairs are the most prone to this problem. Chairs handle a greater load than other pieces—and the load is dynamic. Combine this with the natural tendency for spindles to loosen due to expansion and contraction caused by seasonal changes in humidity, and you're almost guaranteed to have a few repairs to make before concentrating on the finish.

Begin by determining which joints are sound and which need attention. You can use a Quick-Grip Spreader tool to spring apart the loose joints. This tool is similar to a Quick-Grip Clamp, except that it works in reverse—it spreads apart parts for disassembly.

If possible, leave intact joints alone. If you must take a good joint apart, however, inject a little vinegar to soften the glue. Then, use a rubber mallet or dead-blow mallet to tap the joints loose. Always protect the work with a cloth pad to prevent marring.

With the loose joints apart, scrape away the old glue with a chisel and file (Fig. 1). This is important because the new glue won't adhere to the old. Be careful not to remove any wood because the fit won't be as good and the joint will fail when stresses are applied. Then, apply white or yellow carpenter's glue and reassemble the joints.

Don't try to ensure against future joint failure by using epoxy. While this adhesive will work, the joint will be impossible to disassemble if repairs are necessary on other components of the chair at a future date. If the reassembly time will be longer than a few minutes, use hide glue to increase the time before the glue sets.

After applying the glue and reinstalling the spindles, clamp the components together until the glue has dried. Ordinary clamps are of little value for gripping the irregular configuration of this splayed-leg chair. You can use band clamps for the job, or try the tourniquet clamp that was used here (Fig. 2).

1 After spreading apart the loose joints, prepare for gluing by using a chisel and file to clean off the old glue.

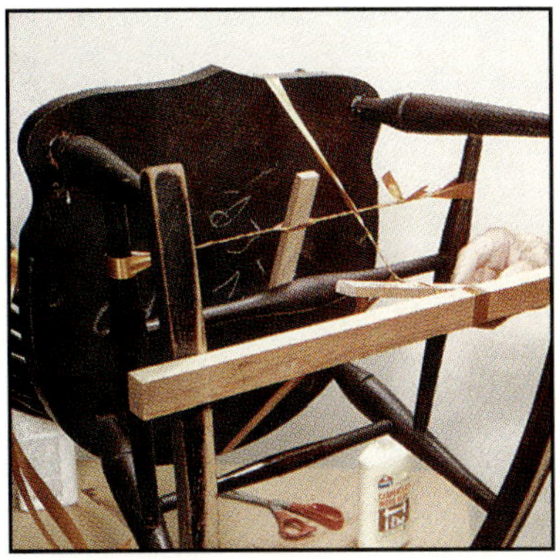

2 Apply glue to the joints and reassemble. Use a shopmade tourniquet clamp or band clamp to hold components together.

Wind a flat cloth band or strong ribbon around the spindles to be clamped. Then, place a stick through the ribbon windings. Rotate the stick to twist the ribbon and draw the spindles together tightly. You also can use rope in place of the cloth band or ribbon. Rope may mar the spindles, however, so be sure to pad them with cloth first.

After the clamps are in place, use a damp cloth to wipe away any excess glue. Be sure to remove all the glue from the original finish.

Restoration

There are several products available for rejuvenating an old finish. First, you need a cleaner such as Formby's Furniture Cleaner to remove dirt, grease and wax buildup, or you can simply use mineral spirits. Check for minor surface imperfections, or a dull appearance. If these are a problem, use a paste polishing compound. Then, apply a paste wax or wipe-on polish to restore the desired luster.

You also can opt to give your chair a complete treatment with Formby's Furniture Face Lift. This kit includes Cleansing Liquid, Buffing Cream, Face Lift Finish, and three applicator pads. The kit is designed for use only on finishes that are sound and not worn through. Before starting with any product, test for compatibility on an inconspicuous area to be sure the finish won't dissolve.

Begin by thoroughly wetting an applicator pad with the cleansing liquid. Then, rub the surface in a circular motion to remove wax and grime (Fig. 3). Apply a liberal coat of buffing cream and buff gently for a few minutes to remove light finish scratches (Figs. 4 and 5). Finally, use a finishing pad to apply the Face Lift Finish. Wipe on a thin, even coat, and reapply after about 4 hours for extra protection (Fig. 6).

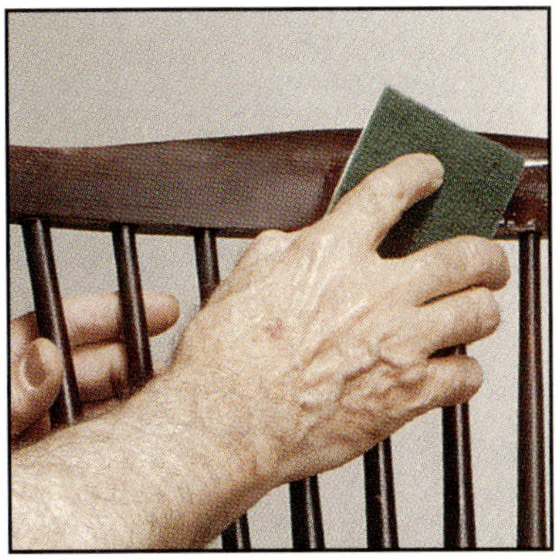

3 Use a furniture cleaner to remove all dirt, grime and old wax. Apply the cleaner with a soft pad in circular motions.

4 To remove minor surface scratches and blemishes, use a polishing compound. Rub each area for several minutes.

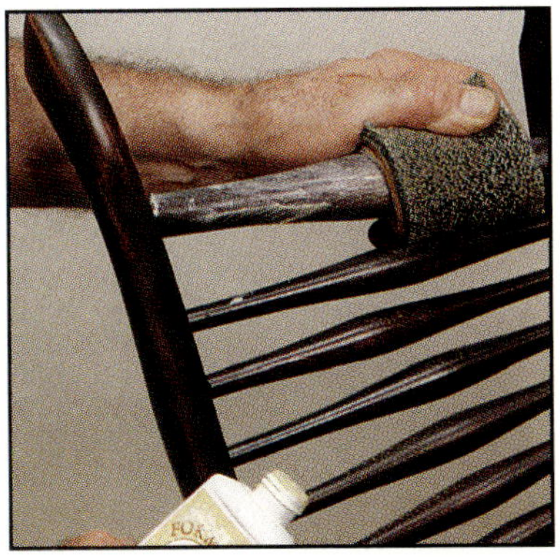

5 To clean up the chair spindles, wrap the cloth or applicator pad around them and polish along their length.

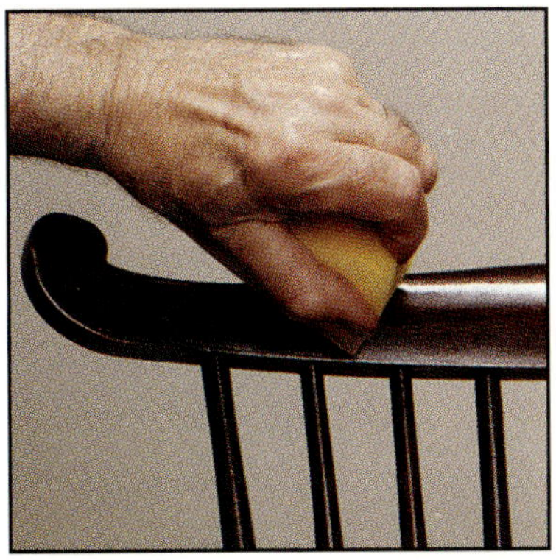

6 Apply Face Lift Finish with the felt-faced applicator pad. Wipe on the finish in thin, even coats.

FINISH REPAIR

If your original finish has a few defects that you just can't live with, a complete refinishing isn't your only alternative. Often, small problems can be made right with a few simple techniques. The materials you need are available through woodworking catalogs and finish supply outlets.

Although blistered and chipped pieces of veneer aren't finish problems, you should take care of them before finishing. To fix blistered veneer, apply heat with an iron. Place kraft paper between the iron and the work, and use medium heat. The heat softens the glue and gentle pressure holds the veneer in place.

If the veneer is chipped, select a sample of the same species, and test stain it to match the finish color. Then, use a knife to trim the chipped area and cut the patch veneer to fit. After gluing it in place and trimming, apply a finish to blend with the original. Veneer sample kits are available through mail-order catalogs and are a good source for patching veneers.

Use a clothes iron with kraft paper underneath to flatten blistered veneer. Keep the iron on medium heat.

Repair chipped veneer with a patch veneer of the same species. Cut patch to fit trimmed area and stain to match.

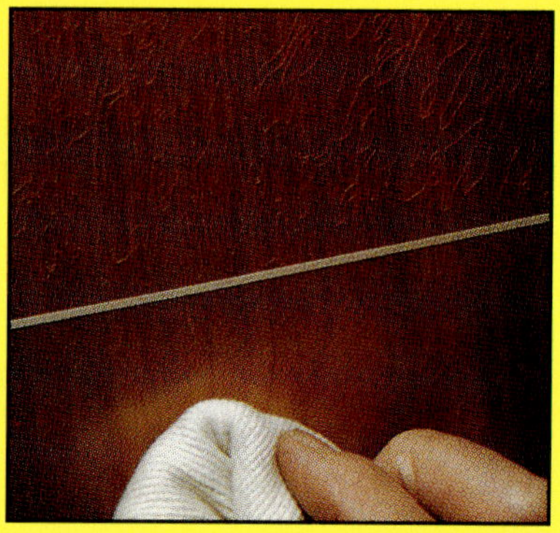

Restore alligatored lacquer by wiping with a lacquer-thinner dampened cloth. Small artist's brush handles fine scratches.

Small scratches and holes also can be filled with a wax pencil. These are available in a range of wood colors.

Use the burn-in method with a shellac stick to fill deep scratches, dents and gouges. Practice first on scrap stock.

Before attempting any finish repair, try to determine the type of finish on the wood. To test for shellac, use a small brush to dab denatured alcohol on an inconspicuous spot. If the finish dissolves, it's shellac. To test for lacquer, repeat the process with lacquer thinner. If the lacquer thinner doesn't dissolve the finish, but just crinkles and lifts it, chances are you're dealing with a standard varnish. If the lacquer thinner has no effect, you're probably dealing with polyurethane.

Scratches are common finish defects. If they're shallow and haven't penetrated the wood—and if the finish is shellac or lacquer—you can blend the finish over the scratch. Using alcohol or lacquer thinner, depending on whether the finish is shellac or lacquer respectively, apply a small amount with an artist's brush to the scratch. Repeat until the finish dissolves and flows together to subdue the scratch.

Alligatored lacquer finishes are characterized by a network of fine surface cracks caused by the expansion and contraction of the wood under a brittle surface coating. To remedy the problem, dampen a soft cloth with lacquer thinner and rub it over the surface. You can repeat the process, but don't overdo it or apply too much pressure to avoid cutting through the finish.

Another way to handle small scratches is to use a wax pencil designed for finish touchups. These are available in a range of wood-tone colors and also can handle small holes. Scratches, dents and gouges can be repaired with a shellac stick of the appropriate color. Called *burning in*, the process uses a special knife called a burn-in knife to apply the shellac stick material to the surface defect.Use a soot-free alcohol lamp to heat the burn-in knife (a grapefruit knife also works). Then, apply the stick to the hot blade held over the blemish, allowing the melted material to drip onto it. Before the patch hardens, use the clean face of the hot knife to compress the material. This process is tricky, so be sure to practice it before working on good furniture. The knife temperature must be just right—if it's too hot, it can damage the surrounding finish.

Use a special liquid abrasive with a felt pad to level the patch without damaging the surrounding finish. Then, apply a burn-in sealer to the area and apply a finish to blend in with the surrounding surface.

Furniture design

A style is a collection of characteristics and general rules for how they're combined in a finished product. In furniture design, styles are defined primarily by shapes, proportions and detailing.

While style names often refer to a period in history, this is not always the case. They also can refer to a philosophy or an influential designer. For example, the term *Federal* refers to furniture that was made during the Federal period while *Chippendale* refers to work of a certain period that bears a stylistic association with the designs of Thomas Chippendale. Of course, you can no longer build furniture that belongs to a historic period, but you can build pieces in the style of a period. In this way, an understanding of styles provides a starting point as well as an appreciation for traditional forms and their impact on design today.

American Colonial

The early American colonists didn't start making elegant furniture the moment they stepped off the boat. It took time to develop a socioeconomic structure to support skilled workers. During this time, it's likely that home-grown woodworking existed on a fairly rough-and-ready level with finer pieces being made in England. It's not surprising, though, that when American workshops became established, they produced work based on current styles across the Atlantic.

Jacobean

The earliest work, dating from about the middle of the 17th century, is referred to as *Jacobean* or more popularly, *Pilgrim* furniture. It's characterized by heavy turnings used for legs and spindles, or split in half and applied to a surface for decoration. This style also features elaborate relief carving, usually of a geometric or floral motif and often accented with applied moldings that divide areas into geometric shapes. The wood is usually oak and/or pine, and painted ornamentation was popular.

A chest of this period, what we might call a blanket chest today, typically used frame-and-panel construction, although the simple pegged, or later nailed, 6-board chest was also evident. As the basic chest with a hinged lid developed, it was enhanced by a shallow bottom drawer. Eventually, the entire chest was filled with drawers and the hinged lid was discarded, creating a chest of drawers. Small, shallow chests, called *desk boxes*, had sloping or flat hinged lids and were used to hold books and writing materials.

In terms of chair design, the Jacobean style is represented by the Brewster chair and the Carver chair. Both are constructed of heavy turned spindles—the Brewster chair differs in the rows of vertical spindles spanning the rails both above and below the seat. Another type of chair, called the *Wainscot* chair, features a back and seat made from flat boards ornamented with carving.

William & Mary

The William & Mary style introduced changes in materials—walnut and maple supplanting oak and pine—and used veneering as a way to create ornamentation through highly figured, naturally decorative wood.

Small desk boxes were placed on stands, and the lid was now hinged at the front so it could be opened for writing. The desk box was also united with a chest of drawers and eventually acquired a cupboard to produce the secretary we're familiar with today.

Although turned legs remain in William & Mary pieces, the profiles are less bulbous and the heavy relief carving of Jacobean designs is replaced by more refined detailing. Drawer openings are frequently accented by thin, half-round strips called *cock beads* and frame-and-panel doors acquire the characteristic arched-top panel based on a S-shaped cyma, or ogee, curve.

Perhaps the most notable furniture type introduced in this period is the *highboy*. This is a chest of drawers placed on a stand. The stand also has drawers and up to six turned legs connected by flat rails sawn to a curved profile. More refined highboys have an arched S-shaped curve motif in the front rail. The stand by itself is called a *lowboy* and is a precursor of today's dressing table.

The transition from Jacobean to William & Mary produced a variety of chair designs. Besides a general refining of detail and proportion, chairs with horizontal curved slats and banister-back chairs with vertical profiled slats became popular.

Queen Anne

Roughly 100 years after the settlement at Plymouth, a new design style, called *Queen Anne*, took the S-shaped curve and made it a more dominant visual component. The most striking example of this is the cabriole leg. Unlike the turnings of the previous styles, the bowed, offset cabriole leg created a smooth, graceful curve that grew from the floor to be continued around the entire piece.

Queen Anne chairs, for example, have cabriole legs at the front and simpler arched legs at the back. The back's central splat is based on a vase shape that further echoes the curves in the legs and back frame.

Queen Anne furniture also features carved shell motifs on the knees of cabriole legs, front panels of highboys and within corner cupboards. Frame-and-panel doors generally feature a half-round arch at the top of each panel. In terms of wood, walnut remained one of the favorites with maple and cherry also in use. Mahogany was beginning to achieve popularity.

Chippendale

Like earlier styles, Chippendale originated in England, and became part of the American furniture scene around the middle of the 18th century. It's rooted in a combination of French Rococo influences. Chinese design and ornamentation and a revival of English Gothic motifs—all held together in forms based on earlier work. The style was given its name in acknowledgement of Thomas Chippendale's work and his book of furniture designs, *The Gentleman And Cabinet-Maker's Director*.

The cabriole leg, broken pediments and arch-top panel doors are a few of the many components carried over from Queen Anne. To these, however, were added detail and ornamentation as yet unseen. Cabriole legs were carved with highly detailed ball-and-claw feet. Straight legs, a Chinese influence, became common on both chairs and tables.

This period also saw the introduction of the breakfront—a large cabinet with a central section flanked by two shallower and narrower side sections. Chests of drawers saw variation in serpentine designs that transformed the traditional flat front into an undulating symmetrical curve.

The wood of choice was mahogany, although walnut, maple and cherry were also used. Highly figured crotch-grain veneering in geometric patterns was a popular means of decoration.

Federal

The years after the American Revolution saw a new style emerging that was founded on a renewed interest in classical forms. The style, a reaction to the heavily ornamented Chippendale, was, to a large extent, introduced to American woodworkers through the work of George Hepplewhite and Thomas Sheraton.

Besides being more geometric, Federal furniture is lighter and more delicate than preceding styles. Details

include fine inlay, reeding, cock beads and refined turnings. Both veneering and painting are used as ornament. Chair and table legs are commonly square in section and tapered. Chair backs are either square cornered or curved and often feature elaborate pierced splats.

Of the chair types associated with the Federal period, one of the most popular is the Windsor chair. The Windsor was actually introduced to America well before this time, but it was in this period that it achieved widespread popularity. The design is characterized by spindle construction, splayed legs and a carved slab seat. Back design ranges from rod-back versions with straight uprights connected by a horizontal member, to oval-back chairs with a continuous bent-back frame. In chairs with arms, the arms may be integral with the bent-back member, or the back may be a separate assembly joined to a C-shaped armpiece. Seat outlines are either convex or accented with the S-shaped curve.

Duncan Phyfe

Some characteristics of Phyfe's work include vase-shaped pedestal table supports with three or four curved, or sabre legs, claw feed and cloverleaf-shaped tabletops. The legs were frequently ornamented with reeding or repetitive floral carvings and multiple beading was a common edge treatment for table- and cabinet-top edges. Broad surfaces such as tabletops and drawer fronts were generally veneered with mahogany, and the pieces were stained dark. Phyfe chairs have a lattice back, often with a lyre-shaped splat.

Victorian

When the Industrial Revolution was making its impact felt on both production techniques and the availability of products, users and makers of furniture were thinking of style less as a slow evolution and more as a library of existing possibilities. Victorian designers used style in a manner similar to the way we use it today—as a means to create cohesive settings based on a variety of influences. Makers began to draw from the past, producing furniture inspired by earlier periods, much in the same way we might make a dining suite based on Queen Anne design elements today.

Notable movements in Victorian furniture drew inspiration from Gothic, Renaissance, Elizabethan and Rococo styles. The makers relied on the ornamentation of a previous period to imbue their creations with a desired aesthetic effect, and heavy ornamentation is one of the hallmarks of Victorian furniture.

Victorian designers produced several new forms of furniture, most notably the circular ottoman, balloon-back chair and the single-end sofa. The wood used runs the gamut from rosewood to oak.

Shaker

The Shakers, a religious society with communities in various locations ranging from New York to New England and throughout the Midwest, produced furniture characterized by a desire for utility, economy and efficiency without sacrificing quality. The result is a clean, relatively unadorned style that, as seen alongside oth-

DUNCAN PHYFE

CHEST OF DRAWERS (1815)

SIDE CHAIR (1815)

VICTORIAN

ROMANESQUE-STYLE BOOKCASE (1840)

ROCOCO-STYLE ARMCHAIR (1860)

ers, appears sparse and institutional. In contrast to elaborate highboys, the typical Shaker chest of drawers is an almost featureless assemblage of flat boards, punctuated by simple turned drawer pulls. The plain turnings of a classic shaker chair are about as far as you can get from the carved cabriole legs and heavy ornamented turnings of mainstream styles. Shaker furniture, however, is anything but styleless, and the apparent emphasis on utility belies a subtle and restrained sense of detail and ornamentation. Even the most elemental pieces often use simple moldings. Chair turnings are sensitively tapered with carefully shaped finials, and the overall proportioning reflects a concern for balance that's rooted in aesthetic concerns as much as utilitarian requirements. The Shakers made furniture from available domestic hardwoods and pine.

Arts & Crafts

The Arts & Crafts movement represented a need to return to basics in design and construction, with an emphasis on utility, simplicity and individual craftsmanship.

Rooted in the work of two English designers, John Ruskin and William Morris, the American movement found expression through Charles and Henry Greene and Gustav Stickley. American Arts & Crafts examples are grouped more by common philosophical goals rather than by design detailing. Where some pieces may show Japanese, Renaissance or Gothic influence, others are characteristically unadorned and rely on functional requirements and joinery techniques to give the work identity. The joints themselves are part of a visual design, supplanting the need for traditional ornamentation. Stickley's furniture, in particular, is typified by straight lines and simple, straightforward joinery. A popular offshoot of the Arts & Crafts movement is the Mission style of furniture. It's characterized by simple rectangular designs, usually built from oak and stained dark.

Art Nouveau

Art Nouveau based its efforts not on copying natural forms and applying them as ornamentation, but by using nature as an inspiration of the entire design.

Art Nouveau is characterized by smoothly curving lines and graceful transitions through the form. The result is an almost sensuous and exotic composition of line. The typical Art Nouveau line begins as a slow S-shaped curve that terminates in a rapid whip-like end. While the intention is natural, the smooth curves and symmetry reflect a synthetic order where the design is a stylistic abstraction of natural form rather than a direct translation.

In America, Art Nouveau furniture never gained the popularity it found in Europe, although the movement was influential in graphic design and architecture. Pieces were, however, made on a production basis, particularly in the early 20th century.

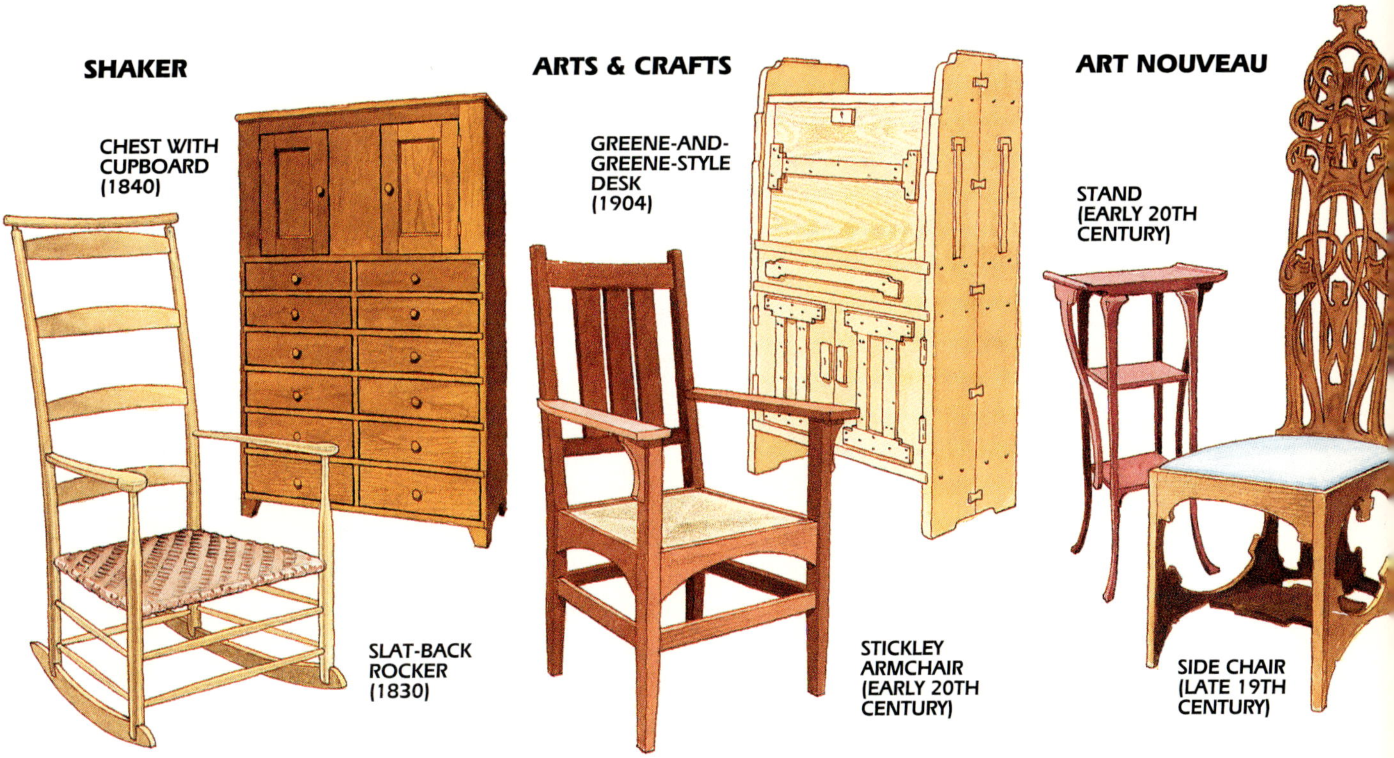

Porch planter

■ Using trees, flowers and shrubs to decorate your home is a great way to add color and warmth. The containers that most plants come in, however, leave much to be desired. The best solution to the problem is to make your own wooden planter boxes. The version shown here is designed for use indoors or on a covered porch. With its galvanized liner, it can handle direct planting. Or, the liner can be left out and the unit used to hold a potted plant.

Select-grade pine is readily available and takes a nice painted finish. If you want an unpainted look, cedar, cypress or redwood would be suitable.

Preparing the Pieces

First, cut 12 pieces of 3/4-in. stock to 2 1/4 in. wide and 24 in. long. Then, using a waterproof glue, laminate sets of three pieces face to face to produce four 2 1/4-in.-sq. × 24-in.-long blanks (Fig. 1). Crosscut the blanks to 20 in. and set aside the cutoffs to use for the finials. Use a jointer or hand plane to true and square two adjacent sides on each post blank, then use the table saw to rip the posts to the 2-in. finished dimension.

Porch Planter was written by Neal Barrett. Lead photo by John Griebsch, step-by-step photos by Neal Barrett. Technical art by Eugene Thompson.

Lay out the locations of the mortises in the posts and cut these with a plunge router and edge guide. It's best to use a spiral upcutting bit, as this type draws the chips out of the cut and plunges easily without burning. Square the mortise ends with a chisel (Fig. 2). Next, switch to a 1/4-in. bit and rout the grooves that hold the edges of the raised panels.

Rip and crosscut 5/4 stock to size for the rails, and lay out the tenons on the ends. Use a dado blade in the table saw to cut the tenons (Fig. 3). Then, adjust the blade height to cut the tenon shoulders. It's best to cut the tenons slightly oversize and pare them to finished dimension. Then, reset the dado blade and cut the panel grooves in the rail edges (Fig. 4).

Glue together 3/4-in. stock for the raised panels, trim them to final dimensions when the glue is dry and then sand, scrape or plane them smooth. Use a plate joiner to aid in aligning the panel boards (Fig. 5).

Cut the raised panel profile on the router table using a vertical panel-raising bit (Fig. 6). Use a tall router-table fence to support the workpiece. Make the cuts in several stages, moving the fence back slightly after each cut. Cut the end grain edges on all panels first. Thoroughly sand the panels with a small sanding block and 120-, 180- and 220-grit sandpaper.

Bore pilot holes in the post tops for securing the finials. Use a doweling jig to position the holes and to keep them square to the post end.

With its galvanized liner, this planter is ready for shrubs and small trees. Without the liner, it handles potted plants.

1 Begin each leg by gluing three 3/4 x 2 1/4-in. boards together. Use waterproof glue, and trim each blank to 2x2x20 in.

2 After cutting the leg mortises with a plunge router and guide fence, trim the ends square with a sharp chisel.

3 Cut the rail tenons with a dado blade. A stopblock clamped to a miter gauge extension ensures accurate repetitive cuts.

4 Reset the dado blade and make the 1/4-in.-wide x 1/2-in.-deep grooves in each rail. Use a push block to move work safely.

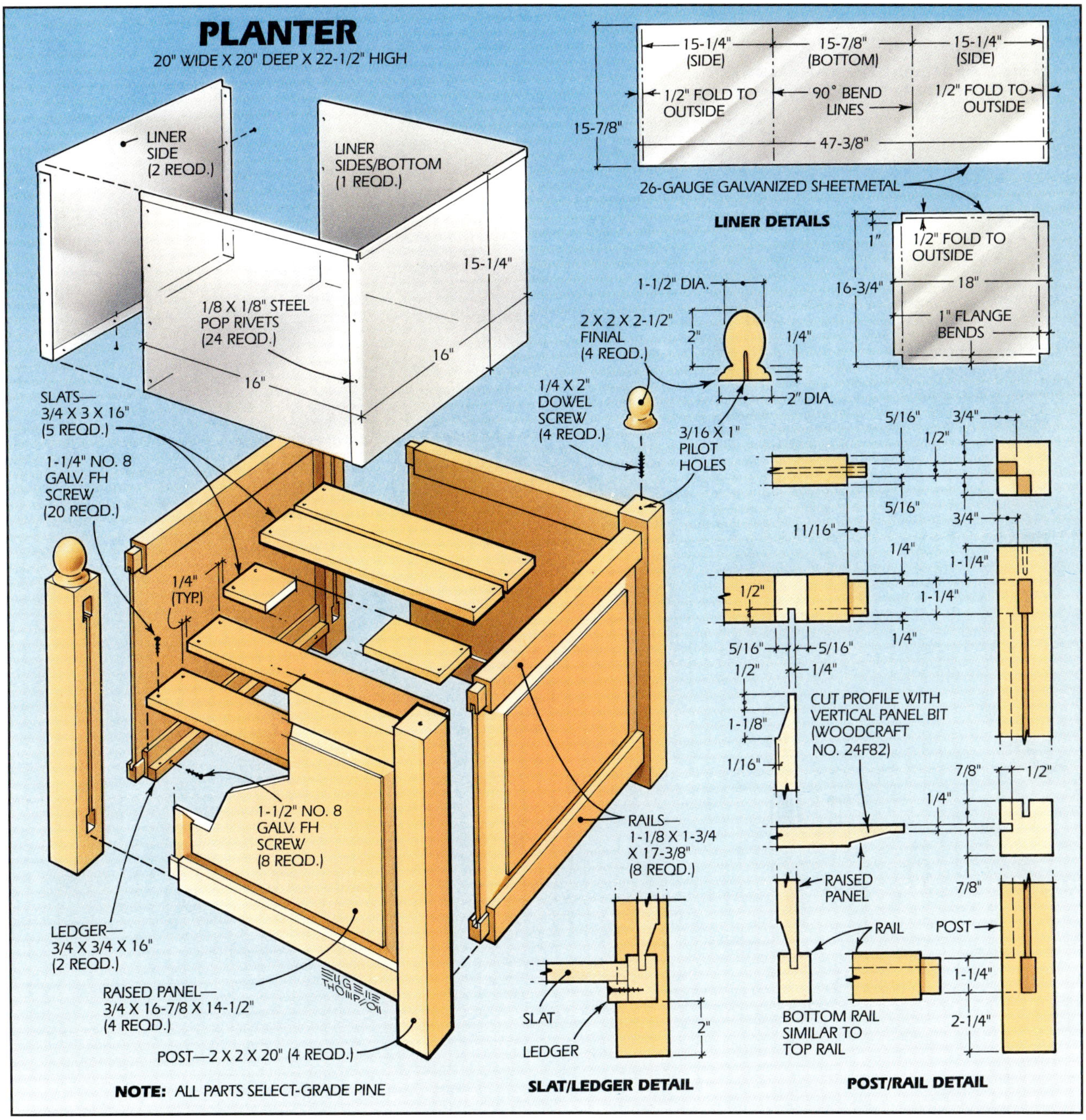

5 Make the side panels by gluing the narrower stock together. Use a plate joiner to ensure good alignment.

6 After trimming the panel to exact size, cut the raised panel profile on a router table with a vertical panel-raising bit.

7 Begin assembly by gluing two rails to one post. Then, slide panel into grooves, add opposite post and clamp joints tight.

Assembly

Apply glue to the mortises and tenons for one side of the planter. Insert the rails into their mortises in one post, and slide the panel into position (Fig. 7). Be sure to avoid getting any glue in the panel groove. Put the second post in place and clamp. Compare diagonals to make sure that the assembly is square, and adjust if necessary (Fig. 8).

Assemble the opposite side in the same manner. Join the two sides and the remaining rails and two panels on a flat surface to avoid a twist in the planter frame.

Cut the ledger strips and slats to size. Bore and countersink pilot holes in the strips and slats. Install the strips to opposite bottom rails using screws and glue (Fig. 9). Then, install the slats with screws only.

Mount one of the finial blanks in the lathe, and use a gouge to turn it to a 2-in.-dia. cylinder. Make a template of the finial profile and transfer the critical transition points of the finial design onto the cylinder. Shape the finial leaving only a small attachment at the top end to hold the work in the lathe (Fig. 10). Sand the piece while in the lathe, then remove, cut off the top stub, and sand it smooth.

Bore pilot holes in the finials and use locking pliers to thread a steel dowel screw in each. Then install the finials on the corner posts and sand the planter. Apply a coat of exterior primer and two or three coats of exterior latex enamel.

Making the Liner

Begin by drawing the pieces on 26-gauge sheetmetal. Use a felt-tipped pen to mark the metal and make the cuts with a pair of heavy-duty shears (Fig. 11).

Mark the bend lines as shown on the drawing. Then, clamp two ¾-in.-thick hardwood strips on either side of a sheet at a bend line at the top edge of the liner. Use the wooden strips as a lever to bend the metal 90° (Fig. 12). Then, use sheetmetal pliers to tightly fold over this top edge and complete the remaining top edges in the same way.

Next, make the two 90° bends in the long strip of metal that forms the bottom and two sides. Finally, make the bends in the two remaining sides to form the tabs that join these sides to the rest of the liner.

Join the pieces together with ⅛ × ⅛-in. steel pop rivets. Use locking pliers or clamps to hold the pieces together while you drill ⅛-in. pilot holes. Then install the pop rivets to assemble the liner (Fig. 13).

For a truly waterproof liner, apply silicone caulk to all interior seams and rivets. Let the caulk cure for 24 hours before filling the liner with soil.

8 Check that the assembly is square by measuring opposite diagonals. If necessary, loosen the clamps and adjust.

9 Install the ledgers to two opposite lower rails with screws and glue. Countersink pilot holes for flat head screws.

10 Use a template as a guide to shape finials. Leave a stub at top end and sand while in lathe. Then, sand stub smooth.

11 Use a felt marker and straightedge to lay out and bend lines on sheetmetal. Make cuts with heavy-duty shears.

12 To bend sheetmetal neatly, clamp hardwood strips at bend line. Then, use strips to bend metal to 90° turn.

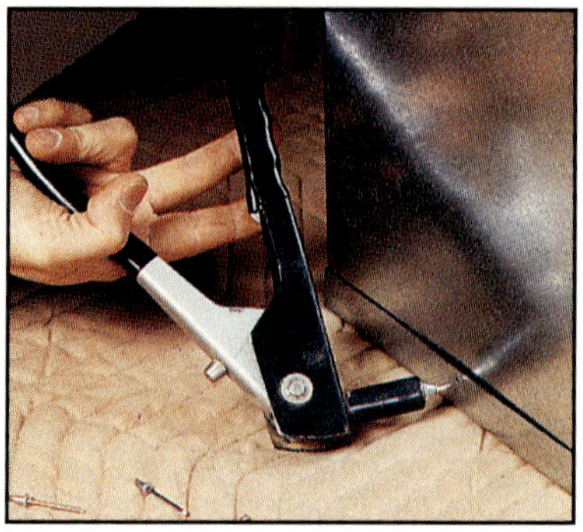

13 To assemble liner, first bore ⅛-in. holes, then install pop rivets. Use silicone caulk to make seams watertight.

Mahogany game table

■ This fold-over game table is a well-bred piece of furniture with a history going back to 18th-century England. Tables of that period had a fold-over top that was supported by a swing-out leg. But this version follows the novel game-table design that evolved in the 19th century. It features an offset top that rotates a quarter turn so that both leaves of the table are supported evenly on the fixed rectangular base.

The table is both functional and decorative, usually being displayed with its folding top resting against the wall. The table has a storage area beneath the top for playing cards, stationery or silverware, should you use it as a small dining table. In keeping with tradition, the table is built from solid mahogany and has a lustrous hand-rubbed finish.

The table is a good project for a reasonably experienced hobbyist, in that it requires lathe work. Lacking a lathe, you can build it with gracefully tapered legs, rather than turned ones.

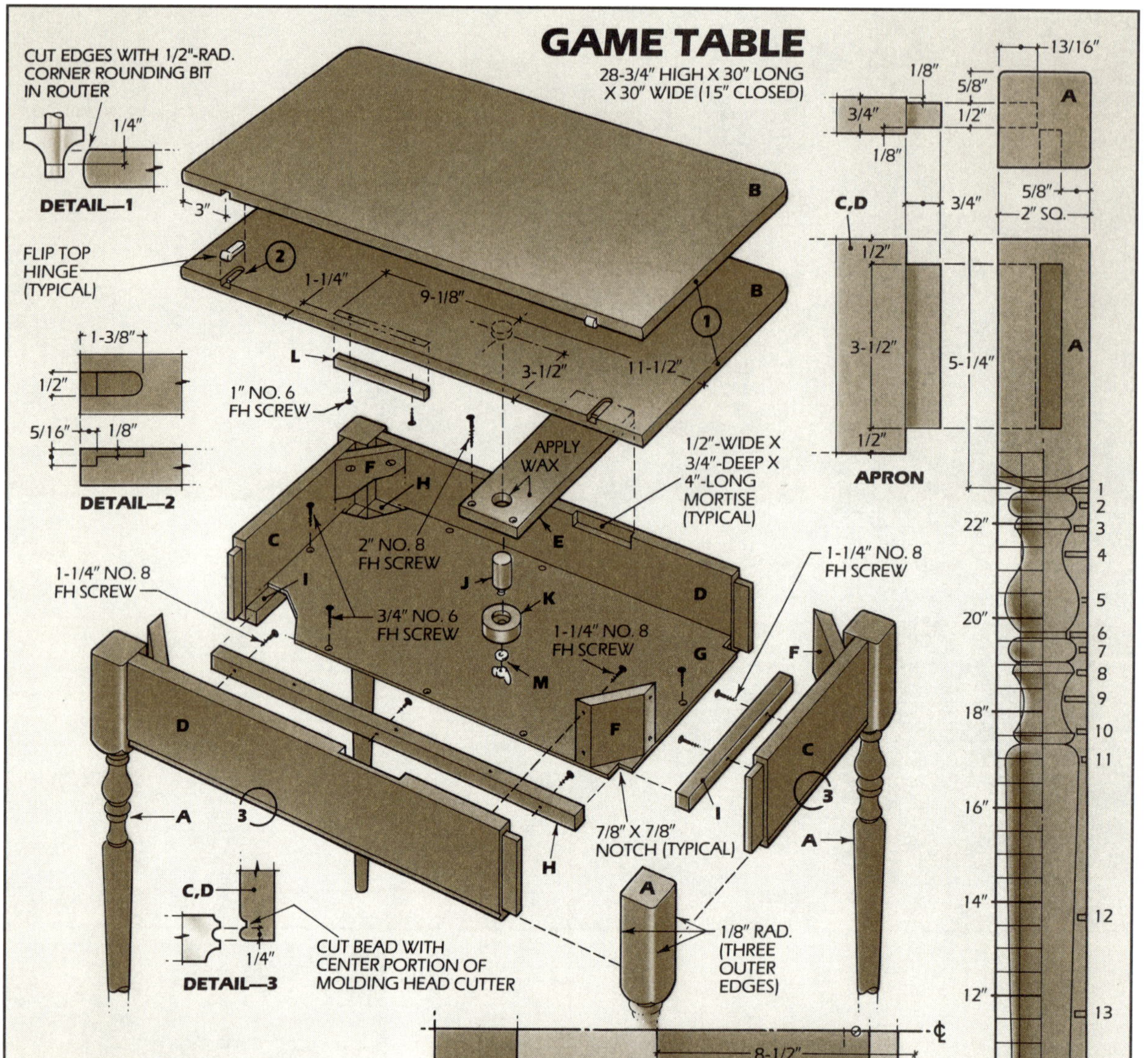

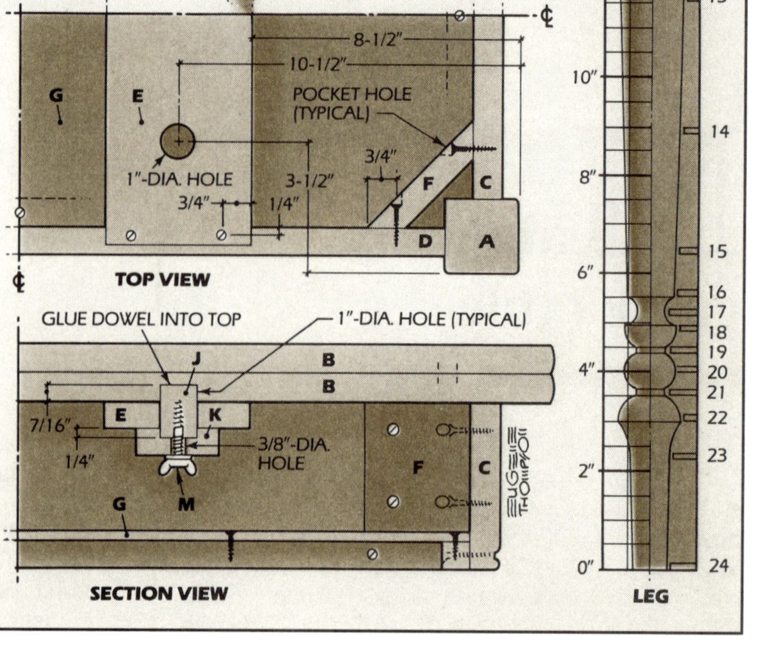

MATERIALS LIST—GAME TABLE

Key	No.	Size and description (use)
A	4	2 x 2 x 28" mahogany (leg)
B	2	¾ x 15 x 30" mahogany (top)
C	2	¾ x 4½ x 11½" mahogany (apron)
D	2	¾ x 4½ x 25½" mahogany (apron)
E	1	¾ x 4 x 12½" mahogany (brace)
F	4	¾ x 3½ x 4" mahogany (brace)
G	1	¼ x 11½ x 25½" mahogany (panel)
H	2	¾ x ¾ x 24" mahogany (cleat)
I	2	¾ x ¾ x 10" mahogany (cleat)
J	1	1"-dia. x 1⁷⁄₁₆" mahogany (pivot)
K	1	¾ x 2¼"-dia. mahogany (cap)
L	1	⁵⁄₁₆ x ½ x 7" mahogany (stop)
M	1	⁵⁄₁₆ x 2" (bolt, washer, nut)

Misc.: No. 20 biscuits; sandpaper; yellow or hide glue; Behlen Solar Lux Stain (Medium Red Mahogany, Behlen product No. B5033A115), Solar Lux Retarder (Behlen product No. B500-00A25): stain and retarder available from Garrett Wade, 161 Avenue of the Americas, New York, NY 10013; shellac; alcohol; paste wood filler; sanding sealer; Deft Gloss Clear Wood Finish; and flip-top hinge from Armor Products, P.O. Box 445, East Northport, NY 11731.

1 Lay out the mortises in the legs. Remove the bulk of the mortise waste by boring holes with a drill press.

2 Clamp the legs to the bench. Using a razor-sharp chisel, pare the sides of the mortise parallel and the ends square.

3 Make a nick using a skew chisel where the square leg turns round. Note the leg pattern taped to the wall.

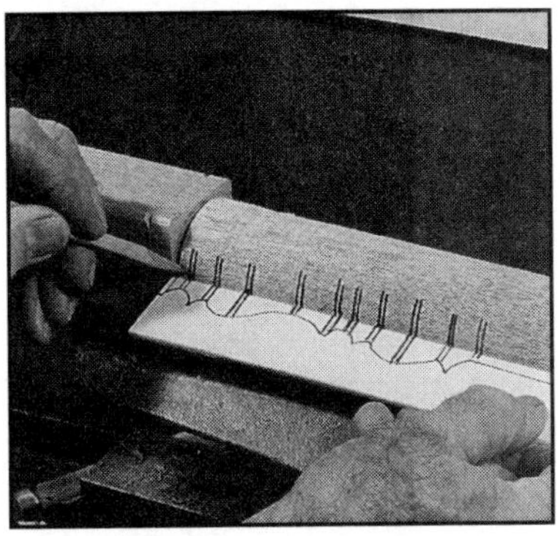

4 Use the half pattern of the leg to mark out the depth cuts that establish the diameters at key points.

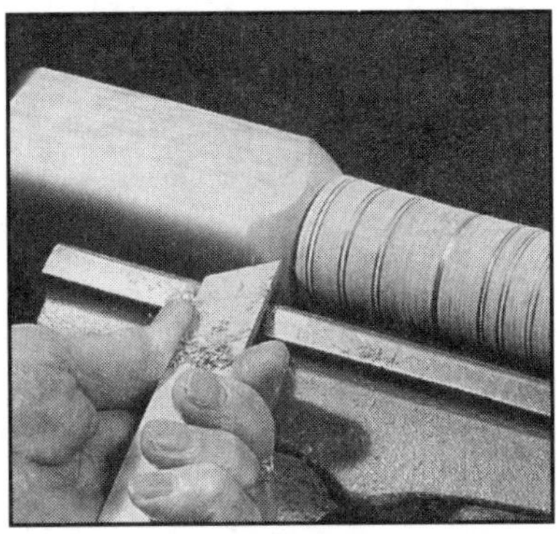

5 Use the skew chisel to turn the round shoulder on the leg. The nick cut made earlier prevents splintering.

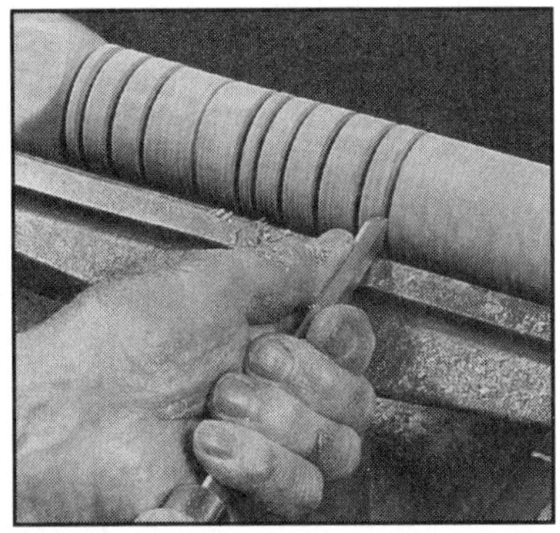

6 Using the parting tool, make each of the depth cuts. Back off from the parting tool occasionally to let it cool.

The Legs

Glue and clamp together a slab wide enough to make four legs. Rip leg blanks from the slab on the table saw.

Next, mark out the leg mortises. Then bore a series of overlapping holes to remove the bulk of the mortise. Pare the mortise to dimension using a chisel (Figs. 1 and 2). Then draw a full-size paper pattern of the leg. Include the diameter sizing grooves at key locations, and hang the drawing behind the lathe.

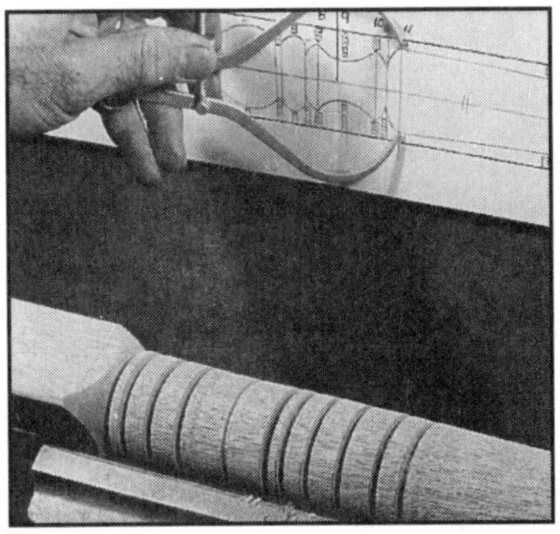

7 Set the caliper to the finished diameter of the leg at a given depth groove. Note the groove number.

8 Measure the diameter of the leg at the corresponding depth groove. Cut the depth groove until the caliper fits.

Carefully center the turning blank on the lathe, because any error here will result in a lopsided shoulder where the square meets the round. To turn the shoulder from square to round, draw two guidelines around the square at $4\frac{3}{4}$ in. and $5\frac{1}{4}$ in. from the top. Hold the skew chisel vertically, toe down and heel up, and make a nicking cut at the upper mark (Fig. 3). This prevents splintering. Next, run in a parting tool to cut the finished diameter of the flat band along the lower guideline.

Now, use the gouge to rough form the cylinder. Starting about 3 in. from the groove, feed the gouge toward the groove to form the round. Then reverse the feed direction from left to right, toward the tailstock to complete the rounding. Pass a wide skew chisel over the cylinder to smooth it.

Make pencil marks on the cylinder at the locations of the depth gauging grooves (Fig. 4). These can be set off with a rule using the drawing for reference or, better yet, with a half-section pattern of the leg drawn on cardboard. This is held to the cylinder to transfer the marks.

Shape the curved shoulder with either the skew or spear-point chisels (Fig. 5). The diameter gauging grooves are next. Use a caliper for checking the grooves, and run in the parting tool to within $\frac{1}{16}$ in. of

9 Shape the remaining parts of the turned section using the gouge, skew and spearpoint chisels.

10 The leg becomes thinner, and not as stiff, as it is turned down. Use a steady rest to prevent chattering.

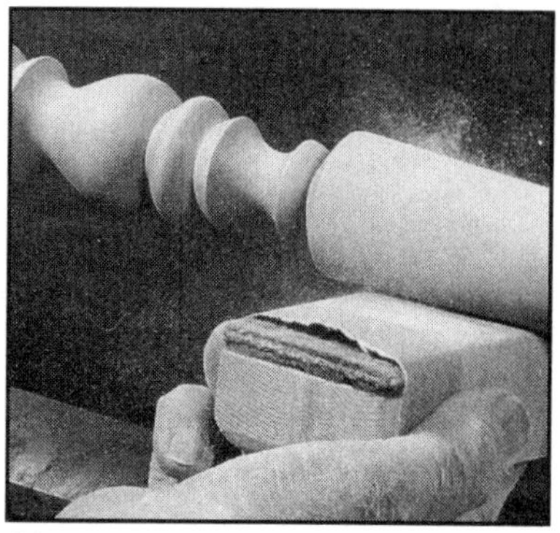

11 Use a felt-pad sanding block and 220-grit paper to smooth the long, tapered portion of the turning.

the finished diameters at the designated locations (Fig. 6). Adjust the caliper to the required setting directly on the drawing (Figs. 7 and 8). Use the roundnose, spearpoint skew chisels and gouge to form the contours (Fig. 9). As the leg becomes thinner, it may chatter. To prevent this, use a steady rest (Fig. 10).

When the shaping has been completed, remove the toolrest, then turn up the lathe's speed to 1000 rpm for sanding. Start with 120-grit paper and work through 150- 180- and 220-grit. Use strips of sandpaper to smooth the contoured areas, but use a felt-backed sanding block when sanding the taper (Fig. 11).

The Top

Rip and crosscut the boards for the top slightly oversize and joint their edges. Then group them for the most desirable appearance while arranging their annular rings alternately facing up and down.

Joining plates were used here to join the boards together, but dowels can be used as well. To cut the plate slots, place the boards on a flat surface in the order in which they will be glued together. Mark the biscuit locations and cut the slots, holding the biscuit joiner and the board flat to the bench (Fig. 12).

Glue and clamp the boards together (Fig. 13). Prevent the panel from bowing under clamping pressure by

12 Use a plate joiner to join the boards for the top. Hold the workpiece and the joiner on a flat, clean surface.

13 Glue and clamp the top panels. Use cauls to keep the assembly from bowing. Waxed cauls will repel glue.

14 Push a cabinet scraper over the panels to remove the dried glue at the joints and to level the panels.

15 While cutting the hinge mortises, guide the router with a simple frame. Clamp and tack nail the frame in place.

16 Cut a notch for the hinge knuckle at the rear of the mortise. Each half of the mortise is notched to receive a knuckle.

17 Cut the ellipse on the edge of the top panels by raising the router bit up so it won't cut to full depth.

using cauls. Wax the cauls' edges where they come in contact with the glue. This prevents the glue from sticking to the caul. After the glue has set, remove the dried glue and small differences in height between the boards using a cabinet scraper (Fig. 14).

Cut the mortise for the flip-top hinge with a router and a ½-in-dia. straight bit. Make a guide frame, and cut the mortises in both leaves at the same time (Fig. 15). The frame is made with four strips of plywood ¼ in. × 1½ in. wide. The size of the frame opening is dictated by the size of your router base. After cutting the mortise, chisel out the notch for the hinge knuckle (Fig. 16).

Cut the radii on the outside corners of the leaves using a sabre saw, then set up the router with a ball-bearing ½-in.-rad. corner rounding bit. To achieve the elliptical edge, adjust the bit so about half its cutting edge projects beyond the base. Shape the edge by making a pass from both sides (Fig. 17).

Finally, use a 1-in.-dia. Forstner or spur bit to bore the flat-bottomed hole that seats the pivot dowel.

18 Cut the apron tenons on the table saw using a dado head. Butt the apron against the stopblock to make the cut.

19 After the tenons are cut, shape the bead on the aprons with a molding head installed in the table saw.

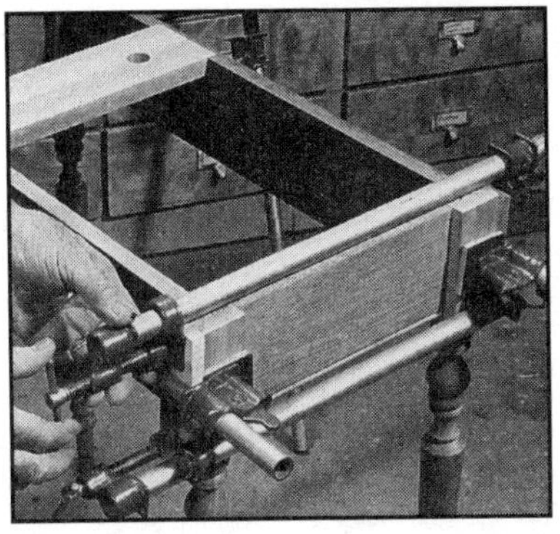

20 Glue and clamp together the aprons and legs in one step. Use blocks under the clamp jaws to prevent marring.

21 Dry assemble the pivot, then position the top on the base to check for movement. Mark the pivot stop position.

Aprons and Assembly

Rip and crosscut the apron stock. Use the miter gauge and an auxiliary fence with a stopblock to guide the aprons as you push them over the dado head in the table saw (Fig. 18). To cut the decorative apron bead, use a molding head in the table saw (Fig. 19).

Next, use a chisel to cut the pivot brace mortises on the inside of the aprons. Dry fit the legs and aprons and bore pilot screwholes in the pivot brace and aprons. Glue and clamp the legs and aprons (Fig. 20), then glue and clamp the pivot brace.

Cut the cleats and the bin's bottom panel to size. Temporarily attach the cleats with screws, then remove them. Cut the pivot dowel to size, then bore the pilot hole and install the hanger bolt in it. Cut a 2¼-in.-dia. disc for the pivot cap, then bore and counterbore the hole for the dowel and bolt. Temporarily install the pivot and the top (Fig. 21). Check the hinge operation, and pivot the top around. Mark the position of the stop. Disassemble the pivot, stop and hinges to allow for finishing.

Mahogany Game Table was written by Rosario Capotosto. Photos by J.R. Rost and Rosario Capotosto. Technical art by Eugene Thompson.

Finish

To obtain the deep rich mahogany color, apply Behlen's Medium Red Mahogany Solar Lux Stain mixed at a ratio of 6 parts stain to 1 part retarder. The retarder helps you apply this fast-drying stain without leaving brush marks.

Apply the stain to one section at a time, then wipe off any excess with a soft cloth. Allow the stain to dry overnight, then seal it with a wash coat of shellac (6 parts alcohol to 1 part 3-pound-cut shellac). Allow the sealer to dry at least 4 hours, and apply a mahogany-colored paste wood filler. If you can't get mahogany-colored filler, use natural-colored filler and add burnt-umber Japan color to suit.

Apply the filler in the direction of the grain using a stiff brush. When the coating loses its wet look, wipe off the excess with a coarse cloth such as burlap. Wipe across the grain to remove the excess, then wipe with the grain using a soft cloth. Allow the filler to dry 24 hours, sand it lightly with 220-grit paper to remove filler residue, then wipe off dust.

Apply a coat of sanding sealer, and again sand lightly. Wipe off the dust with a tack cloth, then apply three coats of Deft Gloss Clear Wood Finish. Allow 4 hours of drying between coats.

Apply sealer to the underside of the lower tabletop and the apron backs. Install the corner braces and the project is complete.

Rocking chair

Rocking Chair was written by Neal Barrett. Photos by Neal Barrett and J.R. Rost. Technical art by Eugene Thompson.

■ There are few things in life more restful than sitting in a well-designed rocking chair. It's hard to say whether the relaxation comes from the rocking motion or the gentle, rhythmic squeak of the floorboards. These days, when most of us have so many demands pulling us in all directions, it's a great pleasure to have a spot dedicated to relaxation.

This chair is built of solid birch, and its construction is a relatively straightforward affair. Since the round back posts are longer than the distance between centers on most home lathes, these were shaped on a router table. The front- and back-seat support rails, as well as the side rails, are cut from ¾-in.-dia. dowels, available at any lumberyard. This rocker is painted but it would look good if it were simply stained and varnished.

Making Posts

Begin the project by making two full-size drawings: one of the front post profiles and another showing how the post and rails intersect. The second should include the rail centerlines.

Cut the blanks for the four posts, but leave the front posts ½ in. long so they can be turned on the lathe. Then, mark the centerlines across the post tops and bore the ½-in.-dia. holes for the finials and dowels.

ROCKING CHAIR

26-5/8" WIDE X 35" DEEP X 43" HIGH

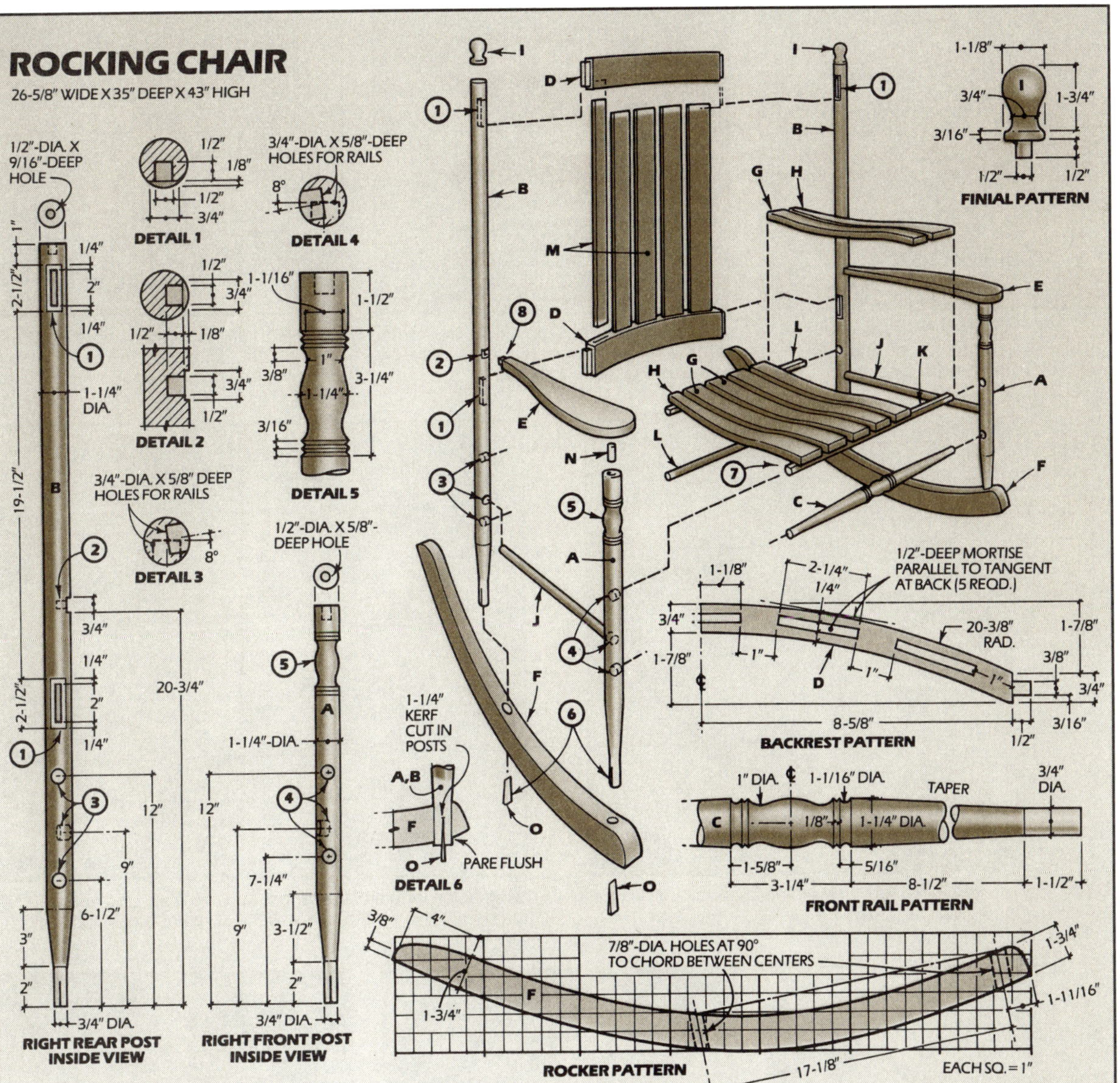

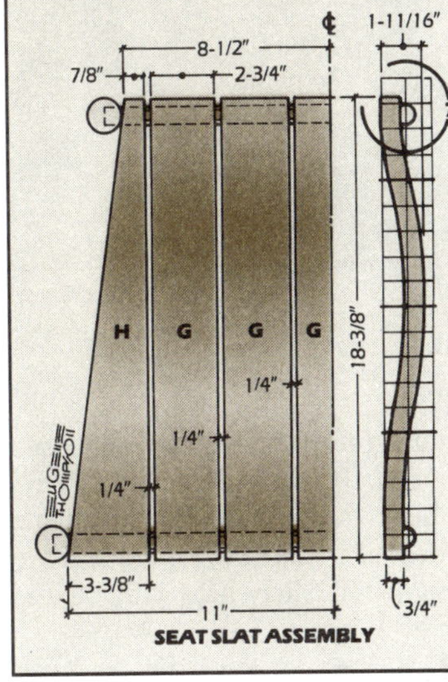

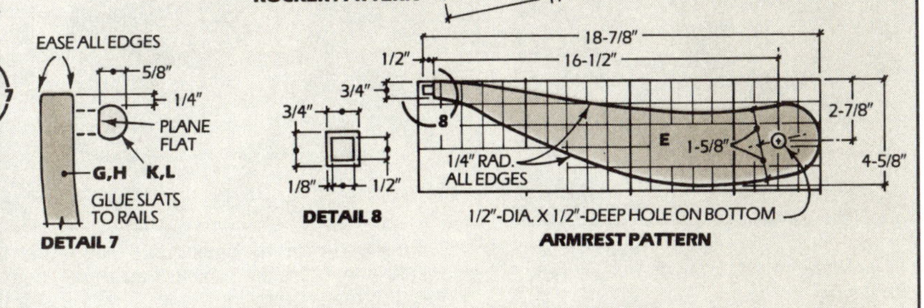

MATERIALS LIST—ROCKING CHAIR

Key	No.	Size description (use)
A	2	1¼"-dia. x 20¾" birch (post)
B	2	1¼"-dia. x 41¼" birch (back post)
C	1	1¼"-dia. x 23¼" birch (rail)
D	2	2½ x 2⅝ x 18¼" birch (backrest)
E	2	¾ x 4¾ x 18⅞" birch (armrest)
F	2	1½ x 6 x 35" birch (rocker)
G	5	1$\frac{11}{16}$ x 2¾ x 18⅜" birch (slat)
H	2	1$\frac{11}{16}$ x 3⅜ x 18⅜" birch (slat)
I	2	1⅛"-dia. x 2$\frac{7}{16}$" birch (finial)
J	2	¾"-dia. x 17⅛" birch (siderail)
K	1	¾"-dia. x 23¼" birch (seat support)
L	2	¾"-dia. x 18¼" birch (back rail)
M	5	¼ x 2¼ x 20½" birch (back slat)
N	2	½"-dia. x 1" birch (post dowel)
O	4	⅛ x ¾ x 2" birch (wedge)

Misc.: Sandpaper, glue, exterior-grade alkyd primer and enamel.

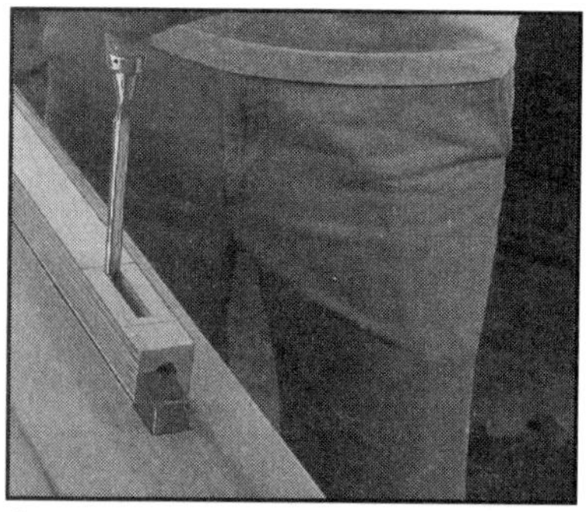

1 Cut the backrest mortises in the back posts with a plunge router, and then chop the ends of the mortises square.

2 Shape the chair posts on the router table using a large rounding-over bit. Make four passes per post.

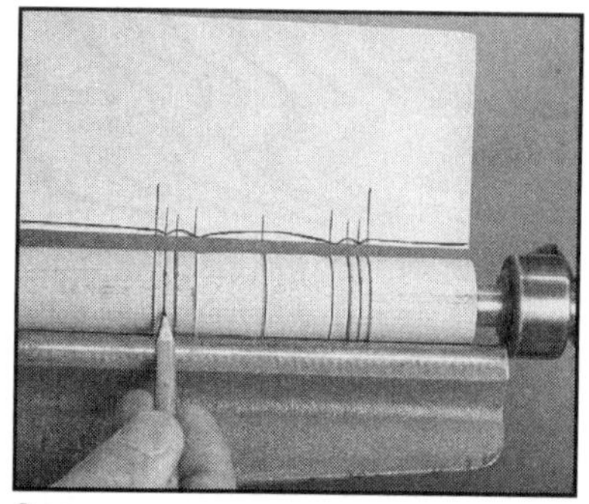

3 Make a template of the decorative bulb. Transfer the shape to the post while it spins on the lathe.

4 The back posts are too long to fit on the lathe, so shape their tenons by hand. Begin by marking the tenon diameter.

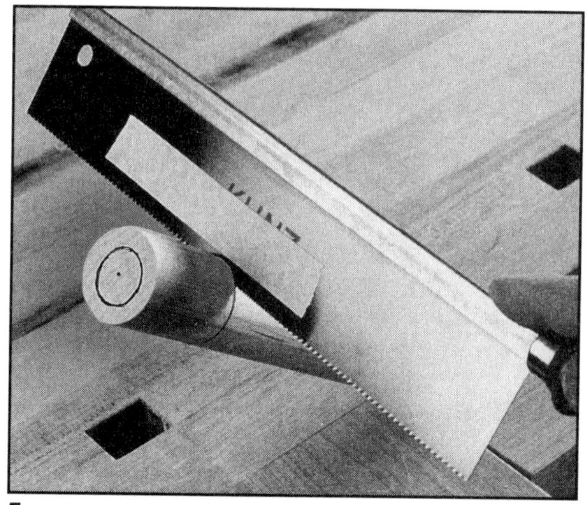

5 Mark the length of the tenon, and then saw on the line. Mark the depth of cut on the saw with a piece of masking tape.

6 Carve the posts to rough diameter with a knife. Then, bring them to final diameter with a rasp.

7 Cut the taper on the back posts using a spokeshave. Turn the post as you work to keep the taper uniform.

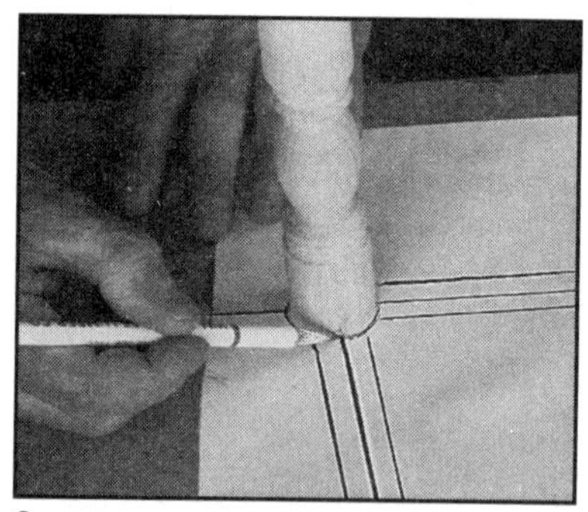

8 Mark the position of the side rails on the front and back posts using a full-size drawing as a reference.

Next, lay out the mortises for the backrests and the front and back rails. Clamp the posts to the workbench, and cut the backrest mortises with a plunge router. Square the mortise ends with a chisel (Fig. 1), then move the posts to the drill press. Using an auxiliary fence, bore the front- and back-rail mortises with the posts clamped to the fence.

Round the four posts in four passes using a ⅝-in.-dia. rounding-over bit in the router table (Fig. 2). Use pushsticks toward the end of each pass to stay clear of the cutter.

Next, make a template of the bulb on the front posts. Mount a front post on the lathe with a live center in the dowel hole. Transfer the layout from the template to the post (Fig. 3), and cut the bulb. Mark the top limit of the ¾-in.-long tenon, and cut the tenon as well as the tapered section above it.

The back posts are too long for the lathe, so shape their tenons and tapers by hand. Mark a ¾-in.-dia. circle on the bottom of each post (Fig. 4). Then mark the tenon length and cut on this line using masking tape on the dovetail saw to mark the depth of cut (Fig. 5).

Carve the tenon to rough size with a knife. Then smooth it to final diameter with a rasp (Fig. 6). Test fit the tenon using a block with a hole bored in it. Then use a spokeshave to shape the taper above the tenon (Fig. 7). Turn the post as you work to achieve a uniform taper.

Stand the front posts on the drawing of the posts and rails. Position the posts so their front-rail holes are aligned with the centerlines for the front rails. Now, mark the position of the side rails using these centerlines (Fig. 8). Stand the back post on the drawing, and repeat this procedure. Extend these marks along the posts, and then mark across the posts to establish the center of the side rail mortises. Bore the rail mortises with the posts clamped to the fence on the drill-press table. Also bore the mortise for the armrests.

Making Rails, Slats and Rockers

Rip and crosscut the blank for the front tapered rail about 1 in. over-long. Turn the blank to size, and cut the decorative center portion to shape. Cut the taper on each side of the center. Because the rail is thin and long, use a steady rest when cutting the taper to prevent the workpiece from

9 The bottom rail is too thin to turn without support. Use a steady rest to keep it stable as it is shaped.

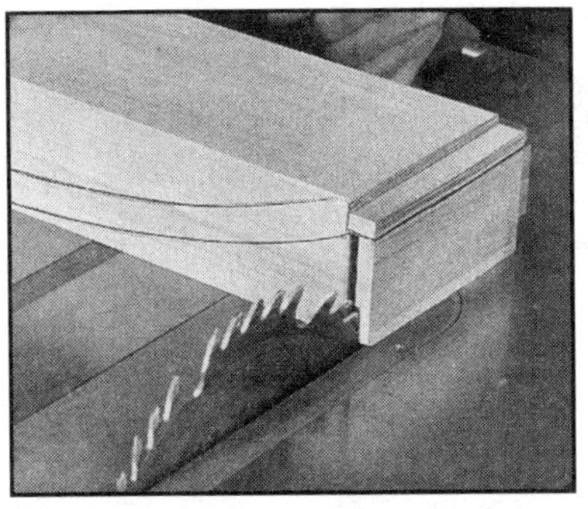

10 Cut the tenons on the backrests using the table saw and miter gauge. Make several passes for each face.

11 Cut the backrests to shape on the band saw. Stay just to the waste side of the line, and feed the workpiece slowly.

12 Remove the saw marks from the outside of the backrest using a block plane and a scraper.

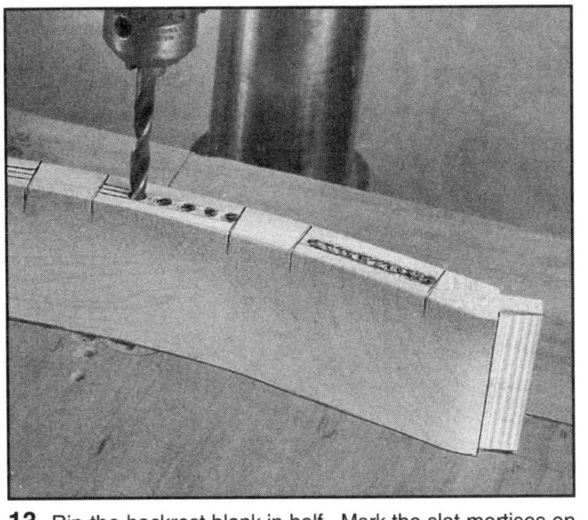

13 Rip the backrest blank in half. Mark the slat mortises on the backrest edge and bore them on the drill press.

14 Press the backrest tenon into the post mortise and trace around it with a knife or sharp pencil to mark the flat.

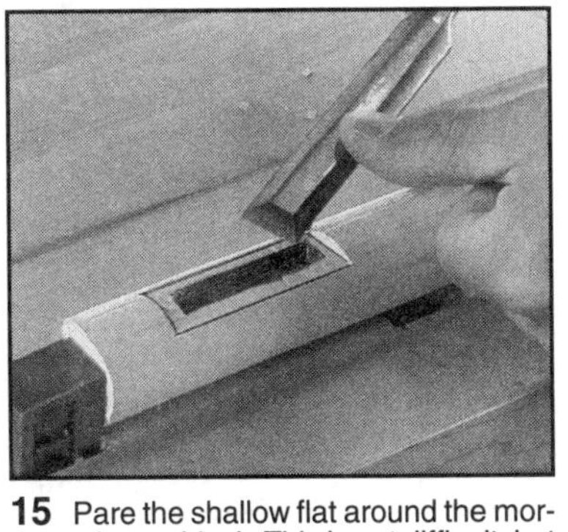

15 Pare the shallow flat around the mortise using a chisel. This is not difficult, but it does require a sharp chisel.

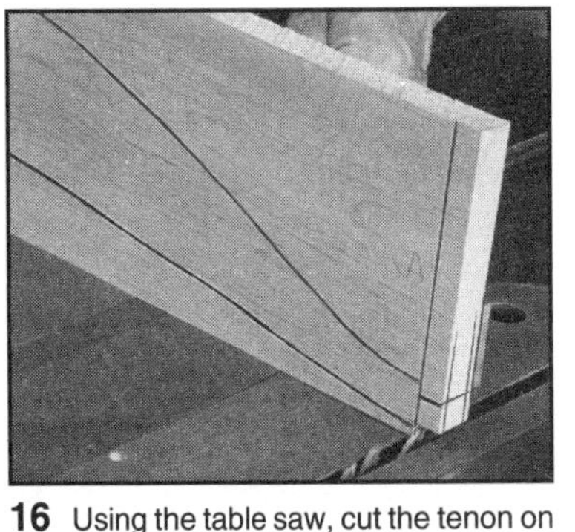

16 Using the table saw, cut the tenon on the armrest. Hold the workpiece on edge against the miter-gauge fence.

17 Prior to boring postholes, mark the posts' positions on the rockers, using a piece of wood and a square.

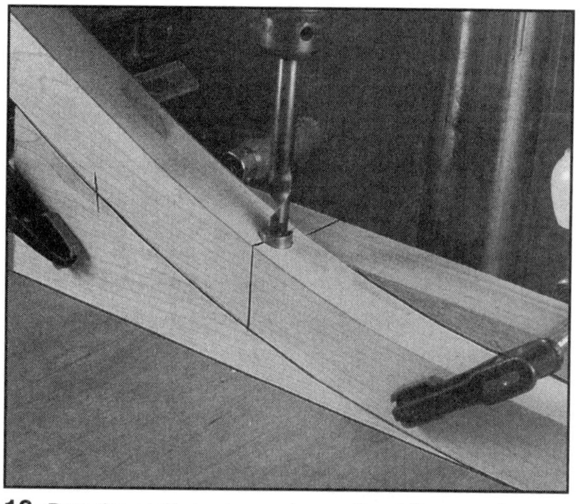

18 Bore the postholes in a rocker on the drill press. Support the rocker with a curved wedge underneath it.

19 Fit the finial's dowel through a block of wood secured to a faceplate. Turn the finial to final shape.

20 The seat support rails are made from birch dowels. Clamp a rail to the bench and plane a flat on one face.

chattering (Fig. 9). Sand the rail on the lathe and crosscut it on the table saw using a miter gauge.

Rip and crosscut a blank that is wide enough to make the top and bottom backrests. Next, lay out the curve on the edge of the backrest, and use the table saw and miter gauge to cut the tenons on the blank (Fig. 10).

Cut the outside curve of the backrest on a band saw. Then remove the saw marks, and refine the shape using a plane and scraper (Figs. 11 and 12). Cut the inside curve, and use a spokeshave and scraper to smooth it.

Rip the blank into two backrests, and lay out the backslat mortises. Remove the bulk of each mortise by boring on the drill press (Fig. 13). Then use a sharp chisel to pare the mortise walls parallel and the ends square.

Mark the tenon shoulders at the top and bottom edge of each backrest, and cut the shoulders with a dovetail saw. Then, dry-fit the backrests to the posts, and trace around each backrest on the post. Using this outline as a guide, chisel a flat surface around the rail mortise (Figs. 14 and 15).

Trace the armrest shapes onto the blanks of ¾-in.-thick stock. Then, use the table saw and miter gauge to cut three sides of each tenon before cutting out the armrest (Fig. 16). Cut out the armrests on the band saw. Then finish cutting the tenons with a dovetail saw. Smooth the armrest edges with a plane and a spokeshave. Then shape the corners with a ¼-in.-rad. rounding-over bit in a router.

Dry-fit the armrests to the back posts and trace the armrest ends on the posts. Cut a flat surface around the post as was done earlier. Then, cut the rockers from a 1¾-in.-thick blank using the band saw, and smooth the cut edges with a plane, spokeshave and scraper.

Note that the holes in the rockers that accept the post tenons are perpendicular to a chord that runs between the hole centers. To mark the proper angle for the holes, cut a block to 17⅛ in. long (the distance between these centers). Place the block from center to center, and use a square to mark the angle along the side of the rocker (Fig. 17). Cut scrap blocks to support the rocker on the drill-press table at the proper angle, then bore the holes

(Fig. 18). Different blocks will be required for front and back holes.

Rip and crosscut the chair-seat blanks, and then cut their edge and face profiles on the band saw. Smooth the slat surfaces with a spokeshave and scraper, and ease the slat corners with a rasp and sandpaper.

Cut the wedge kerfs in the bottom of each post and turn the decorative finials for the top of the back posts. Most of the turning can be done with the finial between centers. To complete the finial, mount it in a "pot" chuck. This device is formed by boring a hole in the center of a wood block mounted on the lathe faceplate (Fig. 19). The turned dowel on the finial's end makes a friction fit in this hole while the top is completed. Glue the finials to the top posts.

Cut the remaining rails from the dowels and plane a flat on the front- and back-seat support rails (Fig. 20). Rip and crosscut the backrest slats' then sand all parts before beginning assembly.

Assembly

Glue and clamp the front rails to the front post and check the diagonal measurements of the assembly (Fig. 21). Then, slide the back slats into the backrests and glue and clamp the back posts to the backrest assembly (Fig. 22).

Next, glue and clamp the side rails to join the front and back subassemblies. Then install the short dowels to the tops of the front posts, and glue and clamp the armrests in place (Fig. 23). Turn the chair upside down, and apply glue to the rocker mortises, post tenons and the kerfs in the tenon ends. Slide the rockers over the tenons, apply glue to the wedges, and tap the wedges in place. After the glue sets, cut the tenons and wedges close to the rocker bottoms. Then trim them flush with a sharp chisel.

Glue and clamp the seat slats to the seat support rails using a scrap piece of plywood between the slats to ensure even spacing (Fig. 24). Finish by applying a good-quality exterior primer and enamel, following the directions printed on the can.

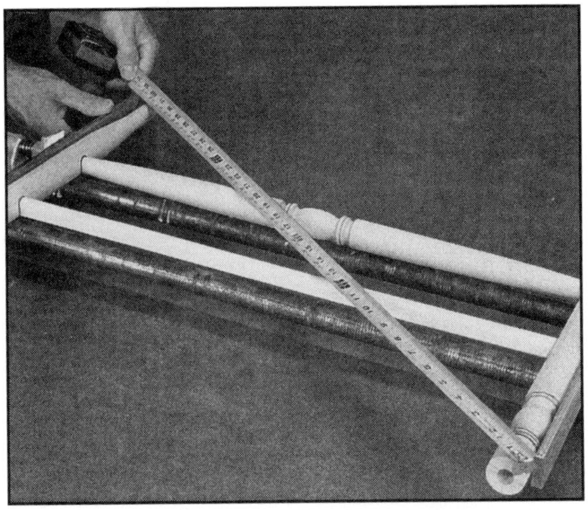

21 Glue and clamp together the front posts spanned by the rails. Check diagonal measurements and let the glue set.

22 Glue and clamp together two back posts spanned by the backrests with slats and the two back rails.

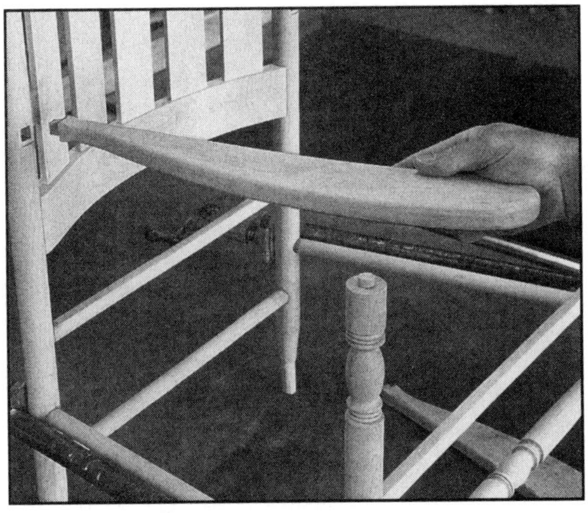

23 Fit the armrests in place after the front and back assemblies have been glued and clamped together.

24 Finish up construction by gluing and clamping the seat slats to the rails. Use alignment spacers between the slats.

Four-Poster Bed was written by Neal Barrett. Lead photo by J.R. Rost with step-by-step photos by Neal Barrett. Technical art by Eugene Thompson.

Four-poster bed

■ The bed presented here is a variation of a Shaker 4-posted design, often called a pencil-post bed because of the thin octagonal posts.

The bed looks good in contemporary homes, but its origins are in the Middle Ages, when canopied beds came into use. Then, woven tapestries were often draped over a heavy frame for both decorative and practical effect because they kept the occupants warm in the absence of efficient heating systems.

The plans here accommodate a queen-size mattress without needing a box spring. If you want to use a box spring, position the framework to yield the proper bed height.

1 Rip and crosscut the post blanks, and use a long straightedge to mark the taper. Also mark the mortise positions.

2 Cut the post mortises before sawing the tapers. Use a plunge router or bore out the mortises on a drill press.

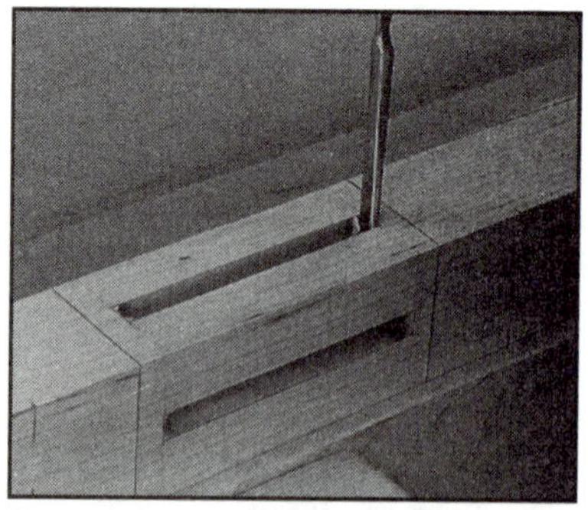

3 Clamp the posts firmly to the bench, and chop the ends of the post mortises square using a sharp chisel.

4 Saw two tapers, then use the marks on the ends of the posts to redraw the tapers on the sawed surfaces.

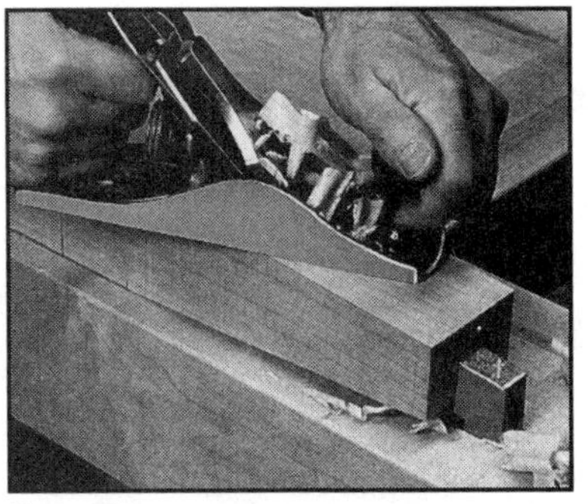

5 Smooth the sawed surfaces and refine the taper with a hand plane. Set the plane to take a fine shaving.

6 Counterbore the bed bolt holes and headboard screwholes in the posts. Use a Forstner bit in a drill press.

The Posts

Begin by preparing the blanks for the bedposts. Glue up stock if necessary, then joint, rip and crosscut the blanks to 2¾ in. wide × 80 in. long. Use a long straightedge to lay out the tapers on each side of the posts (Fig. 1). The taper on the inside edge of the headboard posts begins 15 in. higher than the other tapers. This allows for a square joint with the headboard.

Lay out and cut the mortises in each post at this point—it's easier to do this now, while the posts are straight, than after the tapers are cut. The quickest way to cut the post mortises is by using a plunge router with a ½-in.-dia. straight bit. Clamp the workpiece between bench dogs, and use an edge guide on the router to make the cut (Fig. 2). Cut each mortise in two or three passes to avoid overloading the router. After making each cut, use a sharp chisel to chop the mortise square (Fig. 3).

To make the bed easier to move, its joints are bolted together rather than glued. This construction requires that you bore a hole through the mortise bottoms and bore a matching hole into the tenons on the rails and headboard. Use the drill press to bore the ⅜-in.-dia. holes through the rail mortises and the ¼-in.-dia. holes through the post mortises for the headboard.

Use the band saw to cut the tapers on each post. Note that the tapers are also marked on the posts' ends (Fig. 4). Cut two tapers, then use the marks on the end of the posts to draw the tapers on the newly sawed surfaces. Also, use a roller stand or have a second person help you when sawing the tapers. The posts are simply too long to saw without support.

Use a sharp and finely set hand plane to smooth the cut surfaces and to refine the tapers (Fig. 5).

Next, use a Forstner or multispur bit to counterbore the bolt holes on the outside surface of each post (Fig. 6). Then use a countersink to recess the holes for the headboard screws.

Cut the ⅜-in.-wide chamfers along the tapered edges of each post using a chamfer bit in the router. The chamfers on the inside post corners run the length of the post, while the remaining chamfers are stopped just above the point where the rails join the post. Use a sharp plane or chisel to cut the chamfers at the top of each post.

The Headboards and Rails

Rip, crosscut and joint the stock for the headboard so it forms an oversize blank. Also rip, crosscut and joint the stock for the bed rails and the support rails.

Position the headboard stock so it forms a blank with the grain positioned attractively, then mark it for joining plate slots 6 in. to 8 in. on centers along the mating board edges. Don't position a plate too close to the blank edge—you might expose the plate when cutting the headboard to shape. Hold the headboard pieces firmly to a flat, clean work surface, center the plate joiner on the mark and make the plunge cut (Fig. 7).

7 Rip and crosscut the headboard stock oversize. Cut joining plate slots in the stock, then glue and clamp the stock.

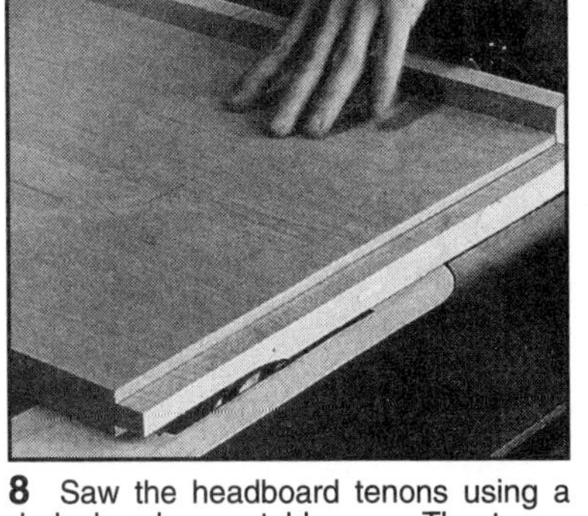

8 Saw the headboard tenons using a dado head on a table saw. The tenon width here requires great accuracy.

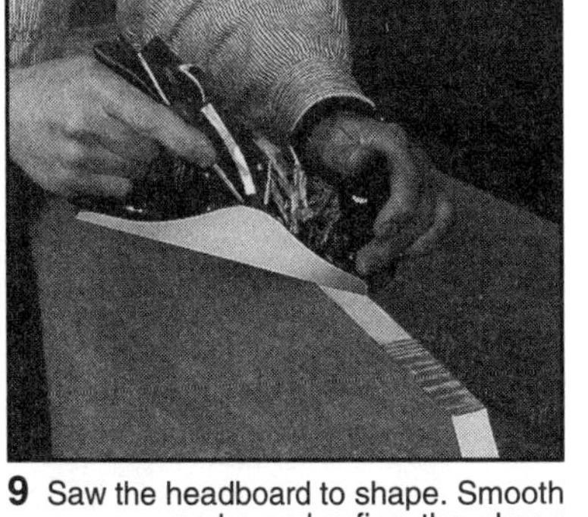

9 Saw the headboard to shape. Smooth away saw marks and refine the shape using a smooth plane and spokeshave.

PENCIL-POST BED

61-3/4" WIDE X
80" HIGH X
86-1/4" LONG

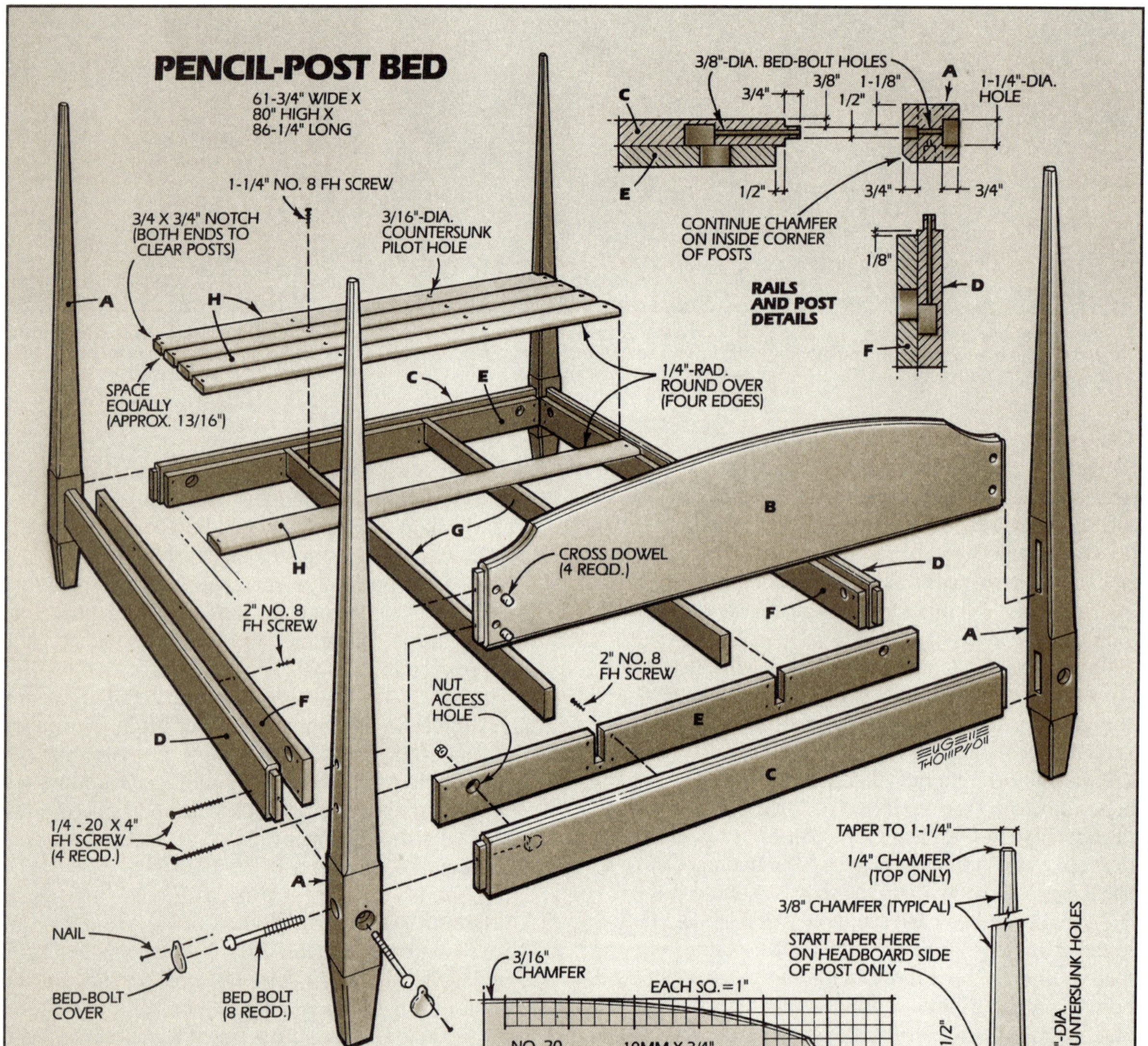

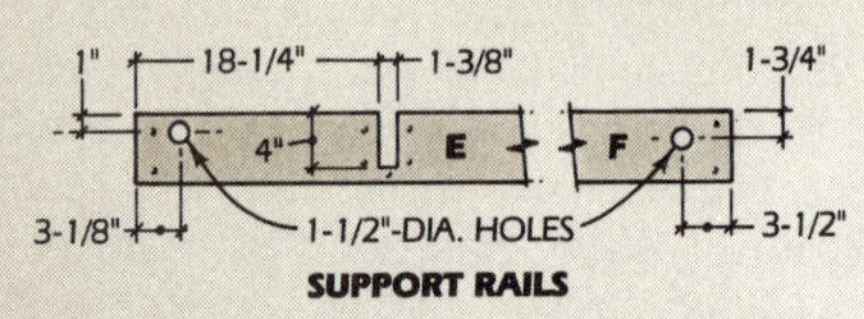

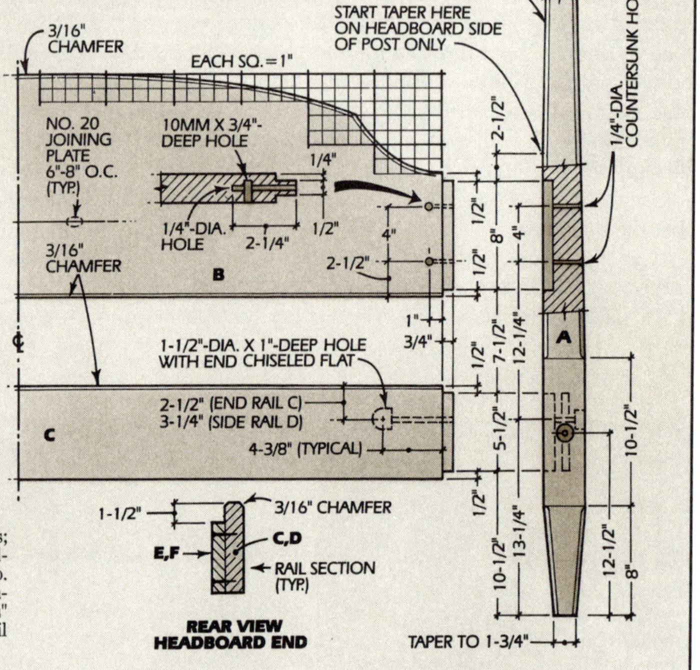

MATERIALS LIST—PENCIL-POST BED

Key	No.	Size and description (use)
A	4	2¾ x 2¾ x 80" cherry (post)
B	1	1 x 16 x 60¾" cherry (headboard)
C	2	1¼ x 6½ x 60¾" cherry (end rail)
D	2	1¼ x 6½ x 80¾" cherry (side rail)
E	2	1 x 5 x 58¼" poplar (end support rail)
F	2	1 x 5 x 79" poplar (side support rail)
G	2	1⅜ x 4 x 80¾" poplar (cross support)
H	14	¾ x 5 x 60¾" maple (slat)

Misc.: 8 No. 6021 bed bolt covers; 8 No. 6010 bed bolts; 1 No. 6012 wrench from Paxton Hardware, 7818 Bradshaw Rd., P.O. Box 256, Upper Falls, MD 21156; 4 No. 31823 cross dowels from Woodworker's Store, 21801 Industrial Blvd., Rogers, MN 55374; 4 ¼-20 fh screws; 1¼" No. 8 fh screws; 2" No. 8 fh screws; Watco Danish Oil Finish; 4/0 steel wool; varnish.

10 With the headboard edges smoothed, mark and cut the shoulders on the top and bottom of the tenon.

11 Use a long bit to bore slowly through the post holes and into the headboard and rail tenons.

Apply glue to the board edges, slots and the biscuits. Clamp the assembly and when the glue sets, plane and scrape it smooth.

The headboard joins the two front posts with two tenons that run nearly the width of the headboard. To ensure tight-fitting joints, it's important that the headboard be perfectly rectangular. Crosscut the headboard blank on the radial-arm saw or table saw. With either machine, be sure you are making a square cut.

Cut the tenons on the ends of the headboard and on the bed rails using the dado blade in the table saw (Fig. 8). The headboard and rails have shoulders on the top and bottom of the tenon. To cut the shoulders on the rails, readjust the blade height on the table saw, stand the rail on edge and cut the shoulder. The headboard shoulders are cut later with a handsaw.

Lay out the curved shape of the headboard, and make the cut with a sabre saw just to the outside of the line. Clamp the workpiece in a vise, and use a sharp and finely set plane and spokeshave to smooth the cut surfaces and work down to the line (Fig. 9). Then mark the shoulders on the top and bottom edges of the headboard tenon, and make the cuts using a dovetail saw (Fig. 10).

Next, using a router and chamfer bit, cut chamfers on the top edges of the bed rails and the top and bottom edges of the headboard.

Dry assemble the headboard and head rail to the posts and clamp the subassembly. Use a long 3/8-in.-dia. bit to bore slowly through the post into the end of the rail tenons (Fig. 11). Use a 1/4-in.-dia. bit for the headboard joints. Bore the other holes for each bolted joint.

Next, lay out and bore the pocket holes for the bed bolt nuts on the inside of the bed rails. Use a Forstner bit in the drill press to bore the holes, then use a chisel to square the sides of each hole, forming a flat surface on which the nut can bear (Fig. 12).

Using a drill press, bore the 10mm-dia. holes for the cross dowels in the back of the headboard. To get the hole in a cross dowel aligned with the hole in the end of a tenon, poke a screw into the tenon and twist the cross dowel with a screwdriver so you can thread the screw into the cross dowel (Fig. 13).

Rig and crosscut the poplar stock for the end support rails. Then, bore the access holes for the rail bolts. Remember to bore the holes so they are offset from those in the outer rails. When the two rails are joined, this allows better access to the rail nuts than if the holes were aligned.

Cut the notches in the end support rails with a handsaw (Fig. 14), and then chop the notches square with a chisel.

12 Use a chisel to cut a flat surface into the hole on the side rails. The bed bolt nut bears on the flat surface.

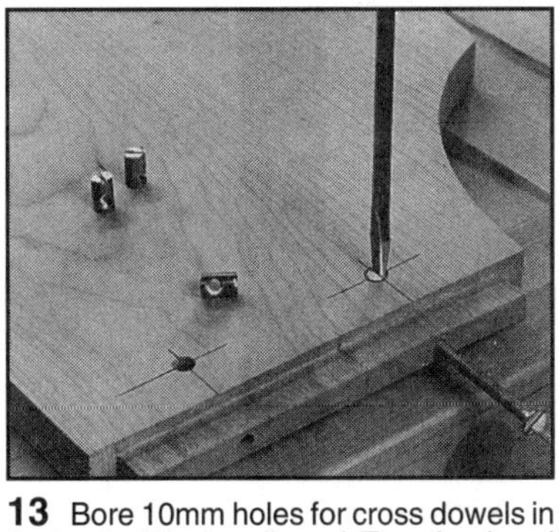

13 Bore 10mm holes for cross dowels in the back of the headboard. Turn the dowel to align its hole with the screw.

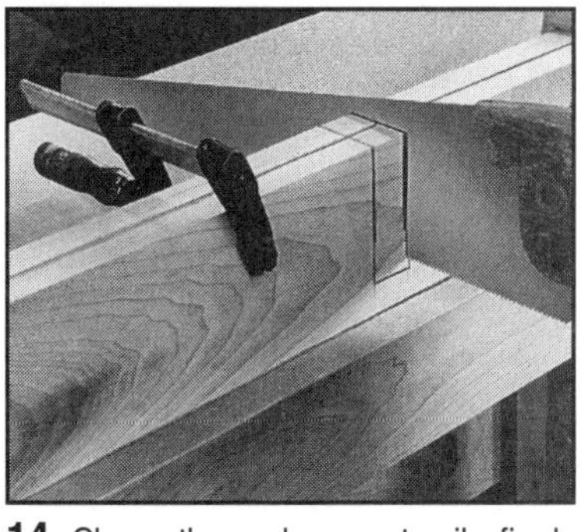

14 Clamp the end support rails firmly together, and cut the cross support notches in them using a handsaw.

15 Fit the head rail and headboard between two posts. Drive screws through the posts and into the cross dowels.

16 Use a bed bolt wrench and an open-end wrench to tighten the connection between the rails and posts.

Assembly

Bore and counterbore pilot holes through the poplar rails to screw them to the cherry rails. Bore a screwhole below the notches in the head and foot rails. Clamp the rails together, and drive screws through the holes.

Screw the headboard to the posts (Fig. 15), and use bed bolts to attach the head rail to the posts. Follow the same procedure for the foot rail and posts. Have an assistant help you bolt together the head and foot assemblies with the side rails. Tighten the bolts using a bed bolt wrench (Fig. 16).

After the frame is assembled, install the cross supports by sliding each into its notches (Fig. 17).

Rip and crosscut the maple bed slats, then cut the notches in the slats at the head and foot of the bed to fit around the posts (Fig. 18). Bore and counterbore pilot holes in the slats, then use a $\frac{1}{4}$-in.-rad. rounding-over bit mounted in a router table to cut the slats' edges. Screw the slats to the cross supports using $\frac{13}{16}$-in. spacer blocks between each (Fig. 19).

Disassemble the bed, and sand all parts with 220-grit sandpaper followed by 320-grit paper. Apply four coats of Watco Danish Oil Finish, using a brush or rag, and let it soak in for 20 to 30 minutes, then wipe it off. Let the piece dry overnight between coats. After the final coat has dried, rub it smooth with 4/0 steel wool. The maple slats need no finish, but a coat of varnish seals them.

Reassemble the bed and nail the bed bolt covers in place. Each cover should be loose enough to swivel.

17 Prepare for installing the slats by fitting the cross supports into the notches that are cut in the end support rails.

18 Cut the slat stock, cut notches in the slats at the foot and the head of the bed so they fit around the posts.

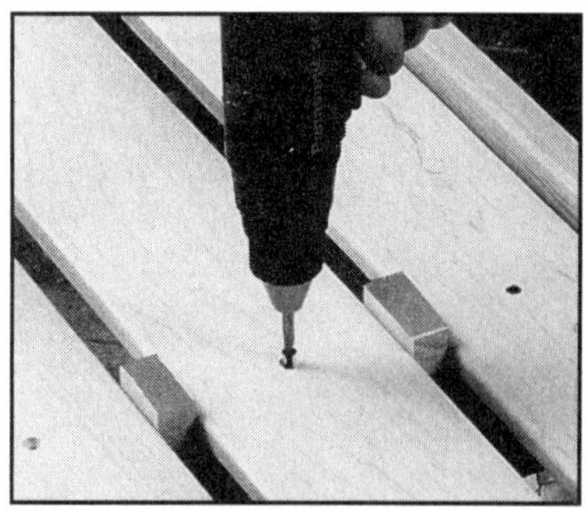

19 Position the $\frac{13}{16}$-in.-wide spacer blocks between the slats, and screw the slats to the cross supports.

Buying hardwood and softwood lumber

Buying Hardwood and Softwood Lumber was written by Neal Barrett. Photos by Rosario Capotosto. Additional photos from Western Wood Products Association and from National Hardwood Lumber Association.

When it comes to buying tools, you know amperage and capacity, you know which manufacturers offer the most for your dollar and you know how to use each tool effectively and skillfully. But tools and skills represent only half the equation—the working half. When it comes to the wood itself, knowing what's available and how to buy it may be a little bit more of a mystery.

You know that there are hardwoods and softwoods, and some boards have knots while others are clear. Unfortunately, lumber isn't sold simply as clear or knotty. Each board is graded and classified according to the nature and number of defects it contains. Having a basic grasp of lumber grading can be the first step to a successful project that doesn't cost you an arm and a leg. If, for example, you're making a simple spice rack, buying the highest grade of lumber may be throwing money down the drain. On the other hand, buying economy 2×6s may be fine for the woodshed roof but a disappointment or disaster when used for a deck railing.

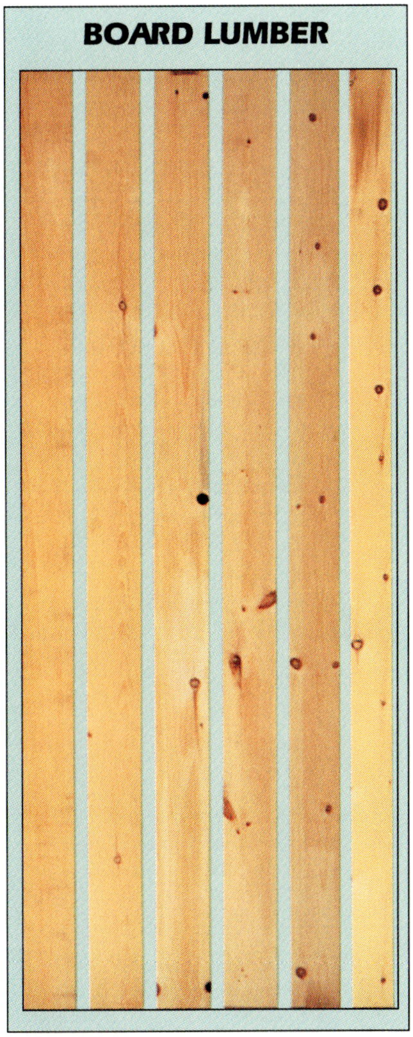

Sample pine boards (from left to right) illustrate the select grades B & Better, C and D, and the common grades 1, 2 and 3.

Structural joists and planks are more than 5 in. wide. Shown (from top to bottom) are select structural and Nos. 1, 2 and 3.

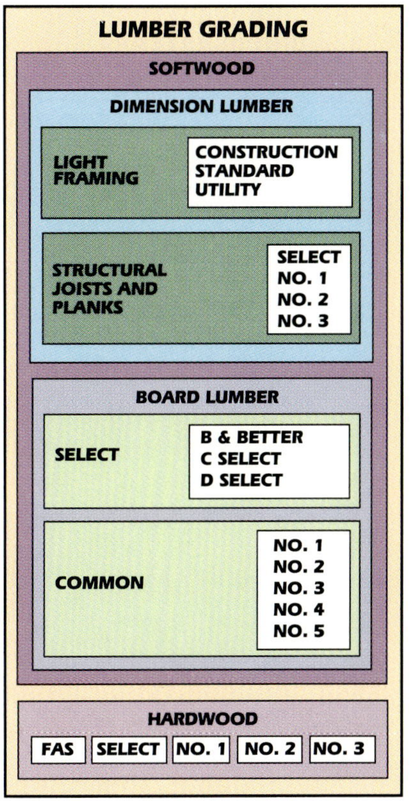

Classes of Lumber

Lumber is organized into three distinct classes and each group has its own grading system. The three main classes are dimension softwood lumber, board softwood lumber and hardwood lumber. For each category, there are particular rules for establishing grade differences and unique subclasses that are based on the usual end use of each product. These rules are quite technical and there is really no need to become familiar with all their intricacies. Though certain grades exist, they are not always carried by many lumber yards. The particular grades available to you will vary with locality, market conditions, labor disputes, weather, distribution systems and even the prevailing political climate.

Setting the Standards

Softwood lumber is graded according to a set of standards set by the American Lumber Standards Committee. These standards are enforced, through inspection, by regional organizations such as the Western Wood Products Association, the Northeastern Lumber Manufacturers Association and the Southern Pine Inspection Bureau, among others. When it comes to hardwood lumber, an entirely different set of grading standards is in force.

A uniform set of rules ensures that the lumber you purchase, of a given grade and species, has met the same criteria as the same grade of lumber anywhere in the country. While this issue may not always seem relevant to the individual consumer, it can prove extremely important to architects and engineers who must specify materials for jobs outside their immediate locality.

Structural Lumber for Framing

When you think of structural framing, you probably picture a 2×4 or 2×6 board. This material is called *dimension lumber*—softwood lumber that has been planed to nominal thicknesses from 2 in. to 4 in. (actual dimensions 1½ in. to 3½ in.). Also included in this classification are 4×4 posts and 4-in.-thick beams.

The grading system for dimension lumber is based on both appearance and strength factors. It is a combination of factors, rather than just one feature, that determines the grade of a piece of lumber. Combinations of different defects may be present in one board but only up to certain specified limits, which vary with grade. The number, size and position of knots and holes, as well as wane (bark on edges), decay, checks, splits and machining defects are all considered. There are also allowable limits for distortions such as cupping, twisting and bowing. Although dimension lumber is classified in several grades, you probably won't find them all available at your lumberyard. The vast majority of outlets stock only two grades of any given product.

Dimension lumber is divided into two main classes. The first is called *light framing*, and includes stock between 2 and 4 in. wide. This class is further divided into three grades: *construction, standard* and *utility.*

Construction and standard grades are suitable for structural, load-bearing uses. While construction grade is a higher classification (allowing fewer and smaller knots), in terms of strength and function, either grade is suitable. Utility grade is the lowest of the three grades, allowing more and larger knots, as well as some waned edges. This grade should be used only for blocking, bracing, or as studs in nonload-bearing walls. In many locations, a fourth grade, called *stud* grade is available. This grade is selected for strength characteristics while allowing certain appearance defects. Stud grade is limited in length to 10 ft.

The second class of dimension lumber is called *structural joists and planks*, and applies to lumber that is more than 5 in. wide. In this group are four separate grades: *select structural, No. 1, No. 2* and *No. 3.*

Any of the top three grades are considered suitable for structural uses such as joists, rafters and studs. When appearance is a consideration, however, either the select structural or No. 1 should be used. No. 2 is used for general construction purposes, and No. 3 is only appropriate where strength isn't an issue.

Besides the grade, lumber is classified by species. In years past, Douglas fir was the lumber of choice for structural applications. Today, however, faster-growing species—such as hemlock, spruce, ponderosa pine and true firs—are widely used for construction. These species are often grouped together into categories such as

LIGHT FRAMING DIMENSION LUMBER

Light framing is a subclass of dimension lumber that includes stock from 2 to 4 in. wide. Shown (from top to bottom) are construction, standard and utility grade.

Hem-Fir. This species group includes hemlock and five true firs.

When examining lumber, you'll notice stamps that indicate the grade, origin, species, moisture content and certifying institution. The symbols and abbreviations used in these stamps may vary, but your lumberyard should have material that explains the stamps used on the lumber it carries.

Softwood Board Lumber

Board Lumber is stock that is widely used in surface applications. While nominal 1-in. stock is the most common (planed to 3/4 in. thick), board lumber is available in nominal dimensions up to 4 in. (planed to 3-1/2 in.). In most situations, the different varieties of pine are the species that are manufactured into board lumber. Other species of softwood, however, including hemlock, spruce and fir, are graded under this classification also.

When board lumber is graded, the better face of the board determines the grade. Again, natural and manufacturing defects are considered, but strength isn't as critical a factor as with dimension lumber.

The highest classification of board lumber is called *select* grade. This grade is divided into three categories: *B & Better, C Select* and *D Select.* All the select grades are commonly used for the most demanding finish applications, with B & Better grade offering the highest quality, followed in order by C and D Select.

The next classification of board lumber is called *common grade*. Common boards are subdivided into five numbered grades. *No. 1 common* represents the highest-quality lumber with a knotty appearance. While this grade is not usually carried as a stock item by lumberyards, it's usually available through special order.

No. 2 common in the grade most often specified for applications where a board with some knots is acceptable. This grade is often used for painted work, since properly sealed knots should not be apparent under a good-quality paint job.

Nos. 3 and *4 common* grades are used for sheathing or subflooring, and any use where appearance is not the primary factor.

No. 5 common is the most economical, but should only be used in situations where neither strength nor appearance is important, such as crating or temporary curtain walls.

In contrast with dimension lumber, grade stamps are often absent on board lumber—especially on the higher grades—to avoid damaging the board surface.

Hardwood Lumber

Grades for hardwood lumber are determined by examining the poorer side of the board and determining the amount and size of clear cuttings that the board will yield.

The highest grades of hardwood are generally sold as one combined grade called *first and seconds*, or *FAS*. Boards of this grade must be at least 6 in. wide and 8 ft. long and yield clear cuttings that are at least 4 in. × 5 ft. or 3 in.× 7 ft. In addition, the overall clear yield of the board must be at least 83-1/3% when judged from its poorer face. Some species have other requirements relating to color (amount of sapwood) or grain.

The next lower grade is called *select*, followed by *common* grade which is divided into subgrades, *1, 2* and *3*. Each lower grade has a smaller size and clear-cutting requirement than the grade above it.

Since hardwood grading is directly related to the size of clear cuttings that a board will yield, it is prudent to plan ahead when shopping for this material. If your project requires large clear pieces, then the highest grade lumber should be chosen. If, however, you will need mostly small pieces, considerable savings can be realized by using a lower grade. As with softwood lumber, most suppliers will only stock one or two grades of material, so it may be necessary to shop around for the most appropriate grade.

Hardwood lumber is typically graded from the poorer side. Oak samples shown (from left to right) represent FAS (firsts and seconds), No. 1 and No. 2.

Mortise-and-tenon joints

Text and photos for *Mortise-and-Tenon Joints* by Rosario Capotosto.

■ Long before plate joiners and doweling jigs—in fact, long before screws were invented—woodworkers relied on simple, strong joints that could be made with basic tools. Of all the joints, the mortise-and-tenon joint was clearly the most widely used when it came to joining wood at right angles. Today, the joint remains the undisputed leader for strength and durability and sets the standard by which modern joining techniques are judged.

As its name implies, the joint is comprised of a mortise, or cavity, cut into one piece and a mating tenon shaped on the other. Besides the simple mechanical strength of this union, the joint provides excellent long-grain contact for gluing. The ability of the joint to resist racking and twisting makes it the choice for chair and table rail-to-leg joints as well as top-quality door and cabinet face-frame assemblies.

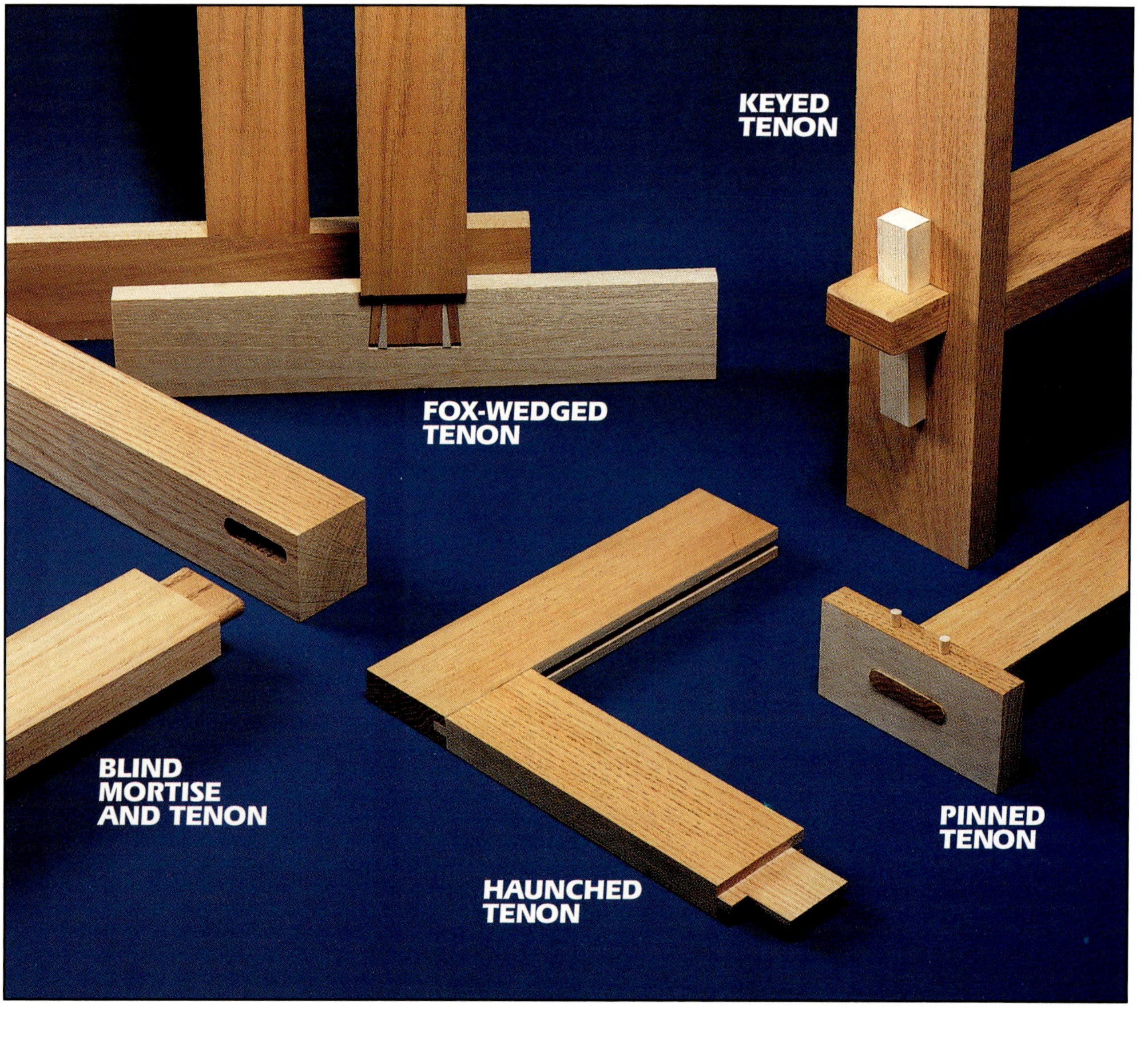

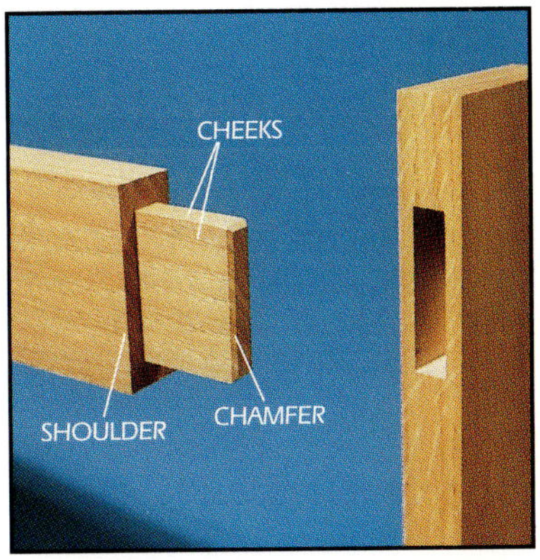

1 Typical tenon is one-third the width of the stock. Cut shoulders square and trim cheeks for snug fit. Chamfer tenon ends.

2 Use a marking gauge to lay out the tenon cheeks and sides of the mortise. Scribe shoulders with a knife and square.

The basic mortise-and-tenon joint is either a blind or a through joint. In a through mortise-and-tenon joint, the mortise extends completely through the stock and the end of the tenon is visible. In a blind joint, the mortise stops short of the opposite face. Other variations include the haunched, wedged, fox-wedged and keyed mortise-and-tenon joints.

A haunched joint is commonly used for corner joints in frame construction. The small hip on this tenon serves to fill the panel groove in door stiles and is also used when there is no groove to resist twisting. The fox-wedged joint is a blind mortise and tenon with internal, hidden wedges that produce a blind dovetail-type joint as the tenon is driven into place. Through-wedged tenons have the wedges driven in from the opposite face. Keyed mortise-and-tenon joints are reserved for nonglued assemblies and knockdown furniture. Here, the tenon projects well beyond the mortised member and is itself mortised to accept a tapered, locking key. Besides being functional, the keyed mortise-and-tenon joint adds some visual interest to the finished piece.

Joint Layout

The design of a basic tenon is important as it affects the joint's strength. The wide surface cheeks of a tenon provide gluing area, and the shoulders, when pressed tightly against the adjoining piece, mechanically resist racking. The shoulders also hide the actual mortise. The ends of the tenon are chamfered (Fig. 1).

When planning a joint, make the tenon thickness about one-third of the stock's thickness. You can increase this to about one-half if the mortise stock is thicker than the tenon stock. Use a marking gauge to lay out both the tenon cheeks and the mortise outline (Fig. 2). Special marking gauges with double pins are available for laying out both sides of a joint at once. Use a square and a marking knife to lay out the tenon shoulders and mortise ends. The scored lines from the marking gauge and knife will serve to guide your chisel cuts as you fit the joint.

The length of the tenon in a blind mortise-and-tenon joint is slightly less than the depth of the mortise. This allows a cavity for excess glue and ensures that the

3 If you don't have a drill press, use a doweling jig and brad-point bit to remove most of the waste.

4 Trim roughed-out mortise to guidelines with a sharp chisel. Keep the sides parallel and square to the stock face.

5 Set plunge router fence to align the bit and use stops to limit router travel. Make several passes to remove waste.

shoulders will seat against the adjoining piece. For a through mortise and tenon, cut the tenon slightly oversize in length—the protruding end will be trimmed flush after assembly.

Always try to cut the mortise before cutting the tenon. It's generally easier to fit the tenon to the mortise than vice versa, particularly if the mortise is formed with bored holes or by routing.

Cutting a Mortise

In the old days, a mortise would be cut with a chisel and a mallet. Although you can still get the job done with these simple tools, it makes sense to use modern power equipment to remove most, if not all, of the waste.

One of the most expedient methods is to use a drill to bore overlapping holes within the mortise outline and then trim the mortise sides to the line with a chisel. A drill press is ideal for this purpose, but a portable drill with a doweling jig to align the holes works nearly as well.

Set the doweling jig for boring holes centered in the mortise outline. Then, use a brad-point drill bit to bore overlapping holes to the required depth (Fig. 3). After the bulk of the waste is removed with the drill, use a sharp chisel to trim the mortise sides flat and parallel to the layout lines (Fig. 4).

Routing the mortise is probably the quickest solution for small shops and is ideally suited for small production runs such as might be required in chair, table or cabinet-door and face-frame construction. Here, the plunge router is the best tool for the job. Equipped with a straight bit of the right size, a plunge router can cut a mortise that requires no trimming by hand. In addition, many plunge routers handle ½-in. shank bits. These heavy bits are available in longer lengths than ordinary ¼-in.-shank bits and therefore are suited to routing the deeper mortises that most furniture projects require.

After laying out the mortise, set the plunge-router edge guide so the bit is aligned with the sides of the mortise. If the mortise width is larger than the bit, align the bit with one side of the mortise. This way, you can complete a centered mortise by making two passes—each referenced against an opposite face.

Next, tack stops to the workpiece to limit the travel of the router to the length of the mortise. If your workpiece is narrow, clamp the stock between two boards to provide a broad base on which the router can ride. To determine the placement of the stops, measure the distance from the cutting edge of the bit to the edge of the base. Then, place each stop that distance from the ends of the mortise.

6 To cut a tenon by hand, first cut the shoulders. Then cut to cheek lines and trim shoulders square with a sharp chisel.

7 With a standard blade in table saw, first cut tenon shoulders. A stop on auxiliary miter-gauge fence positions the work.

8 Use a table saw tenoning jig to cut broad tenon cheeks. Align the work so the waste falls away from the saw blade.

9 Cut narrow cheeks by ripping toward the shoulder. Stop the kerf short of the shoulder and remove waste with a chisel.

10 Use a stop clamped to an auxiliary fence to position tenon for cuts with dado blade. Here, a haunched tenon is cut.

To make the cut, first adjust the depth-of-cut stop on the router and place the tool in position on the work. Push the edge guide firmly against the workface, turn on the power and slowly plunge the router while making a pass from stop to stop (Fig. 5). Don't try to achieve the full depth in one pass. Instead, make several shallow passes until the desired depth is reached.

Once the mortise is cut, use a chisel to square the rounded ends. If you cut a mortise the same size as the bit, you can leave the ends round and shape the tenon cheeks to fit with a chisel and rasp.

You also can rout mortises with a standard nonplunging router. In this case, set up a high fence to guide the router in a straight line. Then, set the bit depth for a shallow cut, turn on the power and lean down the bit into the work. After the first pass, increase the bit depth, make a second pass and repeat the process until the desired depth is reached.

Cutting a Tenon

While a tenon is easier to make than a mortise, you have to take extra care in layout and cutting to ensure that it will fit snugly in the mortise. The simplest way to make a tenon is to cut away the waste with either a handsaw or a radial-arm or table saw. You also can use a handheld router or one mounted in a router table to remove the waste.

To cut a tenon with a handsaw, first lay out the shoulders with a square and a marking knife and the guidelines for the shoulders with a marking gauge. Then, make the shoulder cuts on the waste side of the line. A V cut made with a chisel on the inside of the shoulder lines will help guide the saw.

Next, position the workpiece vertically in your vise and make the narrow cheek cuts, followed by the broad cheek cuts (Fig. 6). Then, use a sharp chisel to trim the shoulders exactly to the lines. Finally, test fit the tenon with the mortise and, if necessary, pare the cheeks for a snug fit. If you're making a tenon to fit a round-end routed mortise, use a chisel and rasp to round the tenon sides.

The most popular tool for making tenons is the table saw. On this machine, tenons can be cut with either a regular blade and a tenoning jig or a dado blade.

To cut a 4-shouldered tenon with a regular blade, begin by making the shoulder cuts. Clamp a stopblock to the miter-gauge fence to position the stock, and then set the blade height for the desired tenon thickness. Make the shoulder cuts on the faces of the workpiece first (Fig. 7). Then, adjust the blade height and repeat the cuts with the work on edge to finish the shoulders.

A tenoning jig holds the work vertically for making the cheek cuts. Tenoning jigs are available from woodworking suppliers or you can make your own. The one shown here rides on the rip fence and uses a clamp to hold the work in place (Fig. 8).

After cutting the shoulders, clamp the stock in the jig and position the jig so the blade cuts on the waste side of the cheek that faces away from the fence. Make sure the waste falls on the free side of the blade.

Cut the narrow cheeks by making partial rip cuts with the blade set high and the stock held flat on the table. Clamp a stopblock to the fence so that the cut stops short of the shoulder (Fig. 9). Then, use a chisel to trim away the waste pieces. You also could use a band saw to cut the narrow shoulders.

To cut a tenon with a dado blade, clamp a stop block to the miter-gauge fence so the shoulder guideline lines up with the dado blade. Then adjust the height of the blade to suit the mortise thickness. After making the first pass, shift the stock over and remove the remaining waste with successive passes. When the broad cheeks are done, cut the narrow cheeks in the same way, readjusting blade height if necessary. Using a dado blade in this way is a fast way to cut haunched tenons (Fig. 10).

Mortise-and-Tenon Variations

Once you've mastered the basic techniques for making mortises and tenons, you're ready to try a few of the many variations of this joint.

To provide extra strength to a mortise-and-tenon joint, drive pins through it to lock the tenon in place. This technique is common to traditional door and frame-and-panel construction and has applications in other situations, as well. A shallow mortise, for example, gains extra strength through pinning (Fig. 11).

11 Use dowel pins to lock the tenon in place. Bore holes in the tenon slightly closer to shoulder to draw the joint tight.

12 When cutting mortises in grooved stiles, use groove as a guide. Haunched tenon fills the gap left by the groove.

13 To make a tapered mortise for a keyed tenon, use an angled block to guide the chisel after the mortise is first cut square.

After cutting and fitting the joint, bore the dowel-pin holes through the mortised stock first. Then, temporarily assemble the joint and mark the hole locations on the tenon. Disassemble the joint and bore the holes through the tenon slightly closer to the shoulders than the marks indicate. The offset holes will draw the shoulders of the tenon tightly against the adjoining piece. Reassemble the joint and drive chamfered dowel pins through the holes, and then trim the pins flush to the surfaces with a sharp chisel, and sand.

Haunched mortise-and-tenon joints are well suited to traditional door construction. Make the mortises after the panel grooves are cut. Use each groove as a guide for the mortise sides, remove most of the waste by boring holes and clean up with a sharp chisel (Fig. 12). When you cut the tenons, dimension the hip on the tenon to fit the short groove that extends past the mortise to the end of the stile.

The mortise and tenon for a keyed joint are cut the same way as a basic joint. First, lay out the main mortise and remove most of the waste with a drill. Bore small holes at the corners to simplify squaring the hole. Then, cut the tenon with a dado blade—in this example, the tenon has only two shoulders. To cut the mortise for the tapered key, first lay out guidelines and cut the mortise square. Then, use an angled guide block clamped to the workpiece to guide your chisel (Fig. 13). Make the slope of the guide block about ⅛ in. over 1 in. After the tapered mortise is done, cut a tapered key to fit. Assemble the joint and tap the key in place with a mallet (Fig. 14).

Wedged tenon joints offer great mechanical strength because the wedges spread the tenon to create a dovetail-type locking effect. To make an ordinary wedged tenon joint, begin by cutting and fitting a through mortise-and-tenon joint. Then, taper the mortise sides using an angled guide block clamped to the stock and cut slots in the tenon for the wedges. Assemble the joint and drive wedges into the slots to lock the tenon in place.

Fox-wedged joints are the blind counterpart to wedged-tenon joints. First, cut and fit a blind mortise-and-tenon joint, making the mortise at least ⅛ in. deeper than the tenon. Use a guide block to undercut the mortise sides slightly so they slope about ⅛ in. over 1 in. (Fig. 15). Saw two kerfs in the tenon that stop about ⅛ in. from the shoulder. Then cut two narrow wedges to the length of the tenon. Make their narrow ends slightly less than the width of the kerf and taper them slightly less than the mortise taper. Finally, apply glue, insert the wedges in the kerfs and assemble the joint (Fig. 16). Use a clamp to draw the joint tight and spread the tenon.

14 Make a pin to fit tapered mortise and tap it in place with a mallet. Here, joint secures trestle table leg to stretcher.

15 Cut a tapered mortise of a fox-wedged joint with a chisel and guide block. Make mortise ⅛ in. deeper than the tenon.

16 Insert wedges in tenon kerfs. Tenon spreads when installed. Cutaway at top shows the locking dovetail effect.

Dovetail joints

Text and photographs for *Dovetail Joints* by Rosario Capotosto.

■ Of all woodworking joints, the dovetail stands in a class by itself. It's not only very strong, but its visual appeal makes it the choice for fine furniture and cabinet construction. Traditional handmade dovetails involve careful layout and painstaking work with a saw and chisel. The payoff, however, is in a great sense of accomplishment and pride of craftsmanship. On the other hand, if speed is a priority, the router and a dovetail jig can be used to cut the joints.

Dovetail variations include the through, half-blind and rabbeted dovetails as well as the sliding dovetail and the half-lap dovetail. The through dovetail is a joint that is visible on both surfaces and the half-blind dovetail is visible only on one surface. The rabbeted dovetail, also half-blind, is commonly used for assembling a drawer that has a rabbeted overlapping front. The sliding dovetail can be used for joining rails to legs or attaching endcaps to breadboard assemblies without glue. The single half lap is useful for assembling narrow-width frame members.

To make the best use of dovetail joints, it pays to know how to make them with both hand and power tools. Except for a few sophisticated router accessories, dovetail jigs produce dovetails of uniform size and spacing. The advantage of doing the job by hand is that you can vary the size and spacing of the dovetails.

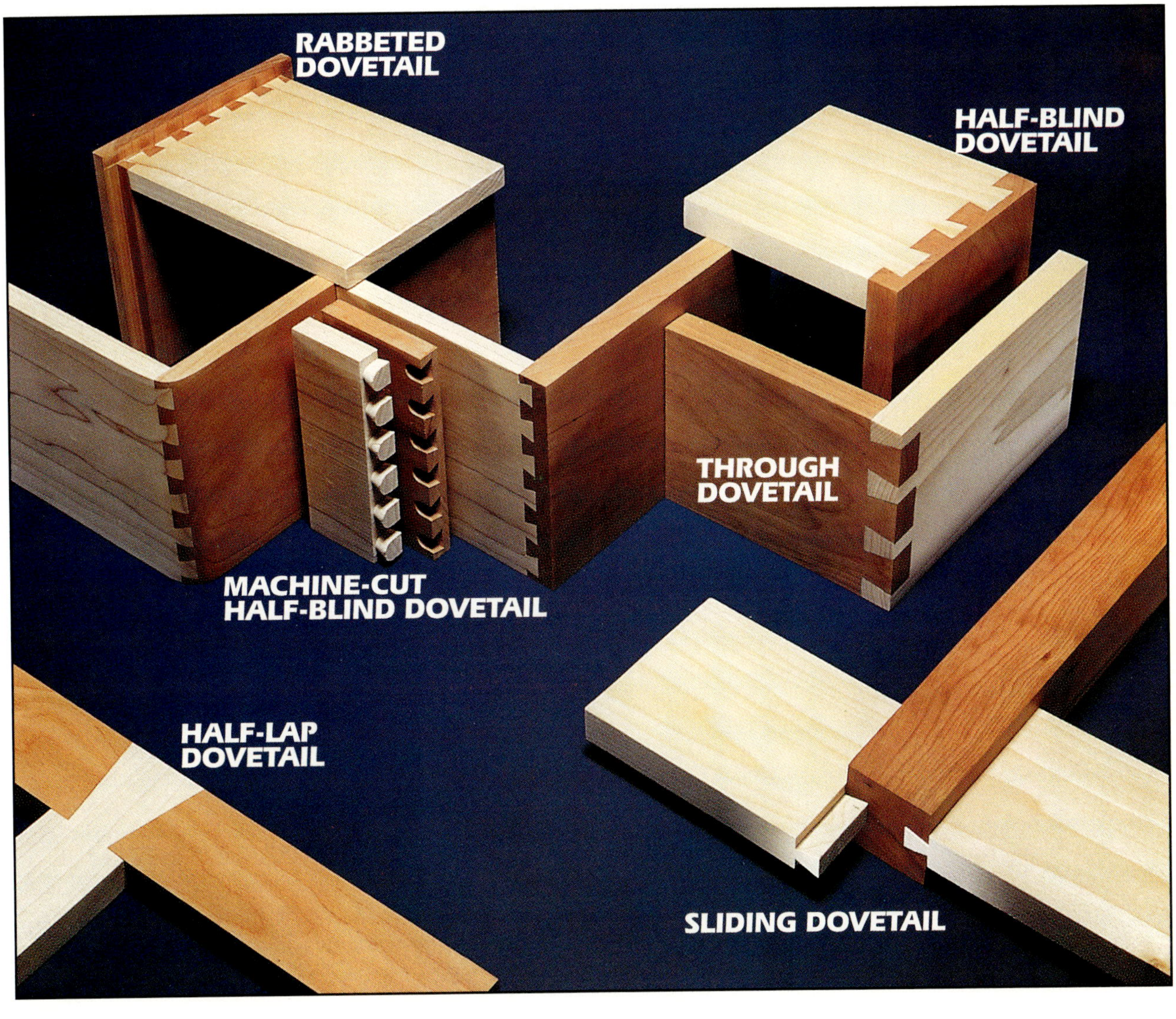

Handcut Through Dovetail

The through dovetail joint is comprised of angled pins that interlock with tapered tails cut on the adjoining piece. Although the entire joint is called a dovetail joint, the term *tail* specifically refers to the angled cuts laid out on the board face. The angled cuts laid out on the end of the adjoining piece are called *pins*. The first and last pins are called *half-pins* because they are sloped on only one side. These need not be half the width of the full pin. For strength and appearance, however, the end pins should never be made too small.

1 After laying out the pin spacing on the face of the stock, use a sliding bevel gauge to mark the dovetail angles.

2 Use a backsaw to begin cutting the pins. Stay to the waste side of the line. A shopmade guide block helps accuracy.

3 After the pin sides are finished, remove most of the waste with a coping saw. Cut almost to the baseline.

4 Clamp a guide board at the baseline and use a chisel to trim the sockets. Trim halfway down, then reverse the work.

5 Align pins with the edge of the adjoining piece and use as a template for the tails. Mark with a sharp pencil.

6 Cut to the waste side of the dovetail lines with a backsaw. Remove waste with a coping saw and trim with a chisel.

Layout

Typically, the slope of the dovetail taper should be within 1:5 through 1:8 in proportion (about 78° to 83°). This and the size and spacing of the pins and tails are variable, as there are no hard and fast rules. As a general guideline, however, use a wider-flare dovetail for soft wood, and where strength is of prime importance, the pins and tails should be about equal in size. When you decide which piece gets the tails, make your decision based on the structural requirements of the object. Because dovetails lock in only one direction—parallel to the piece that holds the tails—plan for the tails to be in line with the greatest stress. In a drawer, for example, the greatest stress is on the front panel in a direction parallel to the drawer sides. Therefore the sides get the tails to mechanically resist the stress on the joint when the drawer is pulled open.

The pins are usually made first, and the completed piece is then used as a pattern for tracing the outline for the tails on the mating piece. To simplify designing the joint, first make a full-size drawing on paper. When sizing the sockets (the spaces between the pins), make sure the width is not smaller than the width of your smallest chisel.

Cut the stock squarely to size and mark a baseline on the face to indicate the depth of the sockets. Make the distance from the baseline to the board end the same as the thickness of the adjoining piece. Use a rule and square to lay out the width of the pins on the outside face of the workpiece. Next, set the T-bevel for the desired angle and mark the angled lines across the end grain to coincide with the parallel pin lines on the face (Fig. 1). Follow by continuing the lines, with a square, down to the baseline on the opposite face of the workpiece.

Sawing

Use a dovetail saw or small backsaw to cut the sides of the pins. Make each cut on the waste side of the pencil line and stop the cuts just short of the baseline (Fig. 2). This can be done freehand, or you can use a simple guide to ensure precise cuts.

The guide used here consists of a small wood block in which a notch is cut that matches the dovetail angle. Cut the depth of the notch to match the pin length. Straddle the guide over the edge of the workpiece and attach two cleats underneath for clamping the guide to the work. You'll need a left and right guide to serve for both sides of each pin. When all the sides of the pins have been cut, use a coping saw to cut out the bulk of the waste. Saw close to the baseline, but not into it (Fig. 3).

7 After cutting the tails for a blind joint, position the work on mating piece and use it as a template for laying out the pins.

8 With pin layout lines in place, hold the backsaw at an angle and follow angled end lines and parallel face lines.

9 Remove waste from pin sockets with a chisel. Make alternating cuts—first across the grain and then with the grain.

Trimming

When the sawing is done, use a sharp chisel to trim the socket bottoms flush to the baseline. A square-edge board clamped on the baseline will help to guide the chisel for precise cuts. Hold the chisel bevel out against the guide board, and tap with a mallet (Fig. 4). Cut about halfway down, and then turn the workpiece over, position the guide board and trim from the other side. If necessary, pare the sides of the pins true to the layout lines.

Cutting the Tails

Begin work on the tails by marking a baseline to match the pin-stock thickness on both faces and edges of the workpiece. Position the pin ends carefully on the face of the tail board, and trace around the pins to lay out the tails (Fig. 5). Use a square to continue the lines across the workpiece end, and mark the waste areas with an X.

Use a backsaw to cut on the waste side of the lines, and stop just short of the baseline (Fig. 6). If you wish, you can use a sawing guide similar to the one used for the pins to guide the tail cuts. Instead of angling the sides of the notch, angle the bottom of the notch and the top and bottom edges of the guide to match the dovetail angle. After the cuts are made, remove the waste with a coping saw and chisel. Test fit the pins and tails and pare the tails, if necessary, until a snug fit is obtained.

Handcut Half-Blind Dovetail

The procedure for making a half-blind dovetail joint is essentially the same as for a through joint except here you begin by cutting the tails. Lay out the depth of the tails about two-thirds as long as the thickness of the pin stock, and cut them with a backsaw and chisel.

Mark a baseline on the pin stock to match the full thickness of the tails. Then, lay the tails in position on the end grain, trace the outline and extend the lines to the inside baseline with a square (Fig. 7). Mark an X on the waste areas.

With the dovetail saw held at an upward angle, make partial cuts on the sides of each socket, following the lines on the end and the face (Fig. 8). Chisel out the sockets using alternate cuts with and across the grain (Fig. 9). Use a narrow chisel to undercut the waste in the inside corners. Two old 1/8-in. chisels reground with left and right skews are ideal for reaching into the tight corners. Then, test fit the joint for a snug fit.

Machine-Cut Dovetails

A router with a dovetail jig provides an easy method for cutting accurate half-blind or through dovetail joints. The most common type of jig uses a comb-shaped template, a guide bushing that is mounted on the router to follow the template and a dovetail bit.

To use a typical dovetail jig, clamp the two adjoining pieces under the comb-shaped template (Fig. 10). Offset the pieces to a distance equal to the average of the dovetail-bit cut width at the top and bottom. Then follow the template to cut the pins in one member and the sockets in the other simultaneously (Fig. 11).

A dovetail fixture of the type shown provides the capability to cut both flush and rabbeted dovetails. Generally, it is necessary to reposition the template and make a second pass with the router to accomplish a rabbeted dovetail. But some fixture models provide optional accessory finger templates that permit cutting rabbeted dovetails in one operation. Other jigs use a straight bit to cut the pins and can produce joints with variable spacing.

10 A typical dovetailing jig cuts half-blind and through dovetail joints. Clamp stock in jig with pieces offset.

11 With dovetail bit and guide bushing in router, follow the dovetail template. Both pieces are cut in one operation.

12 After preliminary groove is cut with a straight bit, use a dovetail bit to rout the dovetail channel for a sliding dovetail.

13 Shape mating piece by routing both sides of work with a dovetail bit. Test fence position on scrap stock first.

Sliding Dovetail

The sliding dovetail, or tongue-and-groove dovetail joint, is an easy one to make, particularly if you have a router table. Shown here is the procedure for making such a joint for a rail-to-leg assembly. Although a dovetail bit is used to make the cuts on the adjoining members, a straight bit is required as well to make a preliminary cut that removes most of the waste in the dovetail groove.

Begin the sliding dovetail joint by making the groove. When working with a typical ½-in. dovetail bit, first install a ¼-in. straight bit in your router and adjust its depth for a slightly shallower cut than the desired depth of the finished dovetail groove.

Adjust the router table fence to position the straight bit's cut in the center of the intended dovetail groove. Then, make the cut. Use a stopblock clamped to the router table fence to limit the length of the groove. Replace the straight bit with the dovetail bit, adjust the depth of cut and make the second pass to form the dovetail groove (Fig. 12).

The tongue is cut by making an endwise pass on each side of the workpiece with the bit kept at the same depth-of-cut position. First, set the fence so that when cuts are made on both sides of the workpiece, the resulting dovetail will slide smoothly into the dovetail groove. Make trial cuts on scrap stock of the same thickness as the workpiece to finalize the fence adjustment.

When the fit is right, make the cuts on the actual piece (Fig. 13). A pushblock is essential to help feed the work safely and accurately. To make the pushblock, cut a notch in the end of a small board. Size the notch equal to the cross-section of the workpiece. The thickness of the block should be greater than the depth of the dovetail tongue.

Single Half-Lap Dovetail

To make this joint with a table saw, first lay out the dovetail by marking the outline of the slopes and shoulders. Next, clamp a stopblock to an auxiliary miter-gauge fence to position the shoulder lines with the edge of the blade. Adjust the blade height and crosscut each edge to cut the shoulders of the dovetail. Readjust the blade height to half the thickness of the stock and make a pass with the work facedown to cut the shoulder for the half lap. With a tenoning jig to hold the work vertically, adjust the blade height so it will intersect the shoulder cut and position the fence to cut the face of the half lap. Then, tilt the blade to the dovetail angle, clamp the stock edge to the tenoning jig and make the angled edge cut (Fig. 14).

Rotate the work 180° to make the second angled cut. Use the dovetail as a template to mark the socket on the mating piece. Adjust the blade to the half-lap thickness and set the miter gauge to match the slope angle. Then, make successive kerfs to remove most of the waste, readjust the miter gauge to the angle of the opposite side and repeat the process. Finish by shaving off the remaining slivers with a chisel (Fig. 15).

14 After the half lap is cut, angle blade and cut dovetail sides. Use a tenoning jig to safely hold workpiece vertically.

15 Cut the adjoining half lap by making successive passes at the dovetail angle from each side. Clean up with a chisel.

Lap and bridle joints

Text and photographs for *Lap and Bridle Joints* by Rosario Capotosto.

■ If it seems to you that experienced woodworkers spend all their time making tightly fit handcut dovetails and chopping through mortises for wedged tenons, it's time to put things back into perspective. Although these revered joints have a place, and their mastery is a goal for any self-respecting craftsperson, there's often a simpler way to get the job done.

It goes without question that the most basic way to join two pieces of wood at right angles is simply to nail, screw or glue them together. Known as a simple lap or overlap joint, this face-to-face union relies entirely on the strength of the fastener or glue.

With a little more ingenuity, however, this mundane lap joint turns into a small family of joints that are both easy to make and relatively strong.

One way to give a simple overlap joint more strength is to notch one member so the adjoining piece fits inside the notch. This improvement adds rigidity as the shoulders of the notch keep the lapped piece from moving from side to side

Unless you're dealing with two pieces of different thicknesses, however, notching one to accept the other won't produce a flush surface. To achieve this, both pieces must be notched—usually half the thickness of

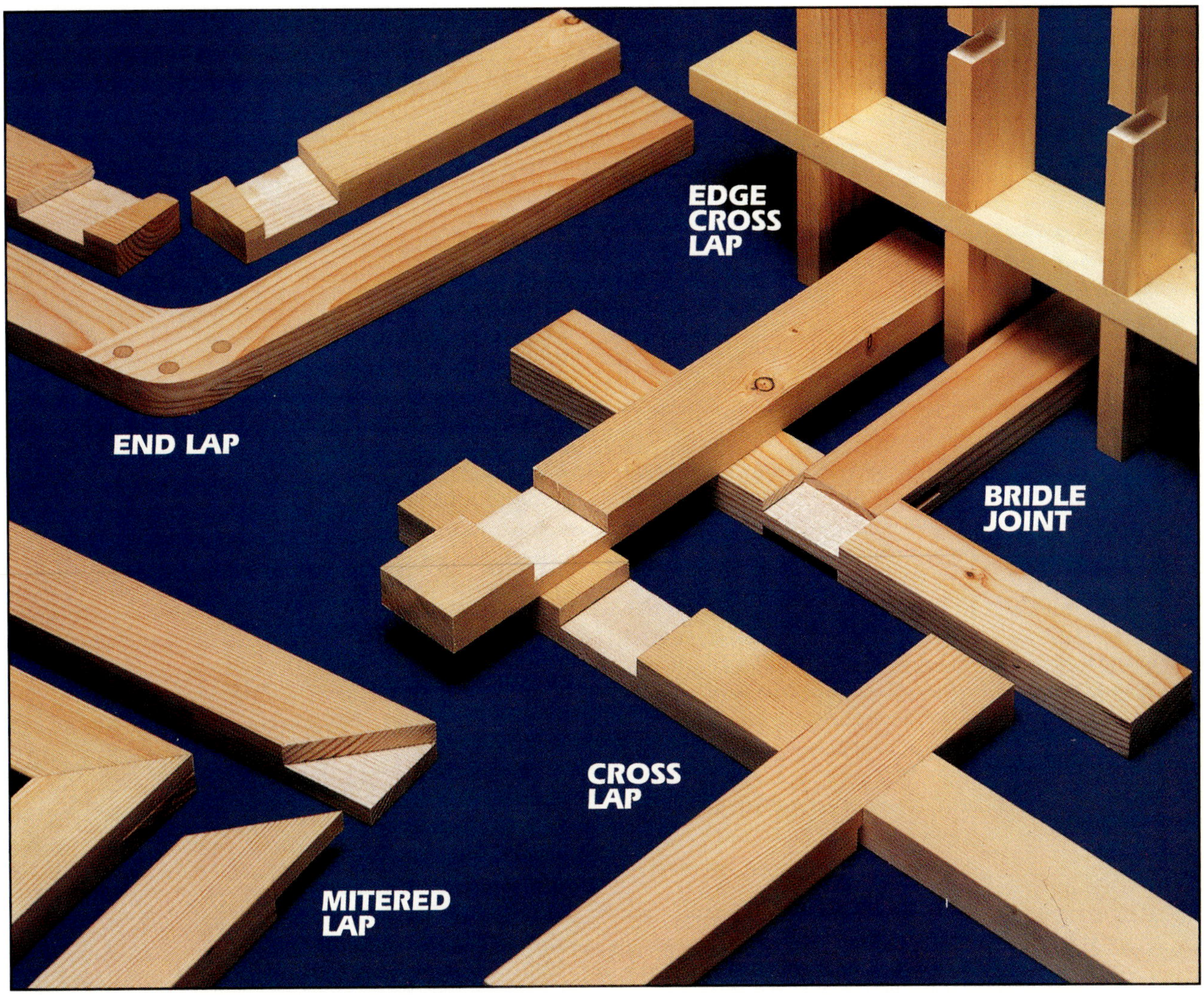

1 Lay out width of half-lap notch by scribing against mating piece with a sharp pencil or knife. Use a square to hold the stock at 90°.

2 After extending lines across edges, use a marking gauge to lay out notch depth. Set gauge at one-half the stock thickness.

3 Use a backsaw to make shoulder cuts with stock held on bench hook. Then make a series of kerfs in the waste area.

4 After prying out the waste with a chisel, pare the notch bottom flat and smooth. Then test fit and adjust if necessary.

the stock. Called a *half lap*, this easy-to-make union has even greater mechanical strength and can be modified to suit a variety of situations.

When used in the middle of a board, the joint is called a *cross lap*. At the ends of two boards, it's called an *end lap*. Egg-crate construction uses the same half lap, but in this case, it's laid out on the face of the workpieces to produce edge cross-lap joints. A mitered lap reinforces an ordinary miter joint by a hidden lap on the back surface.

For an even stronger version that resists a wider variety of loads, choose a *bridle joint*. Here, one member is notched one-third the stock thickness on both faces, and the mating piece gets a deep notch, or slot, along the edge that matches the width of the first piece. Often used as a simple substitute for a mortise-and-tenon joint, a bridle joint can be used at the end or middle of a board and is useful for joining rails and stiles in frame-and-panel construction.

Hand-Cut Half Lap

Before starting to cut a half-lap joint, first lay out the notches with a sharp pencil or knife. Whenever possible, use the actual pieces to mark the cutlines. Align the mating pieces with a square and mark the width of the notch on the faces (Fig. 1). Then, use your square to extend the lines across the edges. Lay out the depth of the notch (one-half the stock thickness) on each piece with a marking gauge (Fig. 2).

Next, use a backsaw to cut the edges of the notch, or shoulders, just to the inside of the lines. Follow by making a series of kerfs to notch depth within the waste area (Fig. 3). Space the kerfs fairly close together—especially if the grain of the stock isn't straight. It helps to use a bench hook to hold the work. A raised and square backstop on the bench hook helps guide square cuts. Then, break out the waste by gently prying with a chisel.

Once the notch is roughed out, smooth and level the bottom notch surface with your chisel, bevel side up (Fig. 4). When both notches are cut, test fit the joint for a tight, flush fit, and adjust the shoulders or depth as necessary.

Machine-Cut Half Laps

To make half laps with a router and straight bit, first make a frame to guide the router (Fig. 5). Space two parallel strips to match the width of both workpieces

5 Use a guide frame to cut half-lap joints with router. Place both pieces edge to edge and cut at the same time.

6 To cut joint on table saw, install dado blade and set height to half the stock thickness. Notch in fence indicates cutline.

7 Cut angled end lap near end of stock—trim overhang after assembly. Notch in fence helps position shoulder cut.

8 For added strength, pin end-lap joint with dowels after applying glue. When glue has set, trim ends flush.

laid edge to edge so you can cut both pieces at the same time. Nail or screw these strips squarely to side strips that limit the notch width. To determine the spacing of the side strips, add the router base width to the half-lap width, then subtract the bit diameter.

Set the bit depth to one-half the stock thickness, make a test joint and check for fit. Note that the position of the finished notch in the jig is indicated by the cut extensions in the two strips adjacent to the stock edges.

To cut half laps on a table saw with a dado blade, first install a wooden auxiliary fence. Set the blade height slightly more than the full thickness of the stock and cut a notch in the fence. Then, lower the blade to half the stock thickness, and make the shoulder cuts aligning the stock with the notch in the fence (Fig. 6). Remove the waste with successive passes.

When cutting square or angled end laps, first make the joint near the end of the stock (Fig. 7). After assembly (Fig. 8), trim the ends flush.

Edge Cross Lap

To cut an edge cross lap on a table saw with a dado blade, first install a tall fence on your miter gauge and adjust the dado blade width to stock thickness. Set the depth of cut to one-half the width of the work. Then, cut a notch in the fence. Disconnect the fence, slide it over a distance equal to the desired notch spacing, resecure it and install a guide block in the fence notch. Make the first cut with the end of the work against the guide block. Then, position each successive cut by placing the last notch over the guide block (Fig. 9) and assemble (Fig. 10).

Mitered Half Lap

The mitered half lap is a novel joint that provides the increased glue area and strength of an end-lap joint while presenting the appearance of a miter joint on one side. The opposite side appears as an ordinary end-lap joint.

To make the joint, first cut one piece of stock squarely to length, and a second at 45°. Then, install an auxiliary fence and set your miter gauge for 45°. As with an ordinary half lap, set the dado blade height to slightly more than half the stock thickness and cut a guide notch in the fence.

Set the blade height at half the stock thickness, align the corner of the square-end piece with the guide notch and make the mitered shoulder cut (Fig. 11). Make repeated passes, shifting the stock after each cut, to remove the rest of the waste.

9 When cutting evenly spaced notches, use guide block secured to fence. Place last cut over guide block to position next cut.

10 Completed edge-lap assembly joins to create egg-crate design. Uniform cutting guarantees accurate alignment.

11 Begin mitered half lap by making a mitered notch on the end of square-cut stock. Align shoulder cut with corner.

12 Set miter gauge to 90° and cut notch on end of mitered stock. Align the shoulder cut with the obtuse corner of the miter.

13 Clamp a stopblock to a wooden auxiliary fence to position shoulder cuts on both faces of workpiece accurately.

14 To cut slot, clamp work with scrap blocks to straddle fence. Make cuts with blade height at width of mating piece.

For the mating mitered piece, set up the fence and guide notch with the miter gauge at 90°. Make the first cut so the shoulder aligns with the obtuse corner of the mitered end (Fig. 12). Then, remove the waste with successive passes.

Because this joint requires resetting the miter gauge and installing a new auxiliary guide fence for each mating piece, it's a good idea to cut all like pieces at once when you're making several joints.

Bridle Joint

The versatile bridle joint can be placed in the middle of a rail or stile, or at the end. When it's at the end, the notched piece becomes a tongue that fits in the slot of the adjoining piece. It's relatively easy to make, provided you align the shoulders of the top and bottom notches accurately.

After laying out the notches on the faces and edges of the work, install an auxiliary fence on your miter gauge and cut a guide notch as if you were making an ordinary half lap. Then, set the dado blade height to one-third the stock thickness. Clamp a stopblock to the fence to position the first shoulder cut. After making this cut, flip over the stock and make the matching cut on the opposite face. Then, readjust the stopblock to cut the other shoulders and remove the waste with successive passes (Fig. 13).

To cut the deep slot in the mating piece, use a tenoning jig or simply clamp the work to scrap blocks that straddle the table-saw fence. First, lay out the slot on the stock edge. Then, adjust the height of a standard blade to match the width of the notched piece.

Precisely adjust the fence to align the cut with the slot guideline. After making the first cut, flip the stock around and make the second cut. Finally, remove the remaining waste by making successive passes, shifting the fence over after each cut (Fig. 14).

When assembling this joint, apply glue and clamp the pieces to draw the notched member tightly into the bottom of the slot. Then, add a smaller clamp to hold the inside faces of the slot against the notch faces.

Making cabinets

Making Cabinets was written by Neal Barrett. Illustrations by George Retseck. Technical art by Eugene Thompson. The veneer used here was obtained from The Woodworkers' Store, 21801 Industrial Blvd., Rogers, MN 55374. The router bit used to shape the raised-panel edges was a Byrom Safety-Raiser bit, No. 363-5802, from Woodcraft, P.O. Box 1686, Parkersburg, WV 26102. The levelers, caps and clips shown are available from Woodland Specialties Inc., 1216 Canal St., Syracuse, NY 13210. The bit and the hinges used are also available from The Woodworkers' Store.

■ One cornerstone of the woodworker's craft is cabinetmaking. Whether the project is a utility tool cabinet, a kitchen cabinet or an entertainment unit, the skills and techniques are much the same. In contrast to the cabinetmaker of yesterday, today's woodworker uses a range of modern materials and tools that both speed construction and offer alternatives in design. One of the most popular styles is called the face-frame cabinet. Here, the door and drawer openings are defined by a rigid flat frame that adds structural integrity to the entire case.

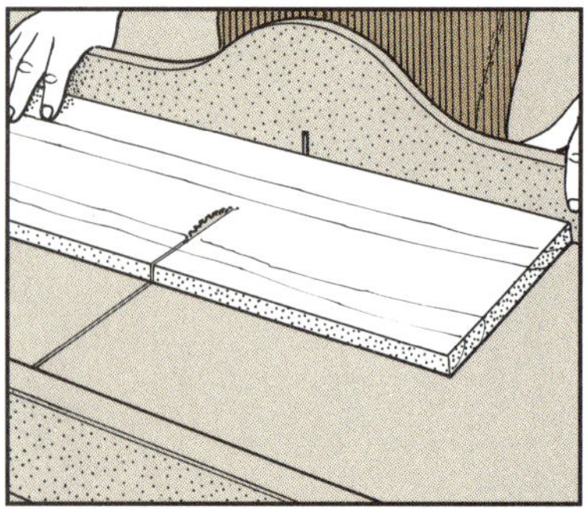

1 After cutting the stock slightly oversize with a circular saw, rip and crosscut to exact dimensions on a table saw.

2 Use a square to lay out the toeboard notches on both side panels of a base cabinet. Cut the notch with a sabre saw.

FACE-FRAME CABINET

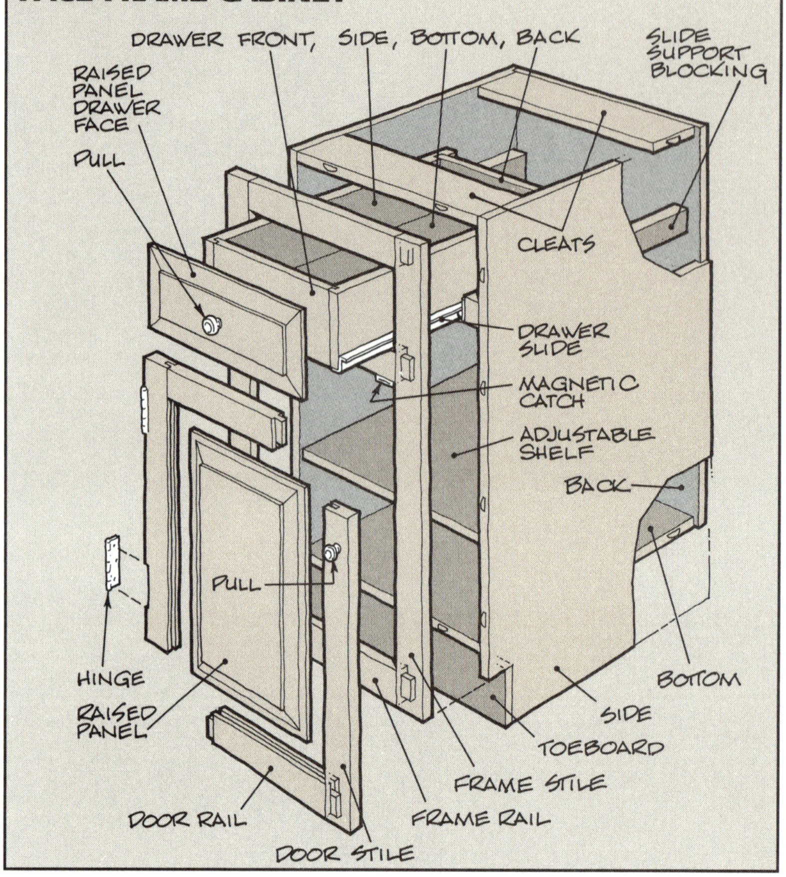

FACE-FRAME CABINET CONSTRUCTION

The updated interpretation shown here is typical of modern face-frame design and you can modify it to suit your needs (see drawing above). It features a hardwood frame-and-panel door, face frame and drawer front. The cabinet sides, back and the remaining drawer components are plywood.

When it comes to joinery, simplified mortise-and-tenon joints for the frame and door were chosen, as were rabbets and grooves to lock the drawer components together. To facilitate the plywood case construction, you can opt for a plate joiner. You could substitute dowels or build the case with dado joints, nail and glue.

While the drawing illustrates the components of a base cabinet, construction of an upper cabinet is similar. Simply omit the toeboard area and drawer-related components, and substitute a plywood panel for the base cabinet cleats that serve for fastening a countertop. Study the plans carefully so that you understand the construction. Then lay out a shop drawing of your cabinet. Make a list of all plywood parts and experiment with various cutting plans to get the best yield from your plywood.

Choosing Materials

The materials for this face-frame cabinet are ¾-in. veneer-core plywood for the sides and shelves, ½-in. plywood for the backs, and ¾-in.-thick hardwood for the face frames, doors and drawer faces. While ¼-in.-thick plywood could be used for the backs to economize on materials, the ½-in.-thick stock provides more rigidity when securing the unit to the wall.

Oak veneer plywood was used for all case parts in the units shown. If you wish, you can use a less-expensive birch or maple plywood for the parts that are hidden when the cabinet is closed.

You'll find hardware, such as hinges, pulls and drawer slides, at most building-supply outlets. Be sure to have your drawer slides on hand before you begin so that you can dimension and position related components appropriately.

Starting Construction

Use a circular saw and straightedge guide, clamped to the panel, to cut each 4×8 sheet into easily manageable pieces. Then use the table saw to rip and crosscut the parts to finished dimension (Fig. 1).

For base cabinets, lay out the toeboard notch at the bottom front corner of each case side and use a sabre saw to make the cutout (Fig. 2).

Lay out the location of joining-plate slots in all plywood parts. While you can use joining plates alone, you can combine them with screws when the case side will be hidden against a wall or another cabinet. This technique eliminates the need for clamping and speeds assembly. Cut the plate slots in the plywood pieces (Fig. 3). Note that it is faster to cut the slots for joining the face frame before you assemble the case (Fig. 4). Be sure to leave the layout marks visible so that you can transfer them to the face frame later.

3 Cut plate-joint slots for joining the cabinet components. A board clamped to side positions plate joiner for case bottom slots.

4 Use your workbench surface to position slots in component edges. Cut slots for joining face frame before assembling case.

5 Use preglued veneer tape to cover bottom edges of upper cabinet side panels. Apply with an iron and then trim flush.

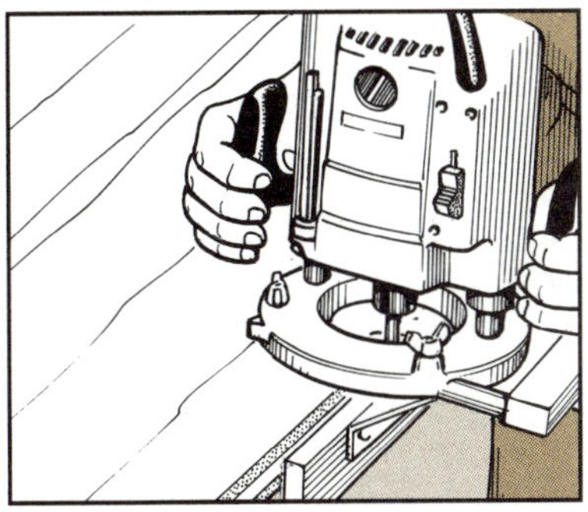

6 Rout the rabbet for the back panel in both cabinet sides. Use a straight bit and a router edge guide to make the cut.

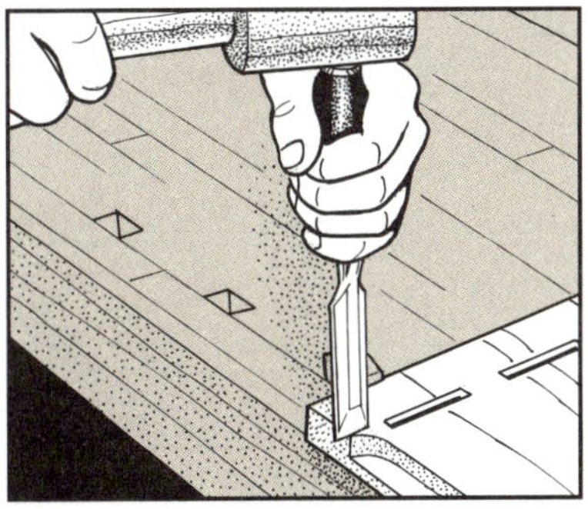

7 Cut a stopped rabbet for the upper cabinet back. After routing the rabbet, trim the end square with a sharp chisel.

8 Clamp case bottom in place and use a template to position holes for shelf pins. Reference template against case bottom.

Since the bottom edges of the upper cabinet sides will be visible, cover them with a preglued veneer edging. Cut a piece about $\frac{1}{2}$ in. oversize and apply with an iron (Fig. 5). Trim the veneer flush with a sharp chisel or utility knife.

Clamp each case side to your workbench to rout the rabbet that houses the back panel. Use a straight bit and edge guide to make the cut (Fig. 6). When building upper cabinets, this rabbet stops short of the bottom edge of the side to align with a rabbet cut along the back edge of the case bottom. Rout to within $\frac{1}{16}$ in. of the stop mark, then use a sharp chisel to square the end of the cut (Fig. 7).

Make a template for the shelf pinholes to guarantee accurate spacing. Clamp the template to the front and back of each case inside face, and bore the shelf pinholes using a depth stop on the drill bit (Fig. 8).

Apply glue to the plate slots for joining the top cleats and case bottom to the sides. Then, clamp or screw the parts together. If using clamps, place heavy cauls across the joints to distribute the pressure evenly. Compare opposite diagonals to be sure that the assembly is square and adjust if required (Fig. 9). Cut the toeboard to exact size, and install it on the base cabinet by gluing it to the front edges of the case sides (Fig. 10).

Cut all parts for the cabinet face frames from $\frac{3}{4}$-in.-thick hardwood stock. Use a dado blade in the table saw to cut the tenons on rail ends. Mark the locations of the mortises in face-frame stiles, and use a router or drill

9 Assemble sides, top and bottom. Use heavy cauls to distribute clamping pressure and measure diagonals to check for square.

press and chisel to cut them. Test fit each joint and adjust as required (Fig. 11).

To assemble the face frame, apply glue to both mortises and tenons and join the parts. Use bar clamps to bring the joints tight, and measure the diagonals to check that the frame is square (Fig. 12). Scrape off any excess glue after 20 to 30 minutes.

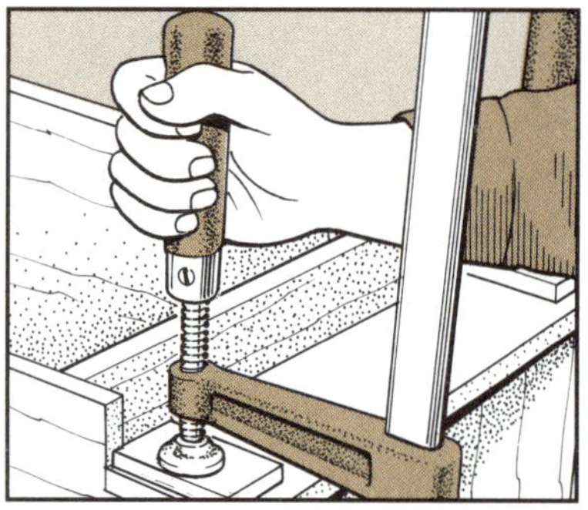

10 Rip and crosscut the toeboard to exact size. Then, apply glue and clamp to the case sides until the glue sets.

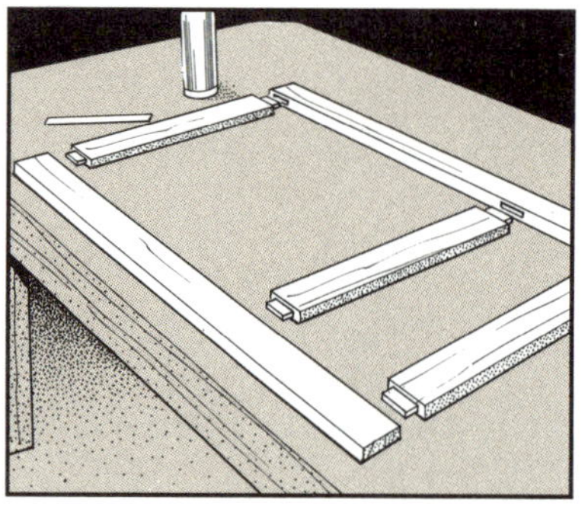

11 After cutting mortises and tenons in face-frame stock, test fit the components. Then, apply glue and assemble frame.

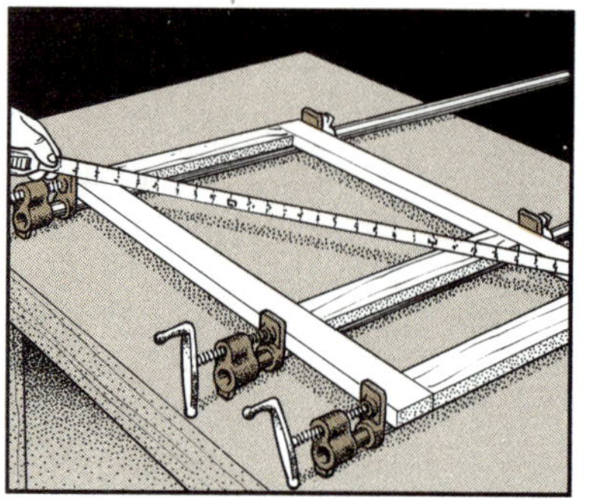

12 Clamp face-frame components together, and check that the diagonals are equal. Remove excess glue after it has set.

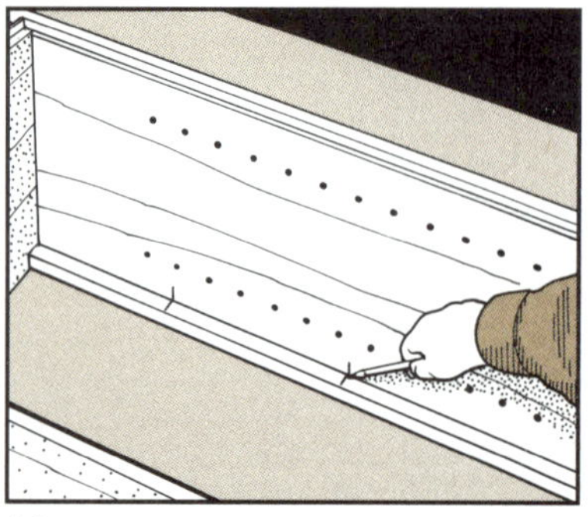

13 Lay case on top of face frame. Then, transfer plate-joint location marks from case sides to face frame for cutting slots.

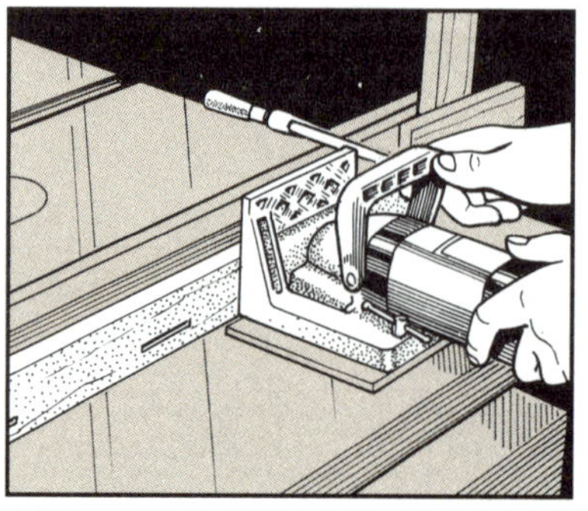

14 Shim base of plate jointer to accurately position plate-joint slots in face frame. Then, make a cut at every slot location.

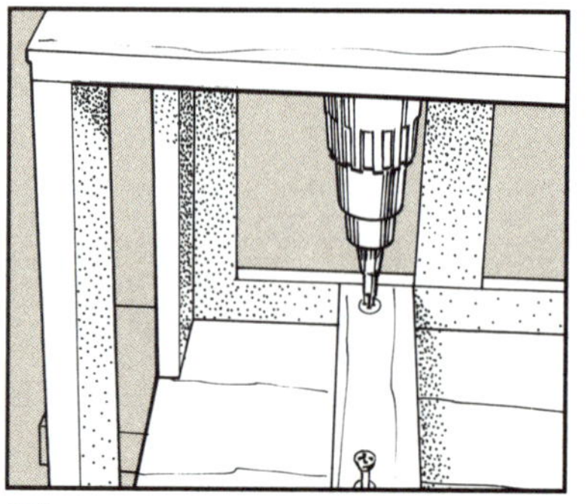

15 Screw drawer slide blocking to the inside of each cabinet. Align blocking with upper edge of face-frame drawer rail.

16 Cut plywood cabinet back panel to fit. Then, apply a bead of glue to rabbets and install back with 1-in. brads.

Place the face frame on your worktable and position the case over it, face side down. Transfer the plate location marks onto the back side of the face frame. (Fig. 13). Cut the joining-plate slots in the face frame, using a shim underneath the plate jointer to position the slots properly (Fig. 14).

Apply glue to the plate slots and case-front edges and attach the face frame to the cabinet. Use clamps to bring the frame tight to the case and let the glue set.

Cut mounting blocks for the drawer slides from poplar, maple or birch, and then screw them in place (Fig. 15). Cut the cabinet back to exact size, and install the rabbets using 1-in. brads and glue (Fig. 16).

Building the Doors

Measure the door opening and allow for a 1/16-in. gap on all sides. Then, compile a list of door parts with finished dimensions. The door uses a 1/4 × 1/2-in.-deep dado along the edge of each stile and rail. This groove holds the panel and also acts as a mortise for the rail tenons. To compensate for dimensional changes due to variations in humidity, trim the panel width 1/8 in. less than the space between the insides of the stile grooves.

You can shape the raised-panel edges with a router bit. Clamp the tall fence to the router table to support the panel and make a series of cuts at increasing depths to achieve the profile (Fig. 17). Sand with 120- and 220-grit paper. Then use a dado blade in the table saw to cut the grooves in the rails and stiles, and the tenons on the rail ends (Fig. 18).

Assemble each door by applying glue to tenons and to those portions of the stile grooves that serve as mortises (Fig. 19). Avoid getting any glue in the rail grooves so that the panel will be free to expand and contract. Join all parts and clamp, cross-measuring to check that the door is square.

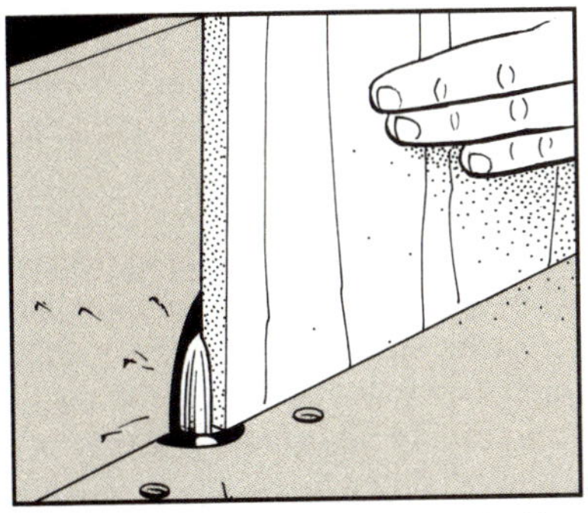

17 Shape the raised door panel with a vertical-panel bit mounted in a router table. Use a high fence to support the work.

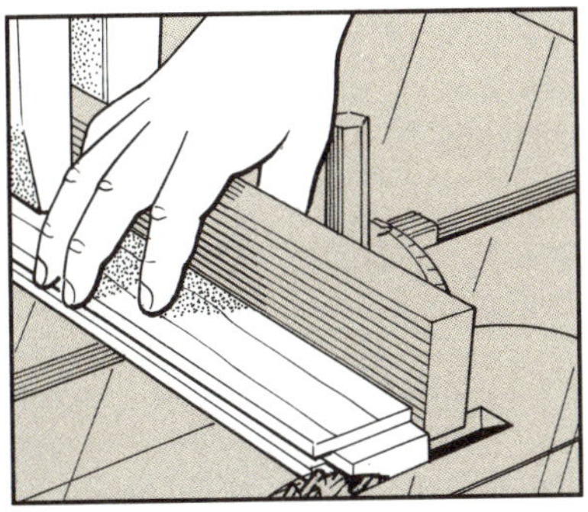

18 After cutting the grooves in the door frame pieces, use a dado blade to shape tenons. Rail tenons fit in the stile grooves.

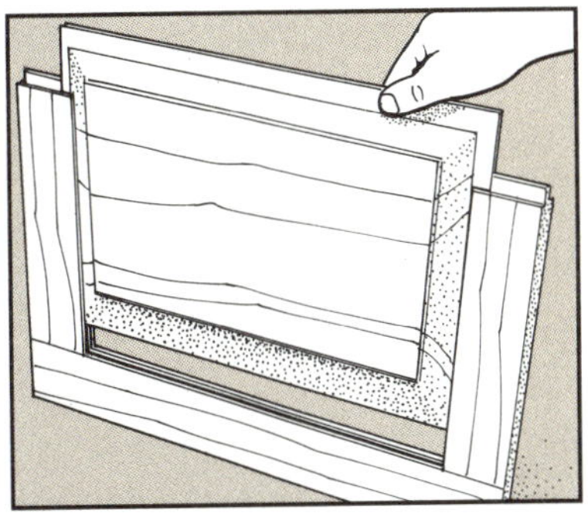

19 Apply glue sparingly to the tenons and assemble the rails with one stile. Insert panel, add other stile and clamp.

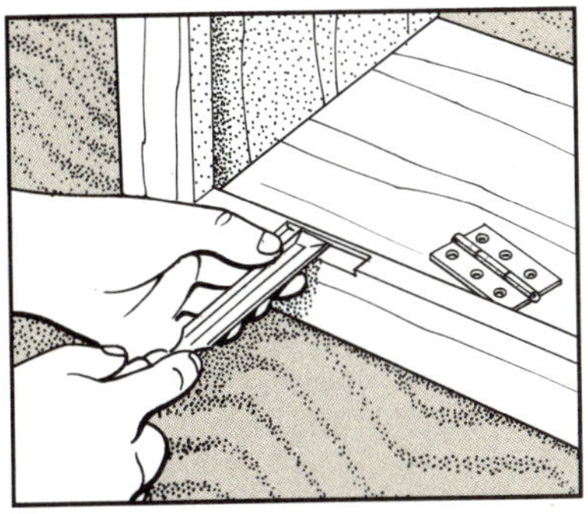

20 Lay out the mortises for the butt hinges on the inside of the cabinet face frame. Remove the waste with a razor-sharp chisel.

21 Install hinges on face frame and position door with $1/16$-in. shims. Then, mark hinge locations on door with a knife.

22 Use a table saw and dado blade to cut the grooves, dadoes and rabbets in the drawer sides, front and back.

Lay out and cut the mortises for door hinges. Use a razor-sharp chisel to cut the mortises (Fig. 20). Bore pilot holes and mount the hinges to face-frame stiles.

Use $1/16$-in. shims to position the door in the opening, and mark the hinge locations on the door stile with a sharp knife (Fig. 21). After cutting the hinge mortises in the door, bore pilot holes and hang the door. Then, bore a pilot hole and mount the door pull, and finish by mounting a magnetic door catch.

Drawer Construction

Use $1/2$-in. Baltic Birch plywood for the drawer sides, front and back and $1/4$-in. birch plywood for the bottom. The drawer face is solid $3/4$-in. oak. Shape the edges using the raised-panel bit, with the bit set lower in the router table than for the door panel. Trim the drawer face $1/8$ in. less than the drawer opening in length and width.

Use a dado blade to cut the grooves for the drawer bottom in the sides and front (the back is cut narrower and the bottom extends under it). Then cut the crossgrain dadoes in the sides for joining the front and back (Fig. 22). Finally, cut the rabbets in the drawer front and back. Assemble the boxes using 1-in. brads and glue. Slide the drawer bottom into place and fasten by screwing into the drawer back with No.5 × $5/8$-in. flat-head screws. Drill pilot holes and mount the drawer face to the box with No. 8 × 1-in. round-head screws (Fig. 23).

23 Clamp the drawer front panel to the assembled drawer box. Then attach the front panel with wood screws.

Mount the drawer slides and install the drawer. Then, mount the drawer pull. Cut and edgeband $3/4$-in.-thick plywood for the adjustable shelf.

Remove all hardware and sand the cabinet with 120- and 220-grit paper. Dust off thoroughly, then apply the finish of your choice.

FRAMELESS CABINET CONSTRUCTION

The real advantage in making your own cabinets lies in their custom construction. You can make kitchen cabinets that precisely fit your particular space and storage requirements, or construct a wall unit that's unlike anything you might buy off the shelf. For the design conscious, custom construction offers complete freedom in terms of style and appearance.

In the diagram below you are shown how to combine the traditional face-frame and panel-door look with modern techniques and materials. For the ultimate in contemporary styling, however, you might want to take full advantage of modern manufactured panels and hardware. The result is frameless cabinet construction.

Frameless cabinets have several advantages over traditional face-frame designs. First, because these cabinets don't have a face frame, they're quicker to build and material costs go down. Second, by using European-style hinges, the entire cabinet area becomes accessible and hinge mounting is simplified. Finally, this type of cabinet allows for a variety of styles and materials. You can combine it with an updated frame-and-panel door design or use sleek plastic laminate for clean, easy-to-maintain surfaces.

To provide just one example of how this type of construction can be used, the cabinets shown were built of 3/4-in. flakeboard that comes covered on one side—the interior surface—with white melamine plastic. The cabinet backs are 1/2-in. melamine on flakeboard. After assembly, all external surfaces and edges were covered with white plastic laminate. Keep in mind that, like all veneered projects, both sides of a panel must be covered to prevent the panel from warping.

When it comes to assembling manufactured panels, a plate joiner is the obvious first choice. Not only is it fast, but the finished stock sizes are easy to calculate because all parts simply butt together. You also can use dado construction, modifying your stock sizes to accommodate the dado depths.

The drawing (see below) highlights the elements of a typical lower cabinet. For upper cabinets, eliminate the drawer components and toeboards and substitute a recessed top for the cleats that secure the countertop.

Before buying any material, complete a simple shop drawing of each cabinet you intend to build. From these drawings, determine the finished dimensions of all case parts. Then, make a cutting list.

Case Construction

Begin by using a circular saw and an edge guide to cut all parts slightly oversize (Fig. 24). Cut the pieces to finished size on your table saw. Use a sharp, carbide-tipped blade designed for cutting plastic laminate to prevent tearout. Then, hold mating pieces together and mark the locations of all joining plate slots in the case sides, bottoms, tops or top cleats and drawer divider rails.

24 Start by cutting all stock slightly oversize in width and length with a circular saw and guide. Cut to exact size on a table saw.

25 Cut plate joints in cabinet sides for joining panels. Position divider slots with guide strip clamped to work.

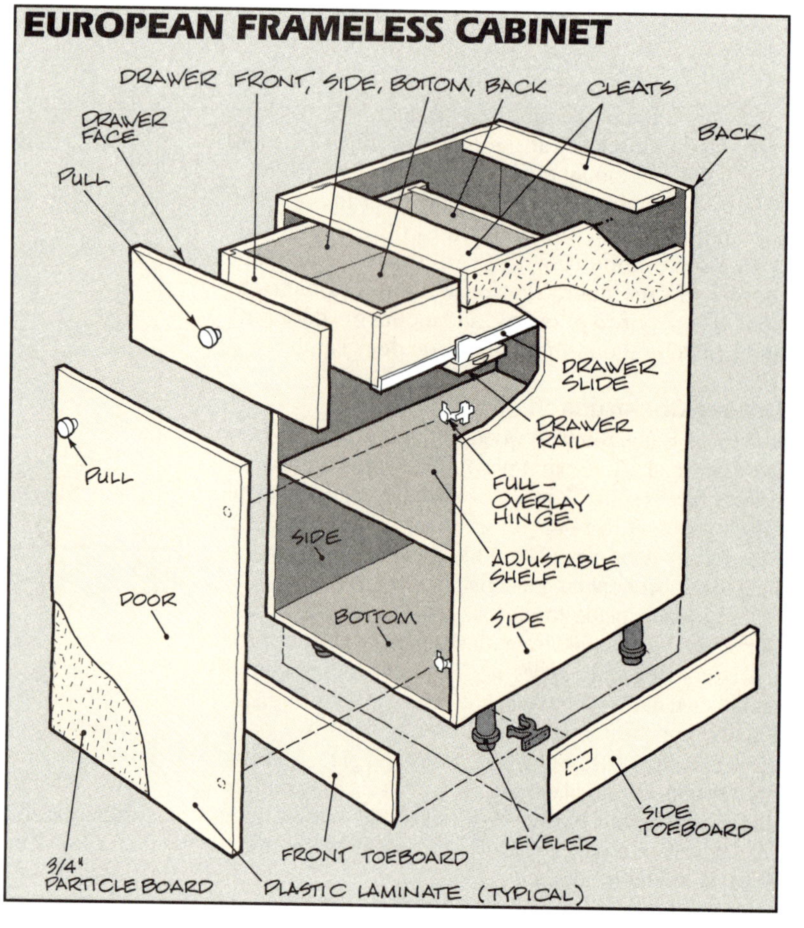

To locate the plate slots for the base cabinet horizontal divider, use a spacer strip clamped to the work at the correct position (Fig. 25). The most accurate way to position the remaining plate slots is to rest both the work and the joiner on a clean, flat surface. Position the top and bottom slots in each side panel by placing both the edge of the stock and the joiner base on a flat surface (Fig. 26). Then, cut the mating slots in the top and bottom panels with the outer face of each piece and the joiner on the flat surface (Fig. 27).

To ensure that the adjustable shelves lie flat, use a template to drill the two rows of shelf pinholes in each cabinet side. Clamp the template in place for each row, and use a depth stop on the drill bit to ensure accurate hole depth.

Since the exterior finished surfaces will be covered with plastic laminate, you can use screws with the joining plates for case assembly. This method eliminates the need for clamping and speeds the work. After the joining plate slots are cut, bore pilot holes for the screws (Fig. 28). Then, countersink the holes so the screwheads will be flush with the panel surfaces.

If you're using a material that will not be covered, such as hardwood-veneer plywood, clamp the cases together instead of using screws. (Edgeband the front edges of all plywood parts before assembly.) You can use screws instead of clamps on any panels that will be hidden by an adjacent cabinet or wall.

Assemble each case by first joining the sides, top and bottom, along with the divider if the case is a base cabinet. Apply glue to the plate slots, insert the plates and join the panels (Fig. 29). Then, screw them together with 2-in. No.8 fh screws (Fig. 30). Immediately after assembly, check to see if the case is square by measuring the diagonals and adjusting if necessary. Then, let the glue dry.

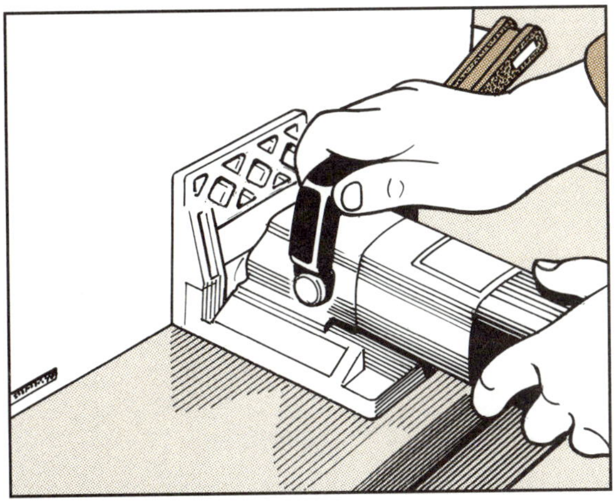

26 Rest edge of side panel and base of plate joiner on a flat surface to position slots for joining top and bottom panels to sides.

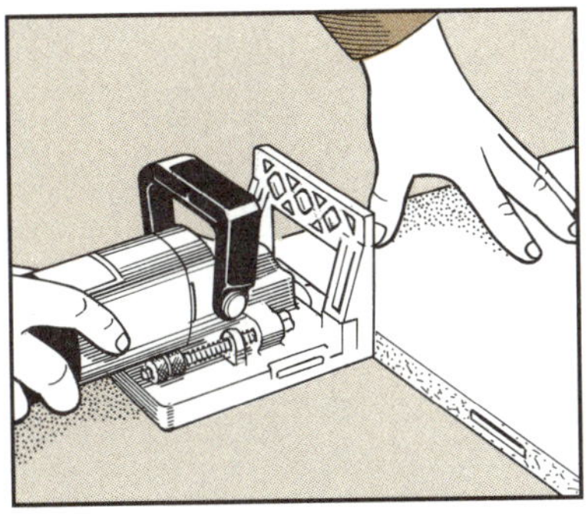

27 To position slots in edges of bottom panel for joining bottom to sides, lay outside face of bottom panel on a flat surface.

28 Bore pilot holes for drawing joints tight with screws. Then, countersink on outside face so screwheads lie flush with surface.

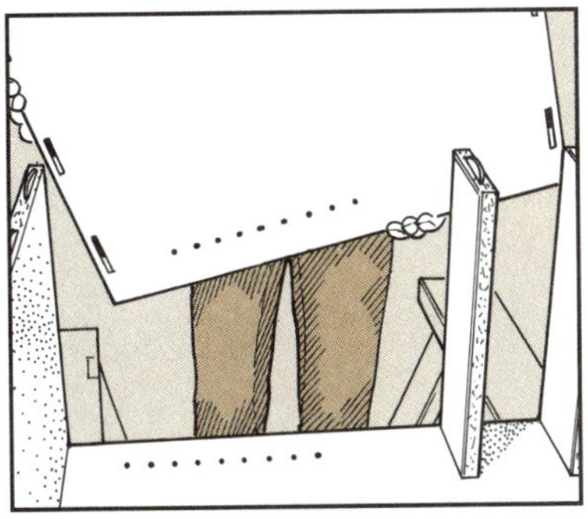

29 Apply glue to plate slots for joining top, bottom, divider and sides. Then, insert joining plates and assemble.

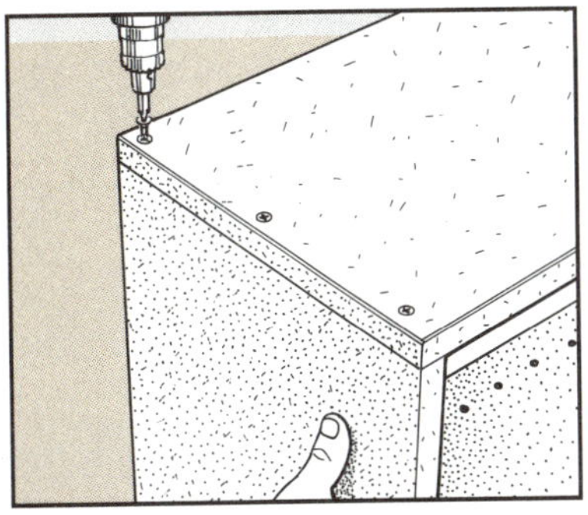

30 Drive 2-in. No.8 fh screws to draw joints together. Screws replace awkward clamps and will be covered with laminate later.

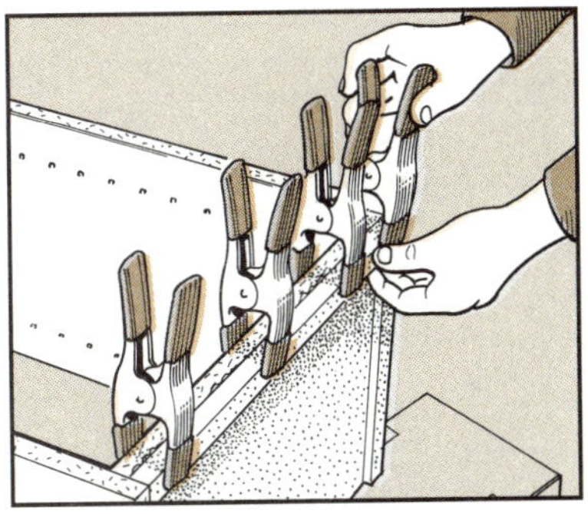

31 Glue a softwood scribing strip to the top front edge of upper cabinet. At installation, trim strip to match case to ceiling.

32 Secure back panel to the side, top and bottom subassembly with $1\frac{1}{4}$-in. No.8 fh screws driven into countersunk pilot holes.

For an upper, wall-mounted cabinet, glue a ¾-in.-thick softwood strip to the top edge so the case can be fit accurately to an uneven soffit or ceiling (Fig. 31). When mounting the finished upper cabinet, hold the unit in place while scribing the exact ceiling contour on the softwood strip. Then, use a sabre saw to trim to the line for a perfect fit.

Finally, install the case back with 1¼-in. No.8 fh screws driven into countersunk pilot holes (Fig. 32).

33 After cutting laminate oversize, apply contact cement and let dry. Then, position laminate and roll with a rubber roller.

Adding Plastic Laminate

To apply plastic laminate, you need a router, a flush trimming bit and a beveling bit. You also need a file for smoothing the laminate edges, contact cement, a few disposable brushes, a cloth roller for applying a uniform coat of contact cement to broad surfaces and a rubber roller for pressing down the laminate.

First, cut the laminate oversize for each surface to be covered. Where edges will be laminated, cut strips 1 in. wide and oversize in length.

For upper cabinets, start with the case bottom. Use a cloth roller to spread contact cement on both the cabinet and the laminate. After the cement is dry, position the laminate and roll over it with a rubber roller to ensure complete bonding (Fig. 33). Then, trim the excess laminate with a router and flush trimming bit.

Next, move to the vertical side panel edges and shelf edges of upper and lower cabinets. Use a disposable brush to coat the edges and the laminate strips (Fig. 34). After it's dry, apply an additional coat to the panel edges because of their porous nature. When the second coat is dry, carefully position the strip over the edge and roll with the rubber roller. Cut the strips for the horizontal edges to exact length, and apply the trim flush with your router (Fig. 35). Use a file to trim the rounded inside corners left by the router bit (Fig. 36). To ensure good contact when laminating broad surfaces, lightly belt sand these surfaces to remove any raised edge banding (Fig. 37).

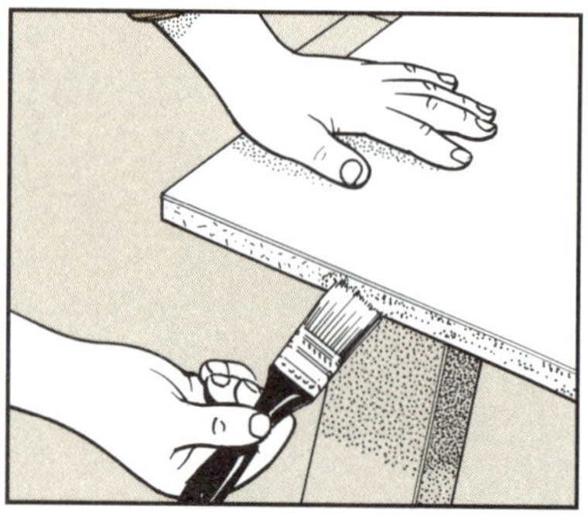

34 Use a brush to apply two coats of contact cement to the edges. Then, coat 1-in. strips, let cement dry and install on edges.

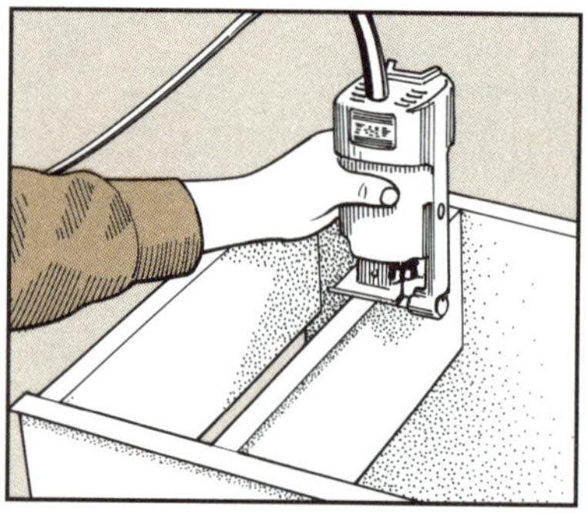

35 Trim laminate strips flush with a router or laminate trimmer and flush trimming bit. Keep router base flat on edges.

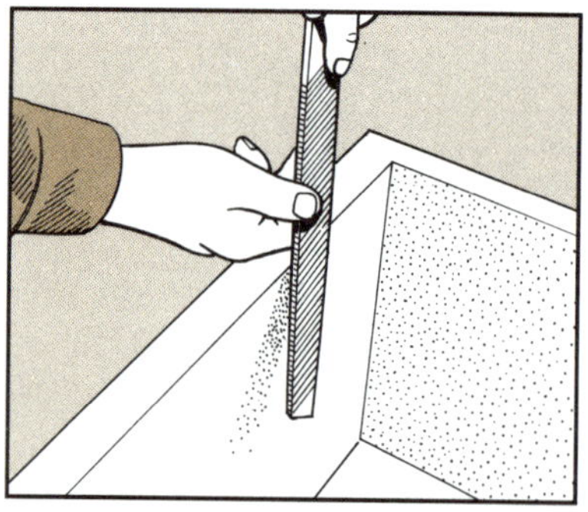

36 Use a file to ensure that laminate edges are flush with surfaces. Then, square rounded inside corners left by router.

37 To ensure that broad surfaces are flat, lightly sand with a belt sander. Apply contact cement to panel and laminate.

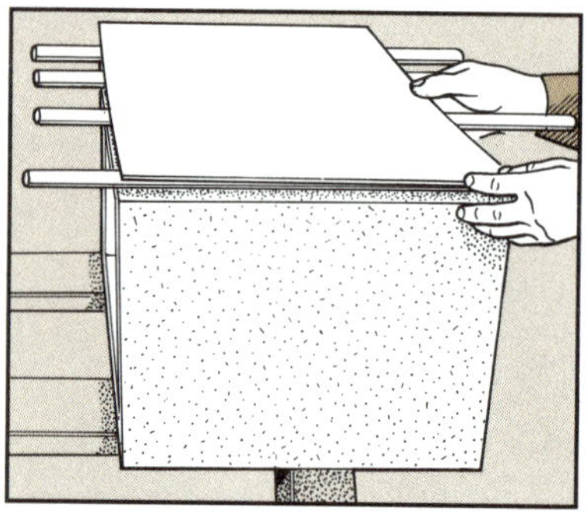

38 When cement is dry, lay dowels on surface and position laminate. Press down laminate as you remove each dowel.

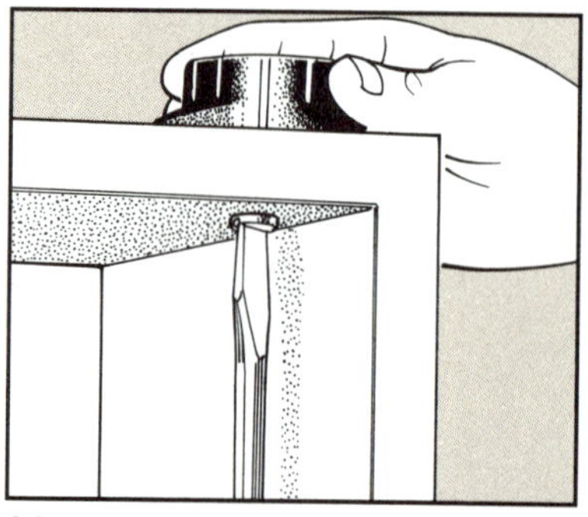

39 After boring holes for cabinet leveler bases, secure with screws from inside. Then, cover screws with leveler caps.

Next, apply the laminate to case sides. First, apply the contact cement, let dry and place dowels 8 to 10 in. apart on the surface. Then, position the laminate on the dowels (Fig. 38). Beginning at one end, carefully remove each dowel to bring the laminate into contact with the core. Use the rubber roller over the entire surface and trim flush.

Use a bevel trimming bit in the router to ease all laminate corners, and use a file to dull sharp edges.

Toeboard, Drawer and Door

To eliminate the need for shimming the cabinet at installation, you can use Blum cabinet levelers in place of a standard toeboard platform. These cabinet levelers mount through the bottom of the cabinet and allow up to 1½ in. of height adjustment at each corner. Accessory leveler caps are available to cover the leveler screws on the inside of the cabinet base. You also can use special clips to mount the toeboards to the levelers. Simply screw the clips to the back sides of the boards and press in place.

Bore 13⁄32-in. pilot holes for mounting the levelers through the case bottom, and attach the leveler base plates (Fig. 39). Install the levelers to the base plates (Fig. 40), and slip on the inside cover caps. After the cabinets are installed, miter the toeboards, install the clips and place the toeboards in position (Fig. 41).

Cut the drawer parts to exact size, remembering to leave appropriate clearance for the side-mounted drawer tracks. Use a dado blade in the table saw to cut the drawer joints, then assemble the drawer box with 1-in. brads and glue. Attach the drawer face with 1-in. No.8 rh screws (Fig. 42), then mount drawer slides (Fig. 43).

European-style hinges require blind 35mm mounting holes on the inside of the door face. First, bore the mounting holes in the cabinet doors (Fig. 44). Attach the hinges to each door using ⅝-in. No.6 fh screws. Drill pilot holes, and mount the hinge base plates to the cabinet sides (Fig. 45). Then install the doors on the cabinets (Fig. 46). Drill pilot holes, and mount the door and drawer pulls of your choice.

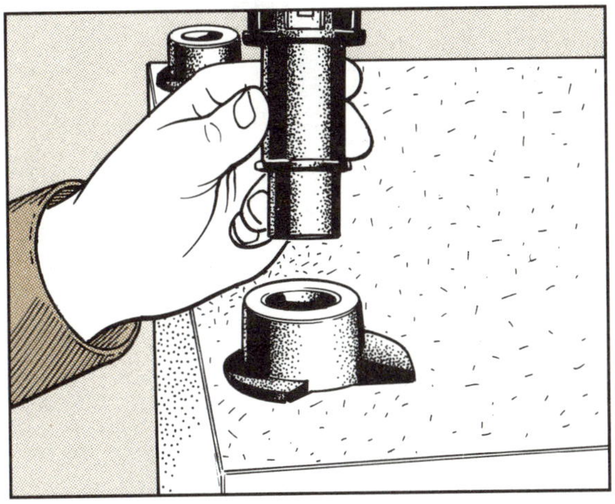

40 Install levelers in leveler bases. Cabinet levelers permit height adjustment at each corner and eliminate shimming.

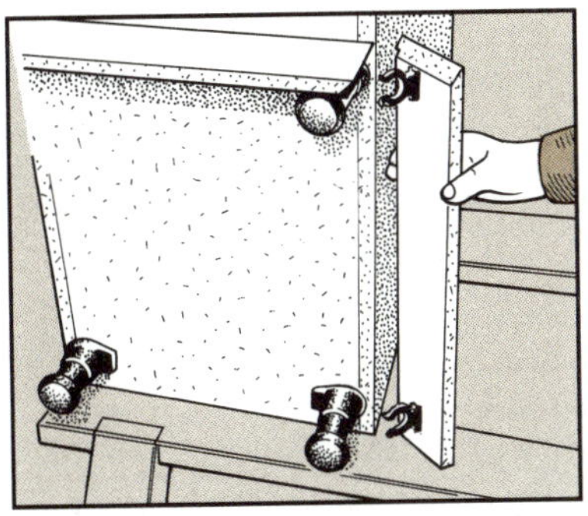

41 Use accessory clips to install toeboard panels to cabinet levelers. Screw clips to mitered panels and snap panels in place.

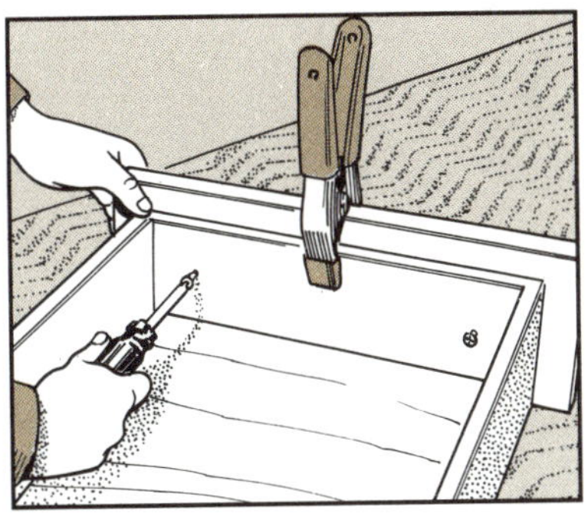

42 After assembling drawer box with 1-in. brads and glue, clamp drawer face in position and attach with round head screws.

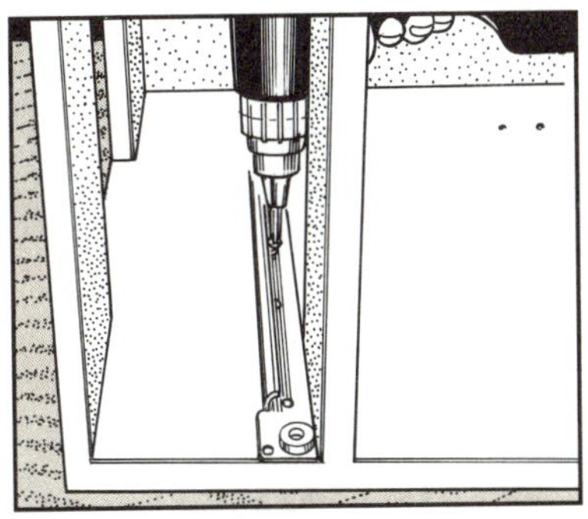

43 Next, attach the drawer slide hardware to the inside of the case side panels and to the drawer sides with supplied screws.

44 Use a drill press and a 35mm bit to bore blind holes on the inside of the door for securing European-style hinges.

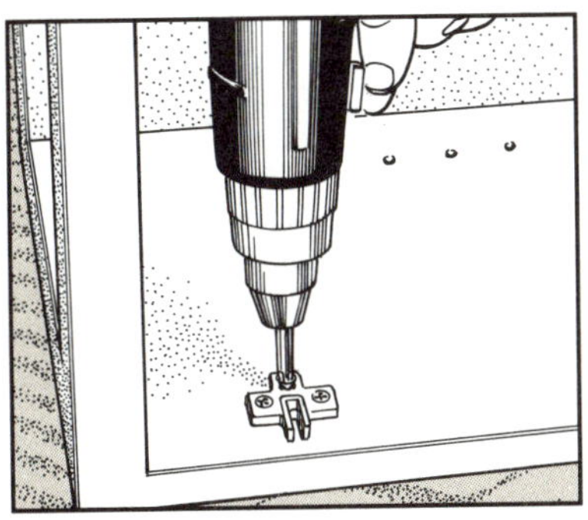

45 Install the hinge base plates on the inside surface of a cabinet side to align properly with the holes bored in the doors.

46 Install the hinges, and adjust for proper operation and fit. Then, install drawer and door pulls to complete the cabinet.

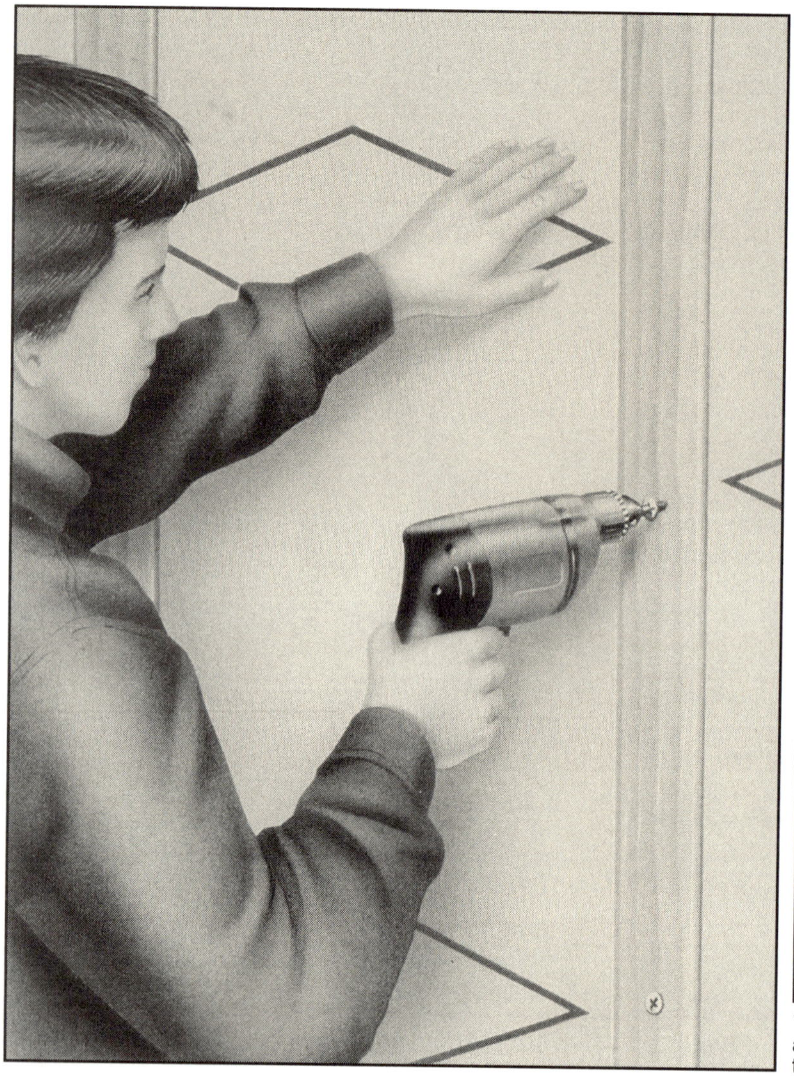

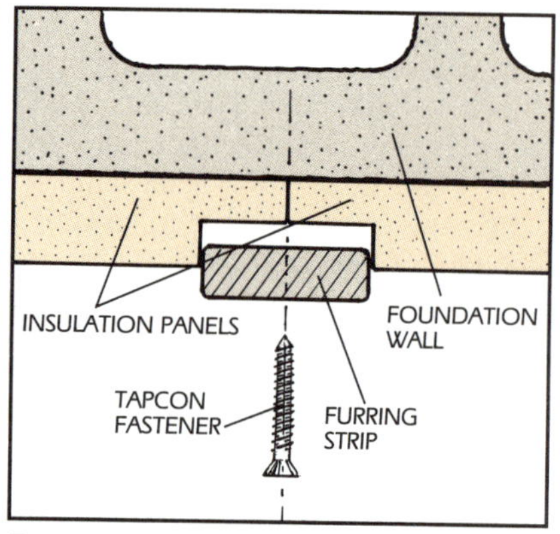

Each rigid foam board has a rabbet—along both long edges—sized to accept a standard piece of furring. The furring strip is attached to the foundation wall using concrete anchors.

1 Begin by cutting insulation panels to size and filling the joist spaces around the top of the wall with these pieces.

Insulating basement walls

Insulating Basement Walls was written by Steven Willson. Illustrations by George Retseck. Wallmate panels are manufactured by Dow Chemical Co. Contact their Customer Information Center, P.O. Box 1206, Midland, Mich. 48674. Information about Tapcon fasteners can be obtained from Elco Industries, Inc., 1111 Samuelson Rd., P.O. Box 7009, Rockford, Ill. 61225.

If you are fortunate enough to have a full basement, you know just how useful this area can be. There's usually plenty of room for doing the family laundry, putting together an extensive workshop, allowing the kids a free-fire zone out of earshot—and even enough square footage left over for storing all that junk you promised to throw away but never did.

A basement has always been a cheap source of extra living space when a family starts to outgrow a house but its bank account hasn't. Turning a basement into a family room or an extra bedroom is a time-honored project and one that just got a little easier.

A new product from Dow called Wallmate was specifically designed to insulate basement walls easily and provide a great support system for standard drywall panels. The idea is so simple, it's hard to believe it's new. Basically, Dow just took its standard Styrofoam product and manufactured it in $1\frac{1}{2} \times 24 \times 96$-in. panels, with a $\frac{3}{4} \times 1\frac{1}{2}$-in. rabbet along both edges. By abutting two panels, the groove that results from the two rabbets matches the size of a standard 1×3 furring strip. To install, just stand the panels against the wall, slide a furring strip into the groove and then attach this strip to the wall. When you're done insulating, drywall panels can be attached directly to the furring.

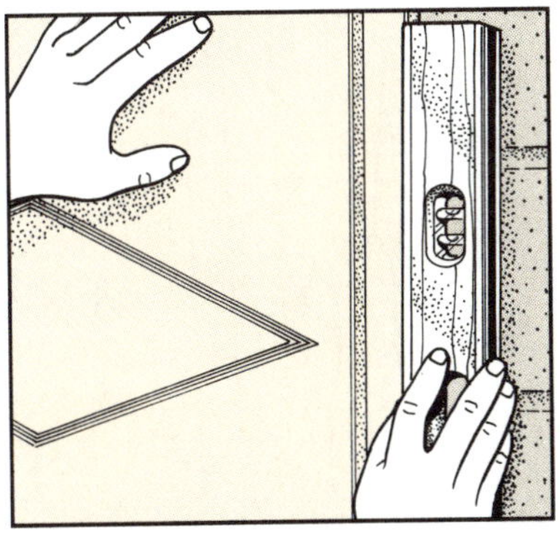

2 Starting in one corner, hold the first panel against the wall and adjust it until its edge is perfectly plumb.

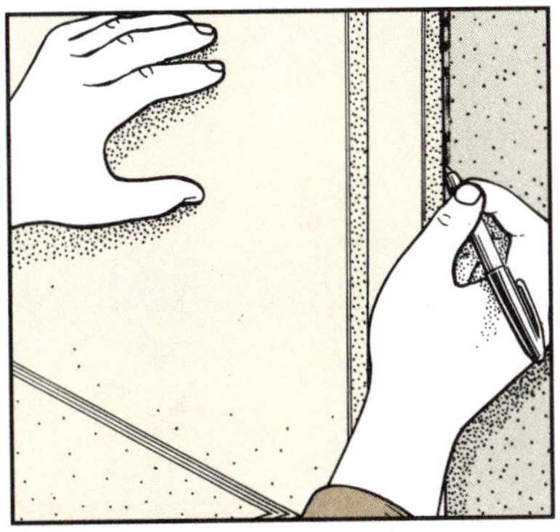

3 While holding the panel in a plumb position, mark the wall alongside the panel to establish a proper reference line.

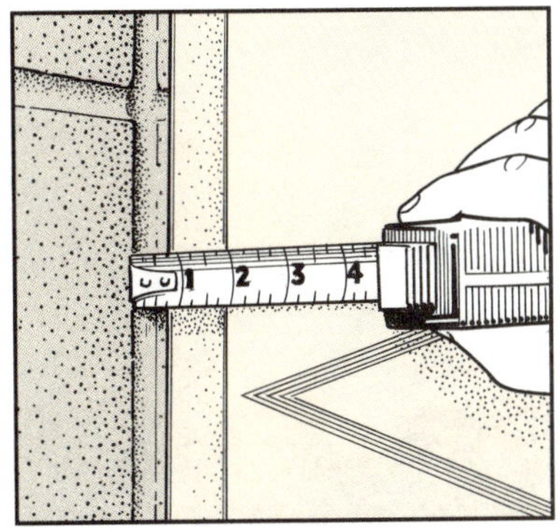

4 With the board still held in its plumb position, measure the gap between the board and the corner at its widest point.

The usual approach that this replaces is the difficult, time-consuming and expensive task of building interior 2×4 walls and filling their stud spaces with fiberglass insulation. In damp basements—which are all too common—there's another benefit: When fiberglass insulation gets wet, it loses its effectiveness as an insulator. Polystyrene panels, like Styrofoam, on the other hand, do not lose much of their insulating power in damp conditions. They have a higher R-value per inch—5 per inch in the case of extruded polystyrene and between 3 and 3.5 per inch for fiberglass. In the case of Wallmate, the panels are R-7.5. And if you double them up, which is very easy to do, you'll get a minimum R-value in your basement of 15.

The only real drawback to this system is attaching the furring strips to your block or poured concrete wall. Masonry nails are very difficult to drive and installing typical concrete anchors is too time consuming.

This installation problem, however, is easily overcome with some clever screws called Tapcon anchors (see detail drawing above Fig. 11). These screws are designed to function in concrete like self-tapping machine screws do in sheetmetal. All you need to do is bore a small-diameter pilot hole with a masonry bit. Then immediately drive the screw into this hole. No matching holes in the concrete and furring are required. Use five screws for each 8-ft. furring strip. It should take you about 3 minutes to install all five.

Of course, you have to pay for this convenience. The screws cost about $25 for a box of 100. But the box does include the proper-size masonry bit for boring the pilot holes, which stays sharp long after you've used up the screws. Between the new insulation boards and these fasteners, you can completely insulate all four of your basement walls in just one day.

Keep in mind that this system is new and therefore requires more than ordinary communication with your local building inspector, especially when it comes to the electrical system. Generally, you cannot install insulation until your electrical cable is in place and inspected. Unfortunately, this insulation is designed to go up before the wiring.

There are several ways to handle this. You could use rigid conduit, metal boxes and metal covers, and simply surface wire the whole job after the insulation and drywall are in place. You also may be allowed to attach the surface

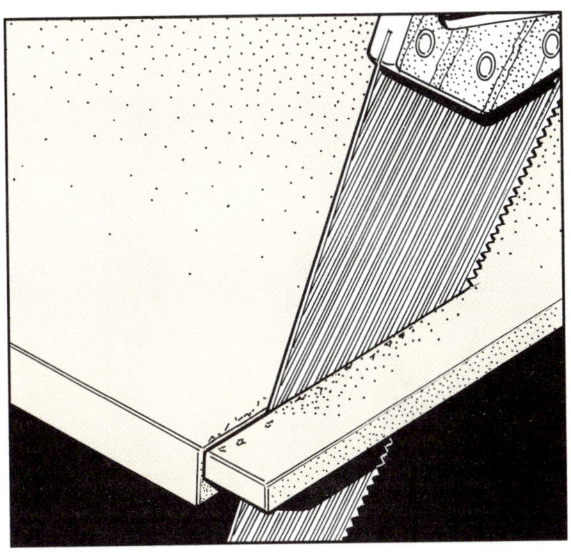

5 Mark the cutline on the back side of the panel, and then cut along the line with a handsaw or sabre saw.

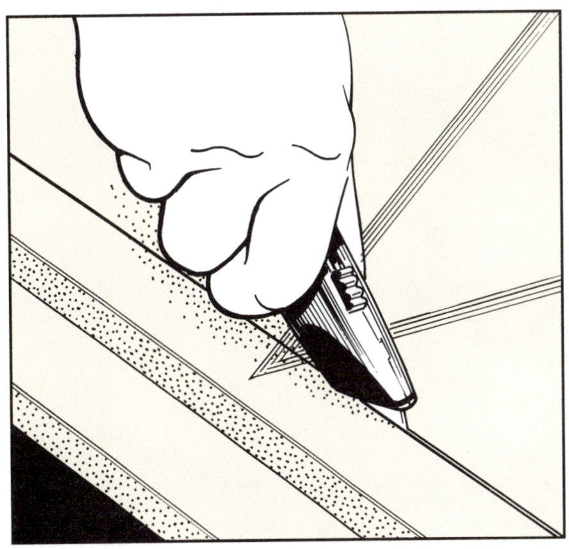

6 Measure the full rabbet width, then mark this width on the front side of the panel. Make the surface cut with a utility knife.

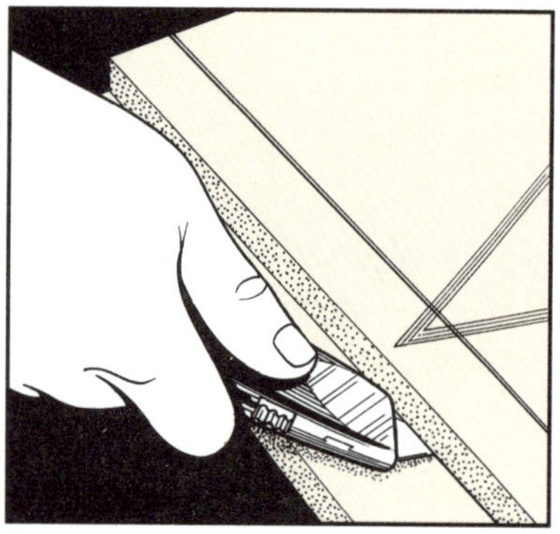

7 Complete the rabbet by making an edge cut with a utility knife. Be sure to use a sharp blade to avoid tearing the foam.

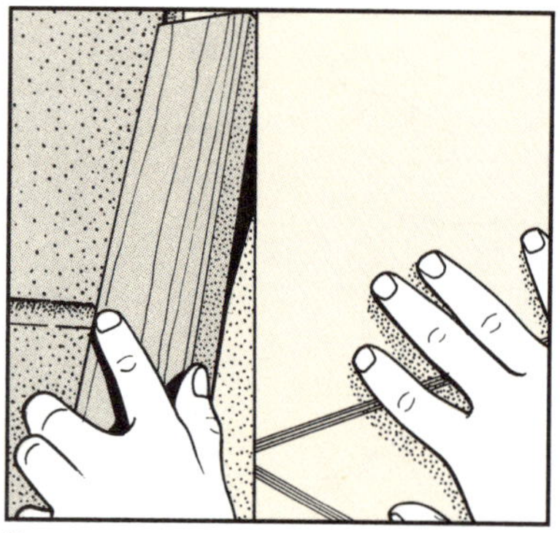

8 Once the panel is cut, hold it in place and check your reference mark. Then slide a piece of furring into the rabbet.

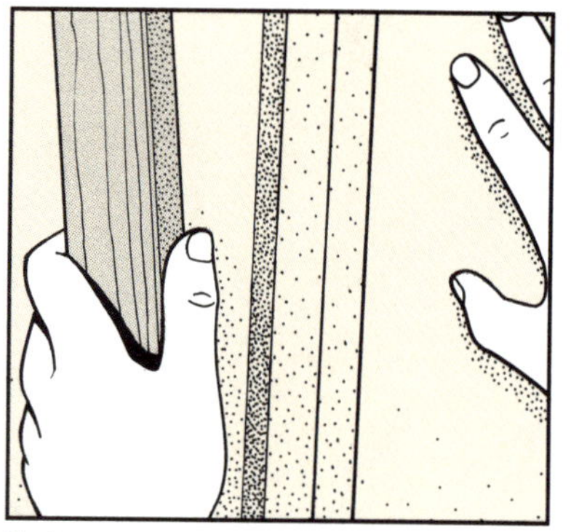

9 Once the first panel is secured, lean a second panel against the first and slide a precut furring strip into the rabbet.

wiring to the foundation walls and then insulate around everything. Or, you may be able to use the system shown here. Just get prior approval for the system you choose.

Where to Begin

You can put all the insulation you want on your basement walls, but if the joist spaces above the walls haven't been insulated, you're not going to save much money on your heating bill. To insulate these spaces, cut up pieces of Wallmate and fill the gaps with them (Fig. 1).

Next, choose one corner for your starting point and push a piece of Wallmate into this corner. Hold a level against the open edge and check for plumb (Fig. 2). Because the position of all the ensuing panels on this wall is based on the alignment of the first one, make sure it's right.

Hold this panel in the plumb position and mark the wall along the outside edge of this panel (Fig. 3). This establishes a reference line for maintaining plumb without needing to hold the level in place constantly. Once the wall is marked, hold the board against the line and measure any gap between the inside edge of the board and the corner at the widest point (Fig. 4). Usually, this is at the top or bottom of the board. Transfer this point onto a panel and mark a line. Then cut along this line using a handsaw or sabre saw (Fig. 5). This material is very easy to cut.

Next, widen the existing rabbet on the face of the first panel so it can accept a full furring strip. Mark this cutline on the surface and make the cut with a sharp utility knife (Fig. 6). Then, make an edge cut with the knife and remove all the waste (Fig. 7).

Once the rabbet is cut, hold the panel in place, check your plumb mark and slide a piece of furring into the rabbet (Fig. 8). Bore a pilot hole about waist high and drive a Tapcon screw into the hole. Then bore the rest of the pilot holes and drive the remaining screws. Use five evenly spaced screws for each 8-ft. furring strip.

Next, lean up a second panel, abut the two rabbets and slide a furring strip in place (Fig. 9). While holding the new panel and furring strip, bore a pilot hole (Fig. 10) followed by a screw (Fig. 11). Continue this process until

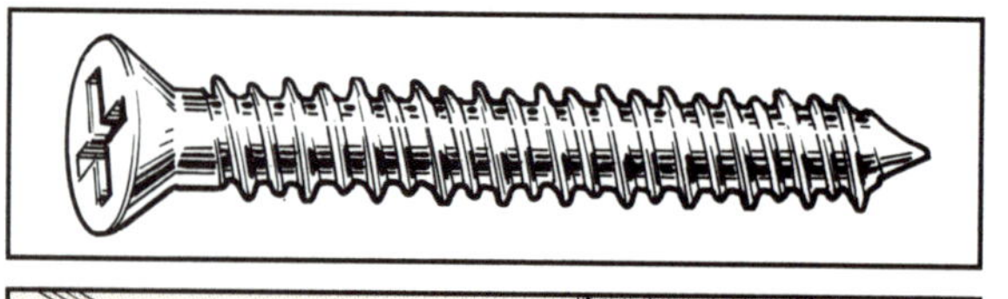

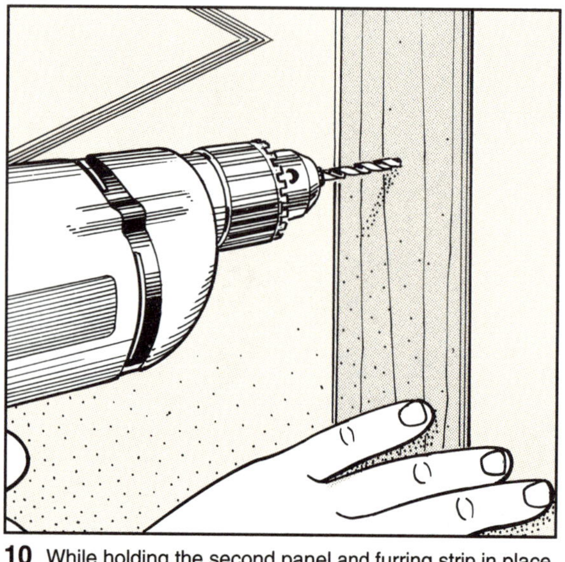

10 While holding the second panel and furring strip in place, bore a fastener hole through the furring and into the wall.

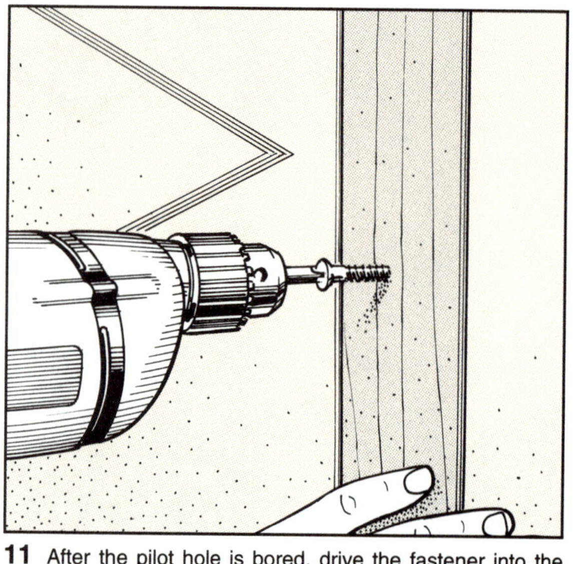

11 After the pilot hole is bored, drive the fastener into the concrete. These screws *(top)* have two threads, not just one.

12 To install receptacle boxes, first cut a board or plywood panel to size. Then trace its perimeter onto the insulation.

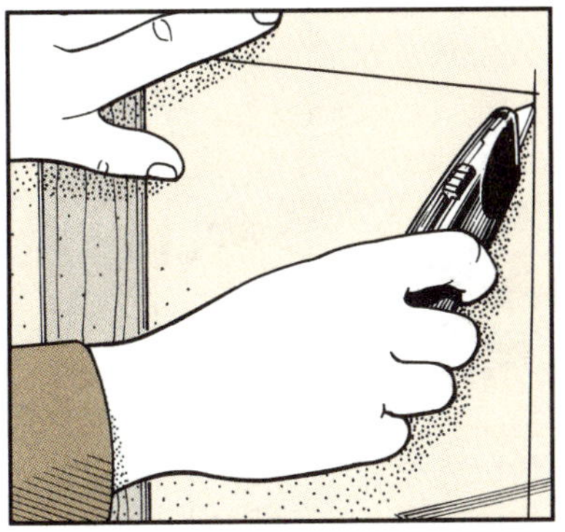

13 Use a utility knife to cut the foam panel. Because the blade can't reach all the way through, make the cut in stages.

14 Attach the board directly to the foundation wall using concrete fasteners. This board must be solidly attached.

the wall is done. Then move to the next wall and plumb the first panel in place, and repeat the same procedures.

Electrical Planning

As mentioned earlier, make sure to check with your local building inspector before undertaking any wiring. If you aren't confident of your skills, hire an electrician to handle this part of the job for you.

Your best strategy is to limit the number of fixtures on the insulated walls. If you are building partitions, locate as many receptacles, switch boxes and wall lights on these walls as the codes will permit, instead of on the insulated walls.

Begin by establishing the location of your electrical boxes. Then determine how far away from the wall the boxes should be attached so that the front of each box will be flush with the surrounding wall when you're done.

In the installation shown here, this calculation was a little complicated because it was planned to first cover the walls with $1/2$-in.-thick drywall and the cover the drywall with $3/8$-in.-thick paneling. It was also decided to use square metal boxes that require cover rings. Because of these requirements, construction started with a $3/8$-in.-thick piece of plywood against the foundation wall, attached a $1\frac{1}{2}$-in.-deep box to this panel; then a $1/2$-in.-deep cover ring was installed on the box. This total depth—$2\frac{3}{8}$ in.—matched the combined depth of the insulation ($1\frac{1}{2}$ in.), the drywall ($1/2$ in.) and the paneling ($3/8$ in.).

This also fulfilled a requirement of the local inspector. Each box had to be mounted on a wood panel large enough for the full box with room left over to staple the cable—which ran to and from the box—firmly in place.

After establishing the proper thickness for your mounting boards, cut them into pieces that measure about 8×12 in. Then trace the shape of each board on the insulation where an electrical box is required (Fig. 12). Cut out the insulation along these traced lines using a utility knife (Fig. 13). Then attach each of these boards directly to the foundation wall using short Tapcon screws (Fig. 14).

Determine the path of your cable and then temporarily attach a straightedge guide to the furring strips to support a router (Fig. 15). Install a $3/4$-in. straight bit in

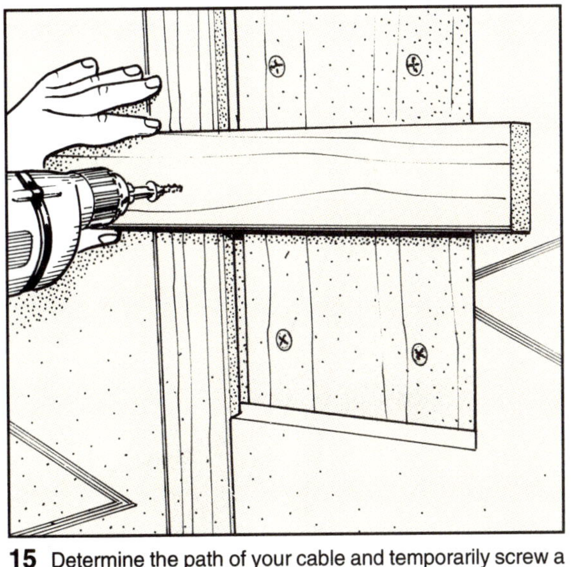

15 Determine the path of your cable and temporarily screw a straightedge guide to the furring strips to support a router.

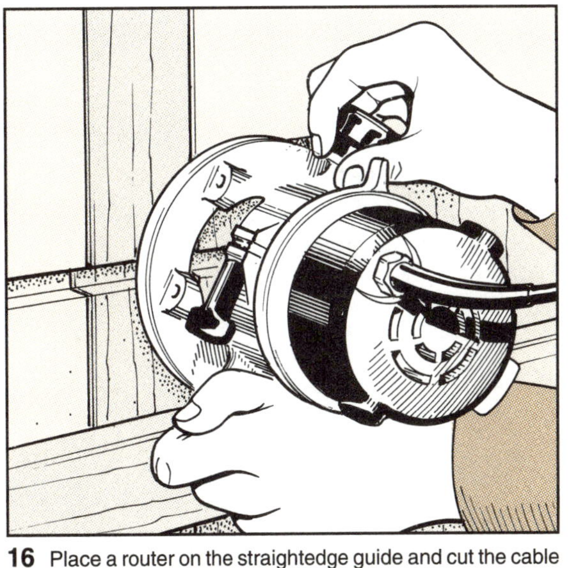

16 Place a router on the straightedge guide and cut the cable groove through the foam panels and furring strips.

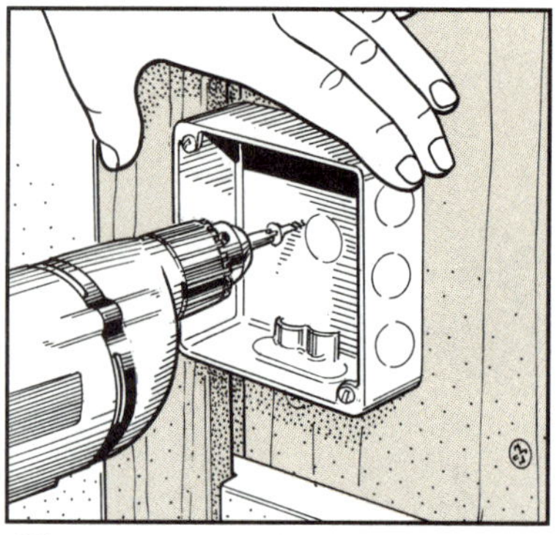

17 Install an electrical box on the board using short drywall screws. Make sure the box is firmly attached.

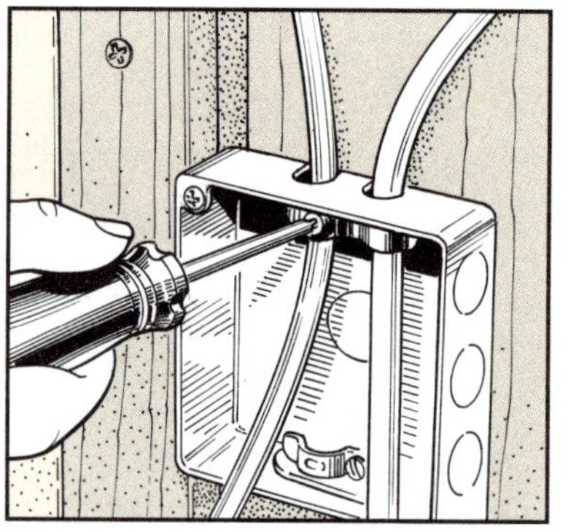

18 Feed the electrical cables into the box and tighten them in place with built-in cable clamps or standard box connectors.

19 Gently staple each cable to the board within 8 in. of the box. Do not tear the sheathing that protects the cable.

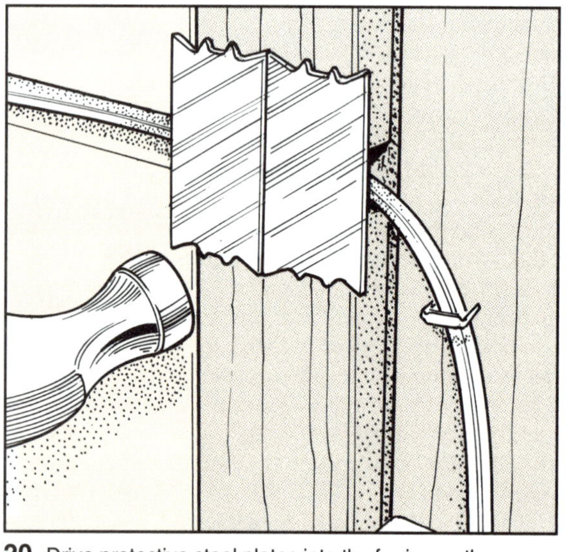

20 Drive protective steel plates into the furring so they cover the cable groove. These plates prevent cable damage.

your router and set the depth to 3/8 in. Then rout a cable groove across the panels and furring strips (Fig. 16).

Once all your support boards are attached and cable grooves cut, install an electrical box on each board using short drywall screws (Fig. 17). Keep the box near the bottom of the board, so you'll have room to staple your cable above the box. Then feed the required electrical cables into the box and secure them by tightening the built-in cable clamps or standard box connectors (Fig. 18). Make sure to staple each cable within 8 in. of the box (Fig. 19).

To protect the cable when it runs over each furring strip, you must install steel plates that bridge the groove and completely cover the cable (Fig. 20). This protects the wire from being pierced by nails or screws used to install the drywall later.

Finish your rough electrical installation by attaching cover plates to the boxes (Fig. 21). Then, after you've passed your rough inspection, just hang and finish your drywall in the usual manner (Fig. 22)—or skip the finishing process and cover the drywall with paneling.

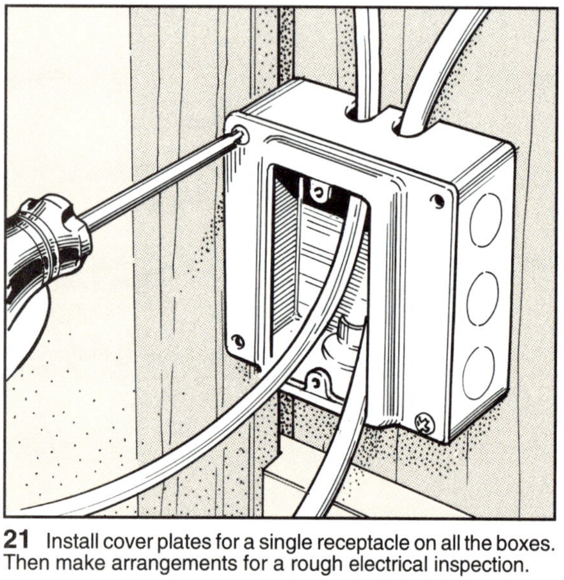

21 Install cover plates for a single receptacle on all the boxes. Then make arrangements for a rough electrical inspection.

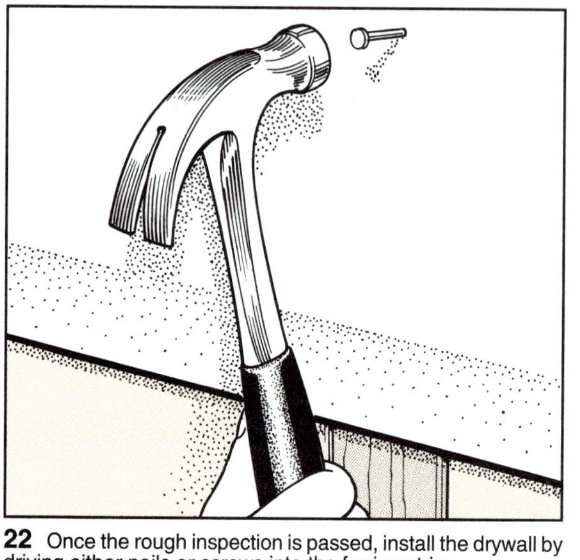

22 Once the rough inspection is passed, install the drywall by driving either nails or screws into the furring strips.

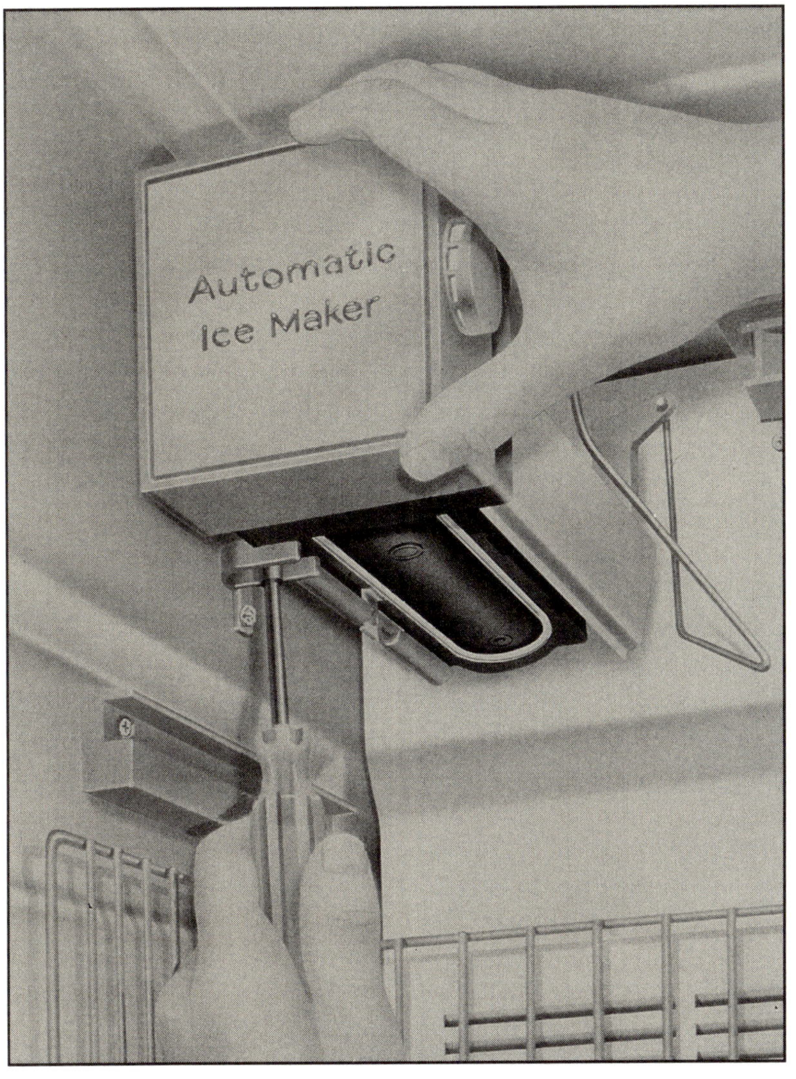

1 Begin by removing the cover plate inside the freezer. Back out the fastening screw, and remove the plate.

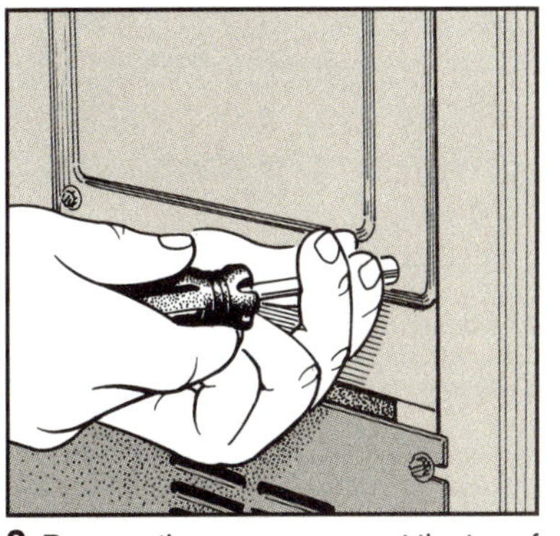

2 Remove the access cover at the top of the refrigerator. Use a nut driver to back out the hexhead screws.

Installing an Icemaker was written by Merle Henkenius. Illustrations by George Retseck.

Installing an icemaker

If you have often wanted an icemaker, but somehow missed the opportunity when you bought your refrigerator, you'll be glad to know that you can install one without much trouble. Installing an aftermarket icemaker kit is easy. It takes less than an hour to complete.

Always choose an icemaker that is the same make as your refrigerator. The Whirlpool icemaker shown is installed in a similar manner as other makes, but you should always follow the instructions of the manufacturer that made your icemaker.

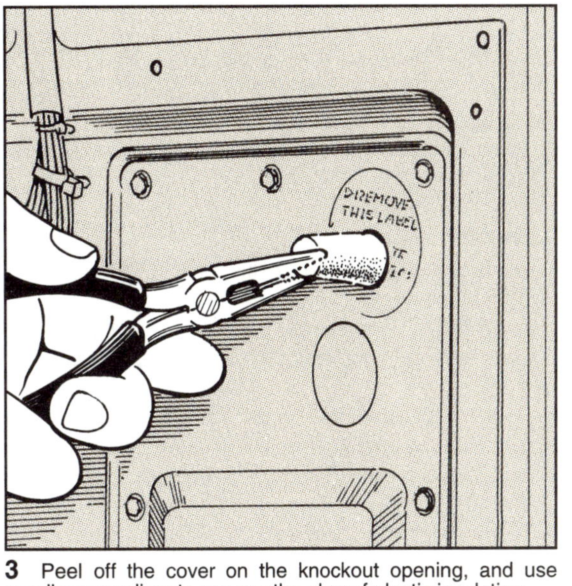

3 Peel off the cover on the knockout opening, and use needle-nose pliers to remove the plug of plastic insulation.

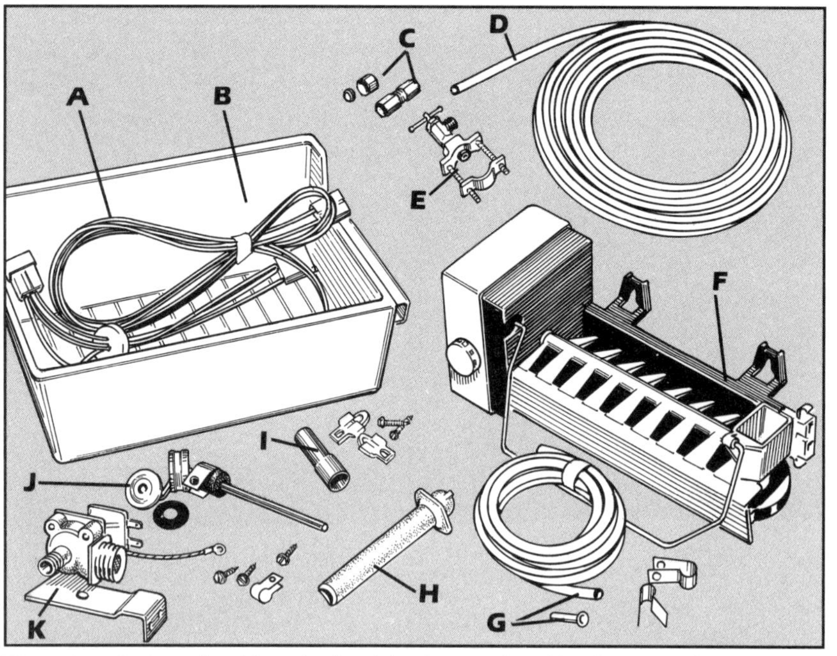

The automatic icemaker kit and related hardware: **A**—wiring harness; **B**—ice bin; **C**—coupling; **D**—copper feed line; **E**—saddle-tap valve; **F**—icemaker; **G**—plastic waterline and insert; **H**—water tube; **I**—water-tube extension; **J**—copper inlet tube and **K**—solenoid valve. Unlabeled parts are screws, clips and fittings.

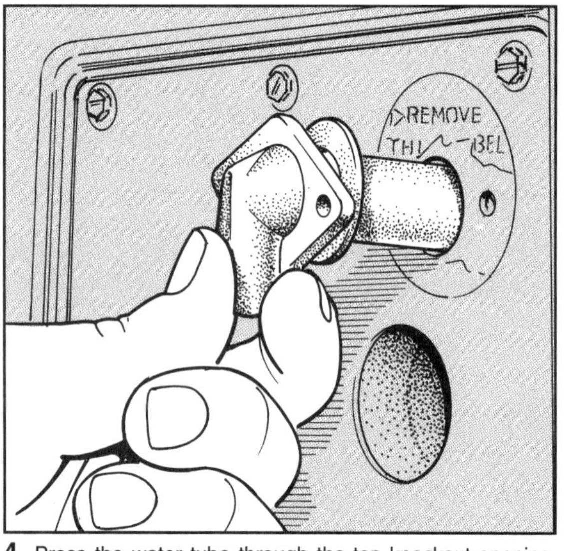

4 Press the water tube through the top knockout opening. Then screw the tube flange to the cabinet.

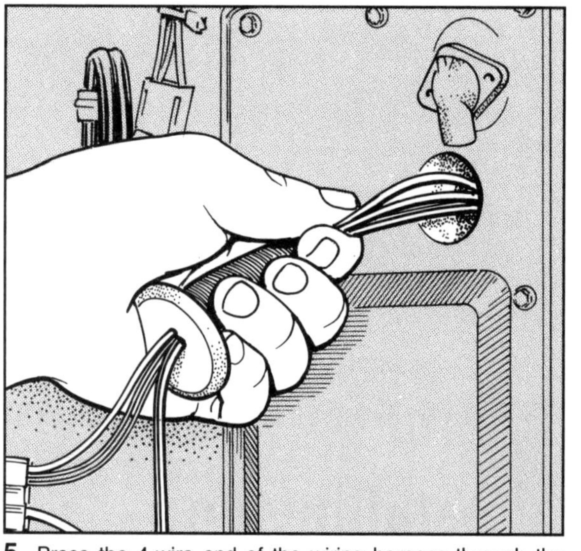

5 Press the 4-wire end of the wiring harness through the bottom knockout. Seat the grommet in the opening.

Assessing Feasibility

While it is possible to install an icemaker in a refrigerator that was not built to accommodate one, it's a complicated retrofit and should be left to professionals. If your refrigerator was built to accept an icemaker, you'll find a rectangular access panel at the back of the appliance, with two knockout openings identified for icemaker use. The appliance also will have a labeled cover plate inside the freezer and several capped screwholes on the adjacent sidewall.

To connect the icemaker, you need access to a cold-water line, either through a sink cabinet or from the basement.

Getting Started

Start by unplugging your refrigerator and pulling it forward. While the icemaker will be mounted in the freezer, most of the work will take place at the back of the refrigerator.

Next, loosen the screws on the cover plate inside the freezer and drop the plate (Fig. 1).

Remove the icemaker access panel on the refrigerator's back and the access panel below it that conceals the compressor (Fig. 2). Behind the icemaker access panel is electrical wiring with a 3-wire electrical slot connector and two knockout openings.

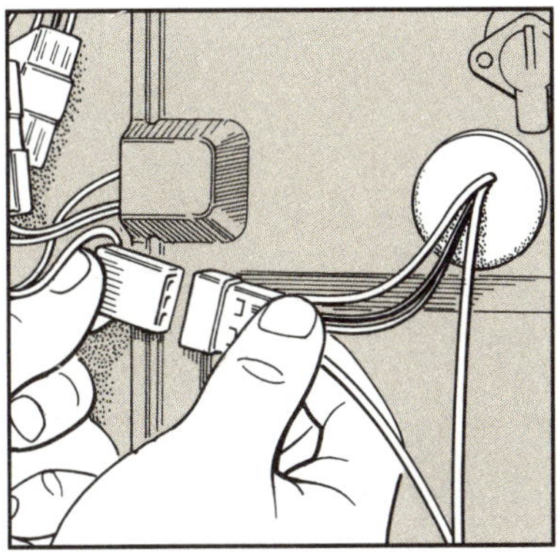

6 Snap the wiring-harness connector to the equivalent connector that was preinstalled on the refrigerator.

7 Place an insert in the plastic waterline, and tighten the line on the solenoid valve with a compression nut.

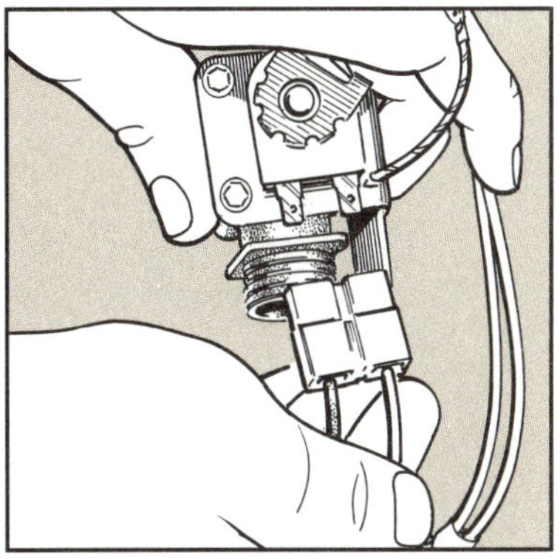

8 Hold the solenoid valve firmly, and press the wire-harness slot connector onto the brass tabs on the solenoid valve.

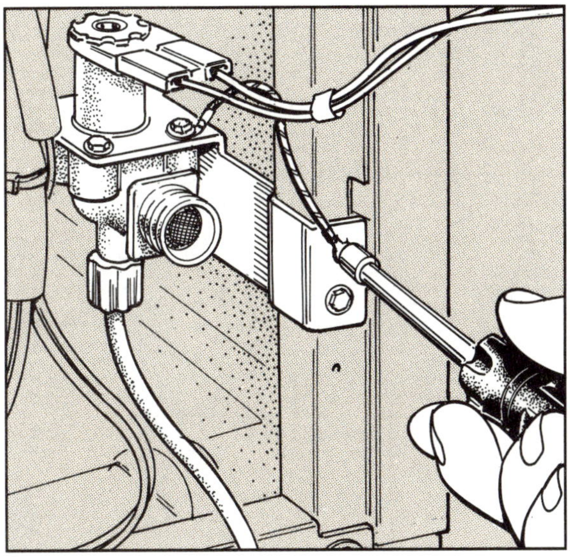

9 Screw the solenoid-valve mounting bracket to the cabinet. Fasten the ground wire with one mounting screw.

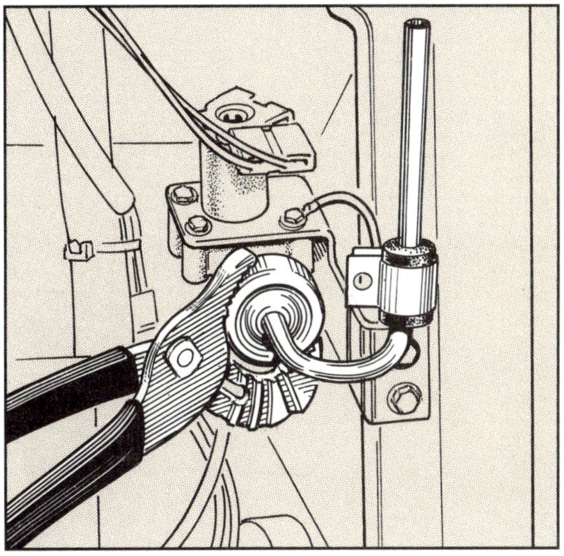

10 Tighten the fitting on the copper water-inlet tube onto the solenoid valve. Screw the tube's clamp to the cabinet.

The knockout openings are filled with a precut plastic insulation that is easy to remove. Just peel the paper cover from the opening and pull out the insulation with needle-nose pliers (Fig. 3). Push the water tube through the top opening, and screw the tube's flange to the cabinet (Fig. 4).

Next, feed the 4-wire end of the wiring harness into the freezer compartment. Push it through the bottom knockout opening, and set its rubber grommet in the opening (Fig. 5). Press the connector on the wiring harness into the equivalent connector that was preinstalled on the refrigerator (Fig. 6). Each slot connector is shaped differently, so there's little chance you'll cross wire the kit.

Next, place a metal insert in one end of the plastic waterline, and push the line into the water-tube inlet port. Hold the line with a band clamp.

Feed the plastic waterline down the refrigerator's back to the compressor compartment. Hold the solenoid valve in place to see how much waterline you need. Put a small loop in the line to prevent it from kinking, and cut the line to length.

Slide a compression nut and ring over one end of the plastic waterline and press a metal insert into the end of the line. The metal insert keeps the line from collapsing as the compression fitting is tightened. Thread the compression nut onto the solenoid valve (Fig. 7). Then, press the remaining wire-harness connector onto the brass solenoid prongs (Fig. 8).

Screw the solenoid valve to the refrigerator cabinet, just inside the compressor compartment. One of these screws also will bind the valve's grounding conductor to the cabinet (Fig. 9).

Next, tuck the plastic waterline and harness wiring into the panel's recessed channel. Then, install the copper water-inlet tube on the solenoid valve, using slip-jaw pliers to tighten the fitting until it feels snug (Fig. 10). Reinstall the compressor access panel.

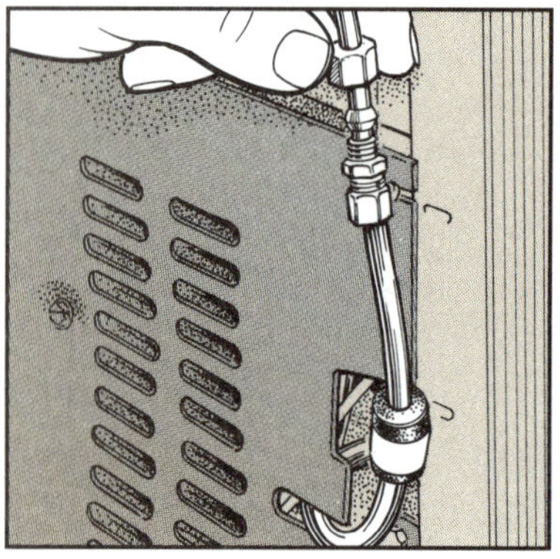

11 Use the brass compression coupling that's included in the kit to join the copper supply line to the copper inlet tube.

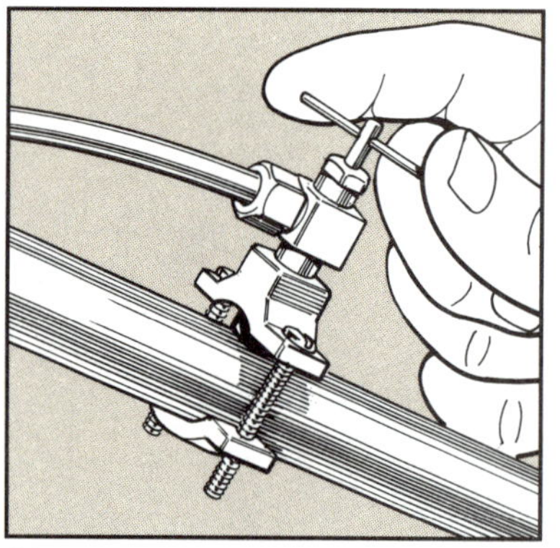

12 Connect the saddle-tap valve to a cold-water pipe, and connect the copper supply line to the valve.

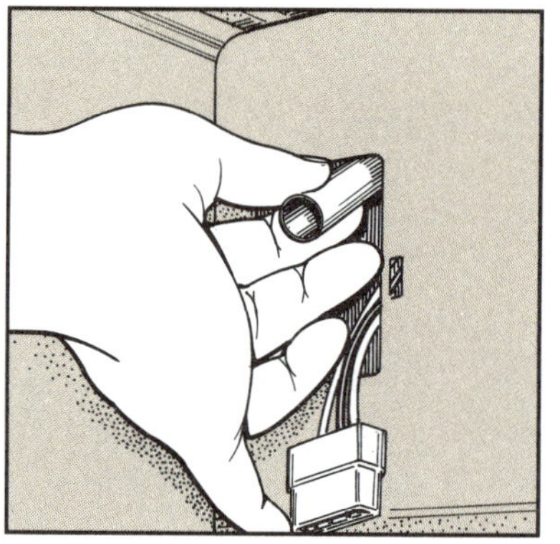

13 Press the water-tube extension spout onto the water tube. The extension should reach well into the freezer.

14 To wire the icemaker, press its slot connector into the connector on the end of the wiring harness.

15 Fasten the icemaker to the wall of the freezer with three hexhead screws that are provided with the unit.

Next, connect the copper feed line to the water-inlet tube using a brass compression coupling (Fig. 11). Slide a brass nut and brass ring from the coupling onto the copper inlet tube. Coat the ring with pipe dope or petroleum jelly, and tighten the nut until it feels snug. Repeat the procedure with the second nut and ring on the feed line. Extend the feed line to the nearest cold-water plumbing pipe.

Mount the saddle-tap valve on the cold-water pipe by tightening the two side bolts. Then, trim the feed line to length and connect it to the saddle-tap valve with the remaining compression ring and nut (Fig. 12).

Working Inside the Freezer

The remaining steps are completed inside the freezer. Begin by sliding the water-tube extension spout onto the water tube, so that the spout reaches well into the freezer compartment (Fig. 13). Then, place the icemaker in the compartment and lock the two halves of the electrical connection (Fig. 14).

To mount the icemaker on the freezer wall, pry off the screwhole caps using a putty knife, and screw the icemaker in place (Fig. 15). Then, level the icemaker by adjusting the leveling screw on the underside of the unit. If your kitchen floor slopes noticeably, check the level again after the refrigerator is pushed back.

With all the connections made, wash out the ice bin and slide the bin under the icemaker. Replace any shelves you may have removed, and install the remaining access cover.

Next, twist the handle on the saddle-tap valve clockwise, so it pierces the pipe. Open the tap by turning it counterclockwise.

Plug in the refrigerator and slide it back. Set the fill-level knob midway between HIGH and LOW, and allow the icemaker to cycle for 24 hours to purge air from the waterline.

Installing a water filter

Installing a Water Filter was written by Merle Henkenius with illustrations by George Retseck.

Water quality is a hot issue these days, and one with an ironic twist. While federal and state agencies are doing more now to improve water quality than at any time in history, many of us suspect that our drinking water has never been more contaminated. The truth is, most water supplies are not as toxic as we might imagine. Still, there are exceptions.

Seventy-five percent of us get our drinking water from municipal water systems, which are subject to stringent ongoing testing and treatment. While this ensures reasonable purity at the source, contaminants, such as lead, can be picked up in the distribution piping or even from the piping in our own homes.

Moreover, a full 25% of us get our water from private or extremely limited public wells. These wells are tested for nitrates and coliform bacteria at their startup, but they are seldom tested regularly thereafter.

Finally, some water, while not health threatening, simply tastes or smells bad, usually owing to a high sulfur content. In other cases, sand or mineral sediment leaves water cloudy and gritty.

Defining Need

No water treatment device should be installed where it's not needed. If you suspect a water problem in your home, check with your local health department about having the drinking water in your home tested. Most can arrange tests that are quite affordable, costing from $15 to $60. If you've recently purchased a home with a private water well, the mortgage company is likely to have required a well inspection and water test. In any case, your health department can suggest the best treatment equipment for your situation.

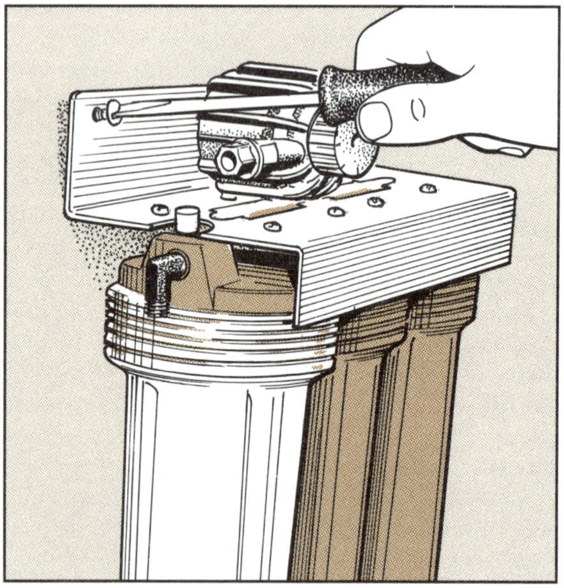

1 Screw filter carriage to cabinet wall using pan head screws. Keep filter housing at least 2 in. from the cabinet floor.

The Filtration Option

There is a wide variety of water purification devices on the market today, ranging from the familiar water softener, to the less familiar reverse-osmosis system. But if your water is marginally high in lead, mercury, trace elements, sediment or chemical compounds (from agriculture and industry), simple filtration can be a reasonable and inexpensive solution.

While point-of-entry systems are available (which treat all water entering a home), a point-of-use system is often an acceptable alternative. The water entering your toilet or the water irrigating your lawn, for example, probably doesn't need to be treated. Because filters reach saturation limits in direct relation to the volume of water that flows through them, filtering only your drinking and cooking water makes sense.

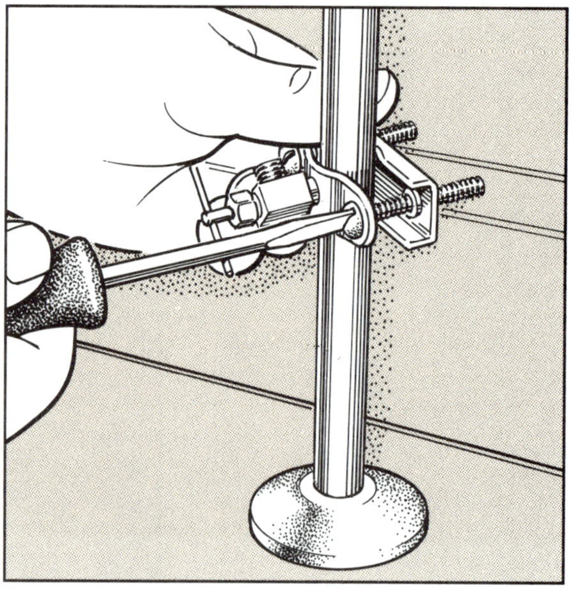

2 After opening the saddle valve to retract the self-piercing point, tighten the valve halves around the supply pipe.

This point is especially important when you consider that saturated filter media actually increase your exposure to contaminants. When a filter medium such as activated charcoal fills up, it can release its contents—in high concentrations—directly into your drinking glass.

3 Connect the supply tubing to the saddle valve using a compression nut, ferrule and tubing insert. Then, tighten with a wrench.

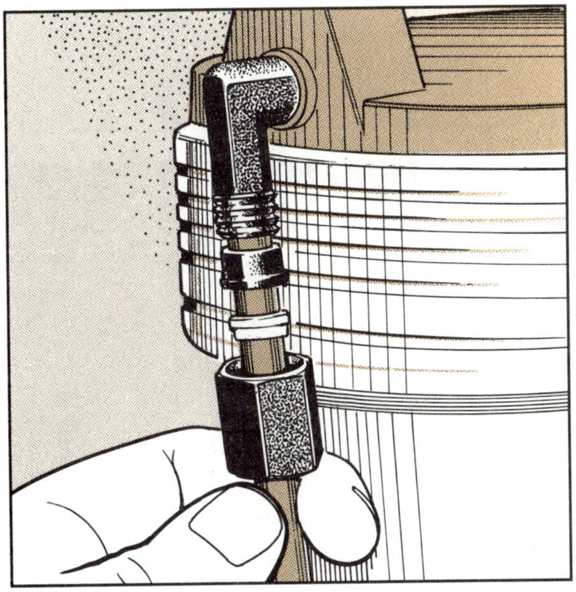

4 Make the tubing connection to the filter assembly with plastic nuts, collars and ferrules. Avoid overtightening the nuts.

Considering Features

The unit shown here is an Ametek 3-filter point-of-use kit, which mounts under a kitchen sink and includes its own sink faucet. It was installed in the fourth deck hole of the sink (the hole often reserved for a spray attachment). Installation is surprisingly simple as the connection to the household water supply is made with a self-piercing saddle valve—identical to those used in icemaker kits. With this type of valve, you can connect the filter assembly with simple tools and without disrupting your plumbing system.

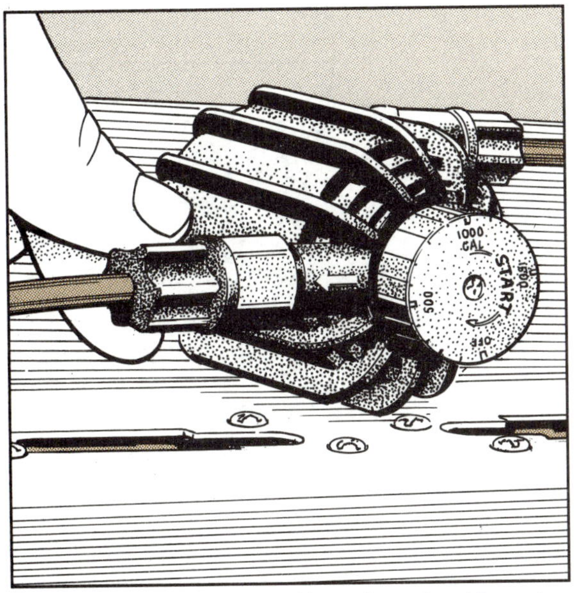

5 Connect a second piece of tubing to the metered flow valve. This tubing supplies filtered water to the unit's faucet.

The Ametek kit consists of a filter carriage with three filter housings. The first filter housing contains a sediment filter, made of spun polypropylene. Polypropylene is bacteria resistant and is able to trap suspended solids as small as 5 microns in size. Replacement sediment filters cost about $3.50.

The second housing contains a granular activated-charcoal filter material, which treats foul-smelling or off-tasting water, and also traps up to 95% of many volatile organic compounds. These are the carcinogenic compounds left behind by agriculture and industry. Granular activated-charcoal filter replacements cost $9 to $11.

The final filter contains powdered activated carbon, plus a metal-absorption resin. Together, they can trap 97% of waterborne lead and mercury. They also filter disease-causing giardia and cryptosporidium cysts, commonly found in surface- and shallow-water sources. Replacements cost $17 to $20.

6 Place the trim flange on the threaded shank of the faucet and insert the shank through the hole in the sink or countertop.

Most importantly, this unit has a metered flow valve. When 1500 gallons of water (roughly one year's use) pass through it, the valve shuts off until you replace the filters. As such, there's little chance of a filter becoming so saturated that it releases contaminants into your drinking and cooking water supply.

Installation

As noted, installation is remarkably easy. You won't even need to shut off the water. Begin by mounting the filter carriage on a convenient wall of the sink cabinet. Use pan head screws to secure the carriage to the cabinet so that it's at least 2 in. from the cabinet floor (Fig. 1).

With the carriage mounted, install the saddle valve on the cold-water supply riser that leads to the sink tap.

With the self-piercing point of the valve threaded back as far as it will go, draw the two sides of the saddle bracket around the riser pipe (Fig. 2). Tighten the two screws evenly, until the saddle valve is secure and can't be turned on the pipe.

Then, trim the supply tube with a sharp knife and connect the tubing between the water supply riser and the inlet fitting of the filter.

The tubing connections are made with compression fittings, consisting of a compression nut, a tubing insert and a nylon compression ferrule. Begin each connection by first sliding the nut and ferrule over the tubing, the slide the insert into the end of the tubing to keep it from collapsing under the pressure of the ferrule. (The plastic fittings on the filter will have outer collars instead of inserts.) Then, slide the end of the tubing into the fitting and thread the nut in place. Don't overtighten

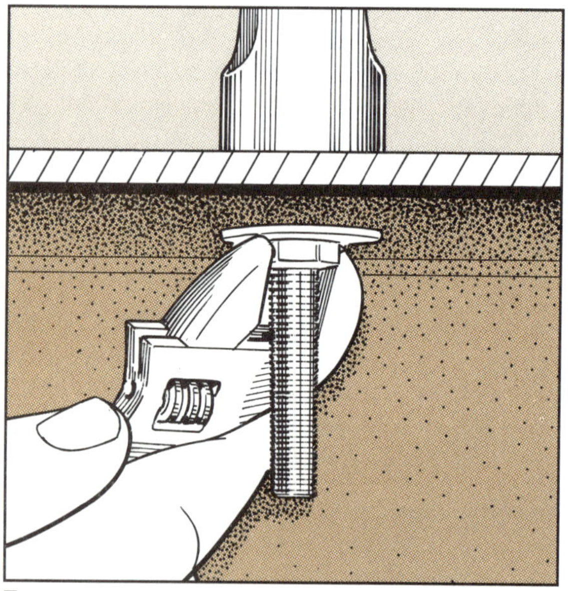

7 To fasten the faucet, first slide a washer over the shank. Then, thread on the jamb nut and tighten the nut with a wrench.

the compression nut—finger tight, plus one or two full turns with a wrench is plenty.

After attaching the tube to the saddle valve (Fig. 3), secure the other end to the filter's inlet fitting (Fig. 4). Once this is done, attach another length of tubing to the outlet of the metered flow valve (Fig. 5).

Next, install the faucet in the fourth sink deck hole. If your sink doesn't have a fourth hole, bore a hole through the countertop next to the sink and install the faucet there. You can also bore a hole through a stainless-steel sink to mount the unit. To mount the faucet, slide the trim flange over the threaded shank and insert the shank into the hole from above (Fig. 6).

Then from below, thread the jamb nut onto the faucet shank and tighten it with an adjustable wrench until it feels snug (Fig. 7). Finally, splice the remaining tubing

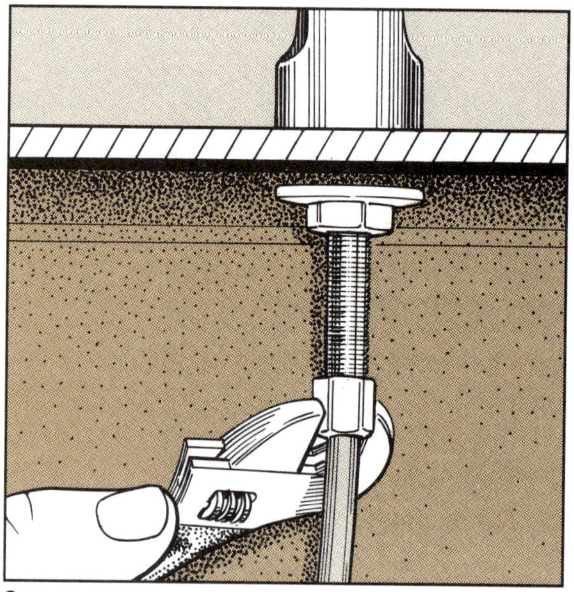

8 Connect the tubing from the metered flow valve to the faucet shank with a compression nut, tubing insert and ferrule.

between the filter's metered valve and the faucet, using compression components (Fig. 8). With all the connections made, thread the saddle valve's tap into the supply pipe until it pierces the pipe. Then, back it out to start the flow of water.

Once in use, this unit's metered flow valve will keep track of how much water has passed through the system. At 1500 gallons, the valve will automatically stop the flow of water, and it's time to replace the filters. After installing the new filters, reset the flow valve to meter the water flow for the next 1500 gallons (Fig. 9).

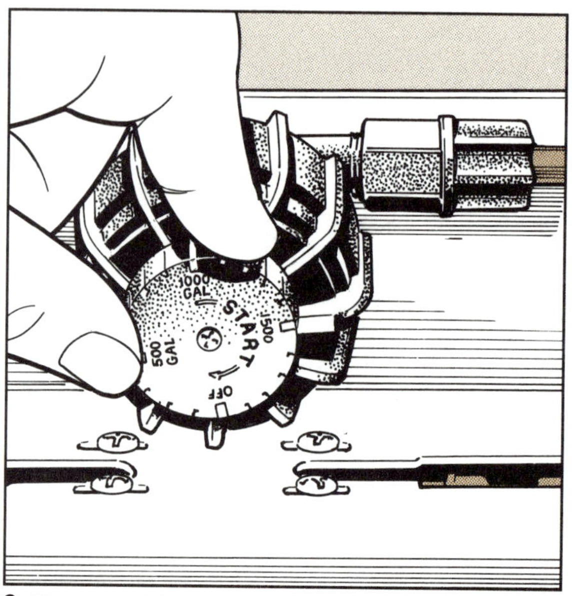

9 The metered flow valve stops the flow of water after 1500 gallons. After installing new filters, reset the flow valve.

Installing a furnace filter

It's no secret that the quality of the air we breathe has been on a steady decline. By-products of manufacturing and power generation, as well as automobile emissions, all contribute to an atmospheric soup that shapes the environment as well as our health.

Installing a Furnace Filter was written by Neal Barrett with illustrations by George Retseck. The unit shown is the Space-Guard High Efficiency Air Cleaner, Model 2200, manufactured by Research Products Corp., P.O. Box 1467, Madison, WI 53701.

1 Use a screwdriver to release the retaining clips that hold the furnace access door in place. Then, remove the door.

2 Remove the existing filter from the furnace and check its condition. If it's a reusable type, clean it and set it aside.

3 Pry off the metal clips that hold the return duct on the furnace. On some installations, you'll find screws.

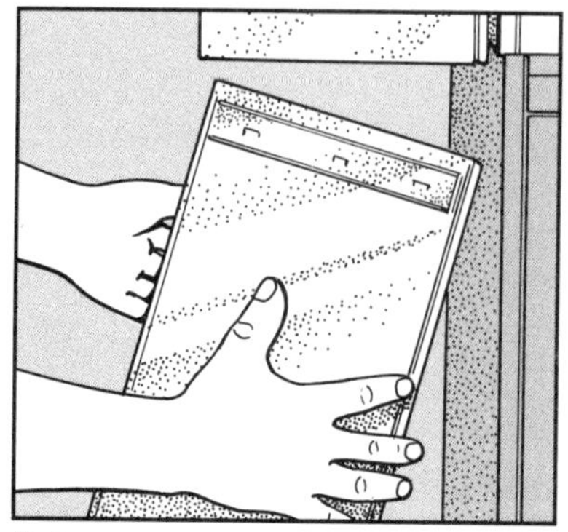

4 Detach a section of ductwork by first releasing the snap joint with a screwdriver. Then, pull the joint apart.

5 Position the air cleaner next to the furnace so the outlet side faces the furnace. Then, slide out the filter frame.

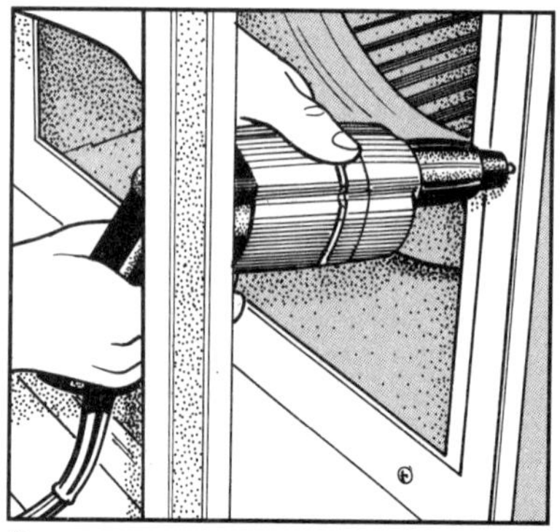

6 Use sheetmetal screws to fasten the housing to the furnace. Power driving with a hexhead driver speeds up the work.

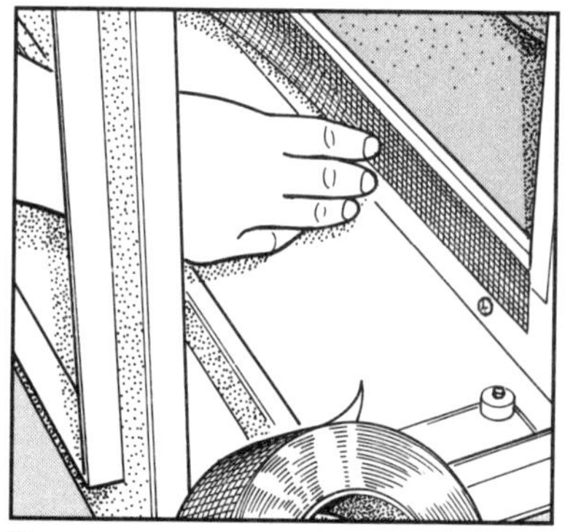

7 After securing the housing, seal all joints with duct tape. Any air leaks will reduce the efficiency of the air cleaner.

Until recently, our homes seemed to be havens from this toxic assault. Within the past decade, however, it's become apparent that even here we are vulnerable to pollution.

The sources of indoor air pollution are many. Products used in construction, such as flakeboard, plywood, certain types of insulation and carpet backer, can emit gases into the home. Tobacco and cooking smoke, skin flakes, viruses, bacteria, animal dander, mold and mildew all contribute to a less-than-perfect environment inside the home.

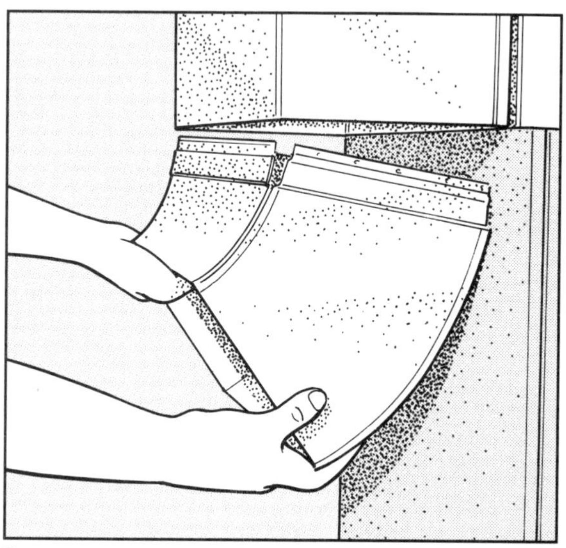

8 Begin rerouting the cold-air return duct to the air-cleaner housing by adding a 45° bend to the existing ductwork.

One way to tackle indoor pollution is to circulate the indoor air through a filter. With a forced-air heating or air-conditioning system, the ductwork, gratings and blower are already in place. Unfortunately, the filters generally installed in these systems are not very efficient in eliminating most of the pollutants. One solution to the problem is to install a supplementary air filter.

Choosing a Filter

The two most common types of air cleaners are the media type and the electronic type. The media type has an accordion-shaped, dense paper filter that catches particles in the airstream. These filters have no moving parts and require no electricity to operate, although the filter medium must be replaced about once a year, which costs about $30 to $40. Electronic cleaners use an electric charge to trap particles on a screen. Although the filters are permanent, they have to be cleaned every two to three months.

Electronic air cleaners remove smaller particles than media filters and are a good choice if you suffer from allergies. On the other hand, they cost three to four times as much as a media-type filter and most manu-

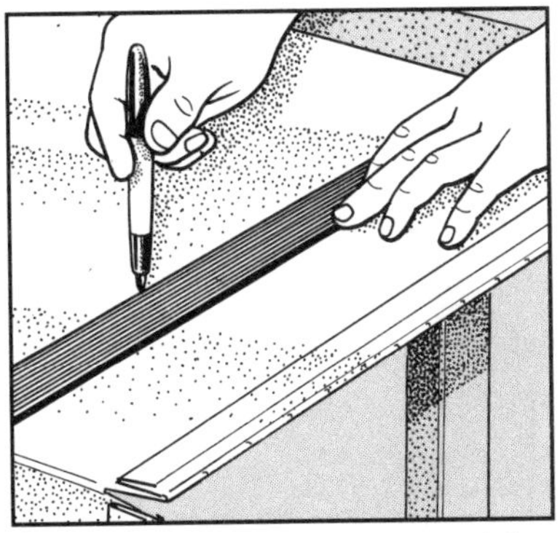

9 Cut a duct by measuring exposed duct length from lower edge of snap joint. Then mark with felt pen and straightedge.

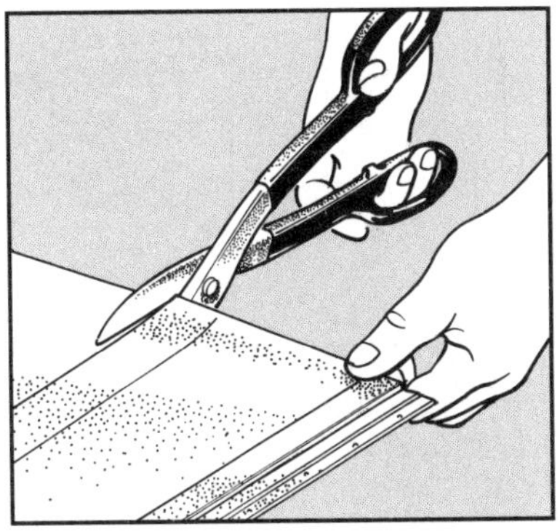

10 Extend cut 1 in. to allow for joining tabs, and cut duct **L** section with metal shears. Beware of sharp edges.

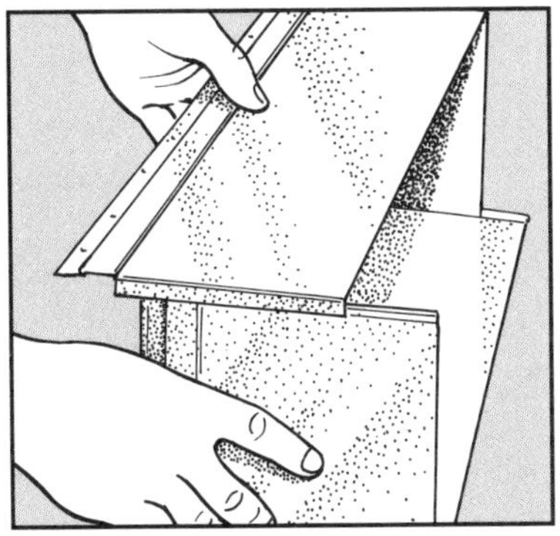

11 After both **L** sections are cut to length, slide them together to complete short straight length of duct.

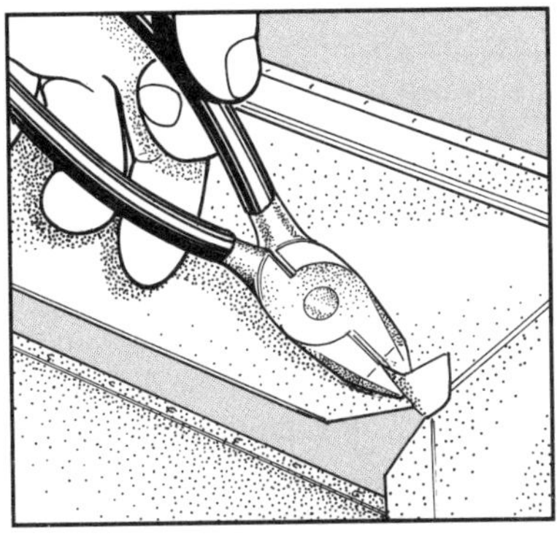

12 Use shears to make small triangular cuts at each corner of the duct. Then, remove these pieces with pliers.

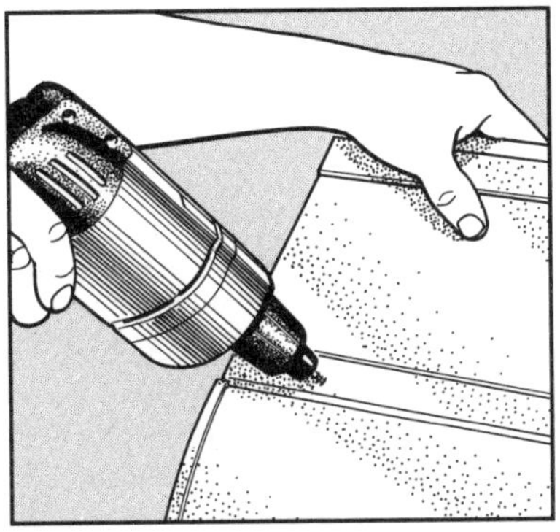

13 Join short duct to a 45° bend by first sliding the cut ends into the snap joint of the bend. Secure with screws.

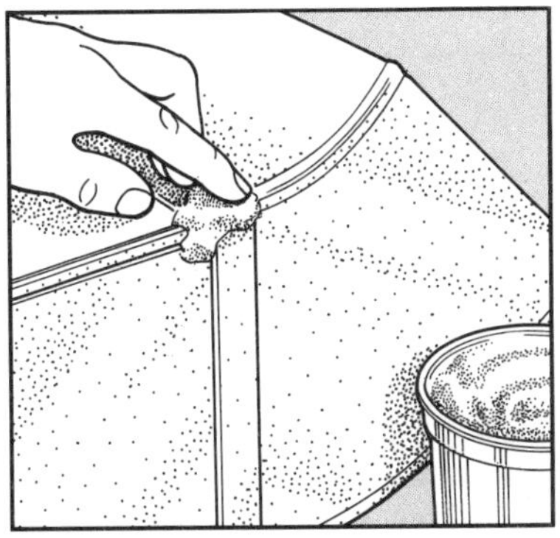

14 Use furnace cement or plumbers putty to fill gaps at joint corners. Then, seal entire joint with duct tape.

facturers won't honor the warranty unless the unit is installed by an authorized technician. By contrast, media-type cleaners cost about $200 and you can install one yourself in about a day.

Filter Location

The air-cleaner unit must be mounted between the furnace and the cold-air return duct so that it filters the air returning to the furnace. Depending on your furnace configuration, the cold-air return may be either on the top, bottom or side of the furnace. Study your layout carefully and determine whether you have space for the air cleaner. In the system shown, the cold-air return duct ran down the furnace side and entered near the bottom. The bottom section of the return consisted of a 4-ft. length of 8×24-in. duct. Because the return duct also contained a humidifier located about 5½ ft. from the floor, it was decided to reroute the lower duct section to make room for the new air cleaner. Note that your air cleaner has an inlet side and an outflow side, and it must be installed in the correct orientation. If necessary, the unit can be turned upside down to achieve the correct relation to airflow.

Getting Ready

To mount the air cleaner on a furnace designed like the one shown, begin by removing the cold-air duct from the furnace. Use a screwdriver or a pair of pliers to turn the locking clips that hold the blower compartment access door in place (Fig. 1). Then, open and remove the door and remove the furnace filter from the blower compartment. If it's a reusable filter, clean it thoroughly and set it aside to be reinstalled later (Fig. 2). If it's a

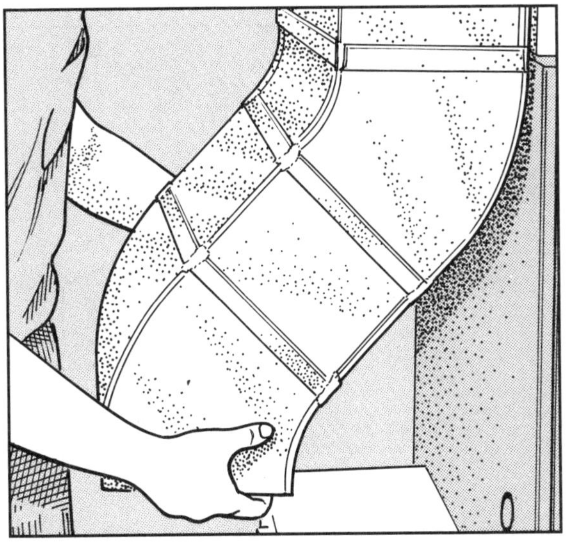

15 Install straight and bent sections on return duct. Measure the straight length needed to reach air-cleaner housing.

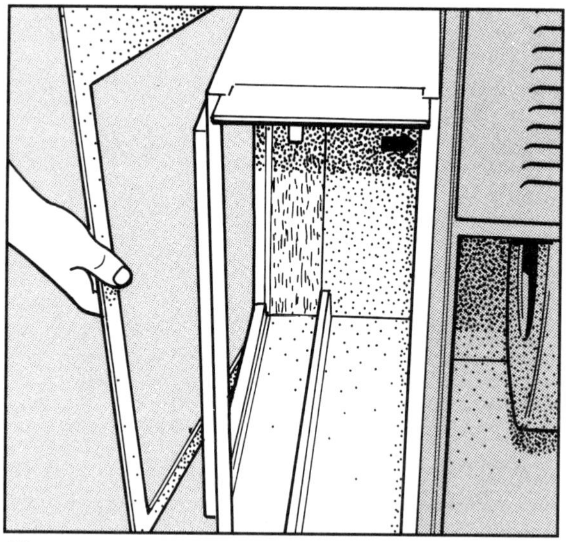

16 Cut opening in duct when duct is disassembled. Hold **L** section against air-cleaner housing and check for fit.

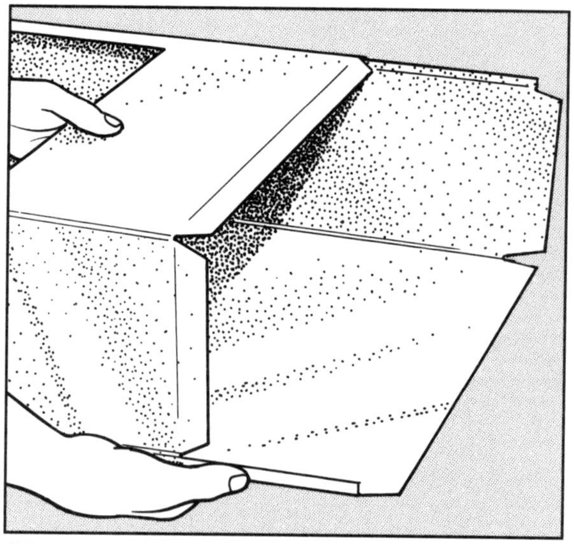

17 Then, assemble L-shaped duct halves by sliding them together. Note triangular corner cutouts in end tabs.

disposable type and it's dirty, discard it and then replace it later with a new one.

Use a flat-blade screwdriver to remove the screws or pry off the sheetmetal clips that secure the cold-air return duct to the furnace side (Fig. 3). Loosen the joint between the last two sections of return duct by prying the snap joints apart. Then, separate the duct sections (Fig. 4).

Installing the Air Cleaner

Position the air cleaner alongside the furnace to provide the most straightforward connection between the duct and the furnace. Open the air-cleaner access door and remove the filter frame (Fig. 5). Use sheetmetal screws to fasten the air-cleaner housing to the furnace and seal the joints with duct tape (Figs. 6 and 7). It's important to seal all joints since the efficiency of the air cleaner depends on the amount of air pulled through the filter medium.

To continue the end of the existing return duct alongside the air cleaner, a 45° bend, a short straight length and an additional 45° bend need to be added. Begin by installing a stock 45° bend to the end of the ductwork. Simply fit the snap-joint ends together and push until the pieces lock in place (Fig. 8).

To make the short straight length, cut a section from longer stock. Note that metal duct is sold in L-shaped sections that must be assembled, and it's easiest to cut the pieces to length before assembly. Determine the exposed length of straight duct required between the two bends, measure from the back edge of the snap joint on one L section and make a mark. Use a yardstick to scribe a straight line across the duct (Fig. 9). Then make a second line 1 in. farther down the duct and cut along this line with metal shears (Fig. 10). The extra 1 in. of

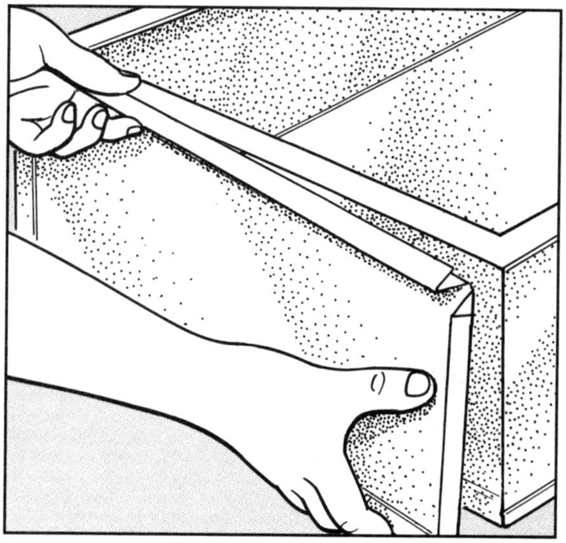

18 Slide the endcap in place and secure it with sheetmetal screws. Then, seal joints with duct tape to prevent air loss.

19 If the duct must slide over an adjacent section, use sheetmetal pliers to bend out tabs. Screw joint together after assembly.

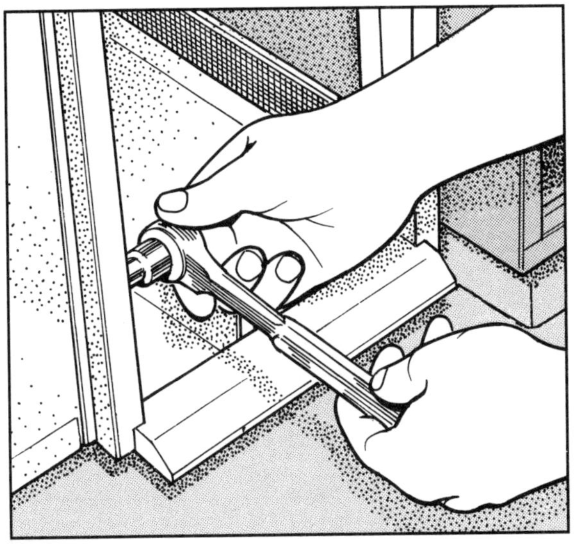

20 A ratchet wrench is best for driving sheetmetal screws that connect air-cleaner housing with return duct.

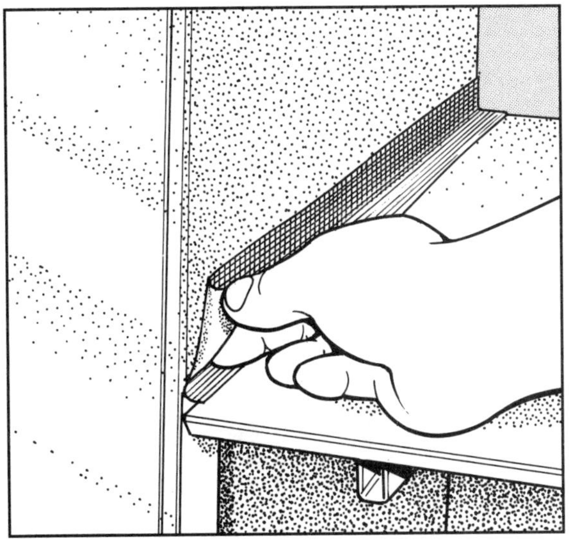

21 After all ductwork is in place and secure, check for any unsealed or open joints and cover with duct tape.

metal will form a tab to interlock with the adjoining piece of duct.

After cutting both L sections of the duct, slide the halves together (Fig. 11). Then, use shears to make small triangular cuts at each corner of the cut end of the duct, up to the first layout line. Use pliers to remove these corner pieces (Fig. 12). The cutaway corners facilitate joining this section with the next.

Join the cut end of the straight section to the second 45° bend and secure the joint with sheetmetal screws (Fig. 13). Use furnace cement or plumbers putty to fill any gaps in the corners and seal the entire joint with duct tape (Fig. 14).

Install the straight section and 45° subassembly to the initial 45° bend already in place (Fig. 15). Then measure the length of the duct necessary to reach the air-cleaner housing at the bottom of the furnace. Remember to allow an additional 1 in. for joining tabs. You might be able to use your original section of duct by cutting it shorter and enlarging the opening to match the air cleaner.

Cut the opening in the duct to fit tightly over the flange on the intake side of the air cleaner. Check the fit of the opening before assembling the duct (Fig. 16). While the section is in place, drill pilot holes for securing the duct with screws after the duct is entirely assembled.

Join the two L sections (Fig. 17) and make triangular cuts at the corners, as before. Install a duct endcap at the bottom end of the duct and secure with sheetmetal screws (Fig. 18). If this last section must slide over an adjacent section, use sheetmetal pliers to gently bend the joining tabs outward to ease assembly (Fig. 19).

Slide the duct in place and join to the previous section and to the air-cleaner housing with sheetmetal screws. A ratchet wrench is handy for tightening screws in confined locations (Fig. 20). Remember to make sure all the joints are sealed with duct tape (Fig. 21).

Install the filter media in the filter frame as directed by the manufacturer. Locate the pleat spacers as required (Fig. 22). Then slide the filter frame into the housing and close the air-cleaner door.

Install a clean furnace filter in the blower compartment and replace the door. Then, turn on the furnace blower, let it operate continuously for about 15 minutes and check that the installation is functioning properly.

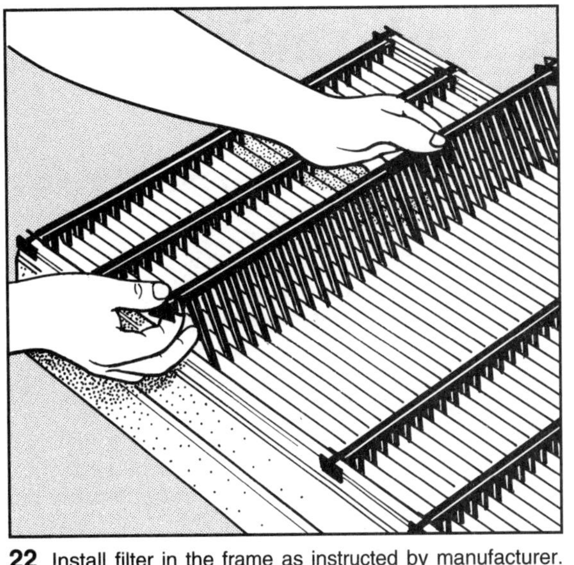

22 Install filter in the frame as instructed by manufacturer. Position pleat spacers as required to maintain filter shape.

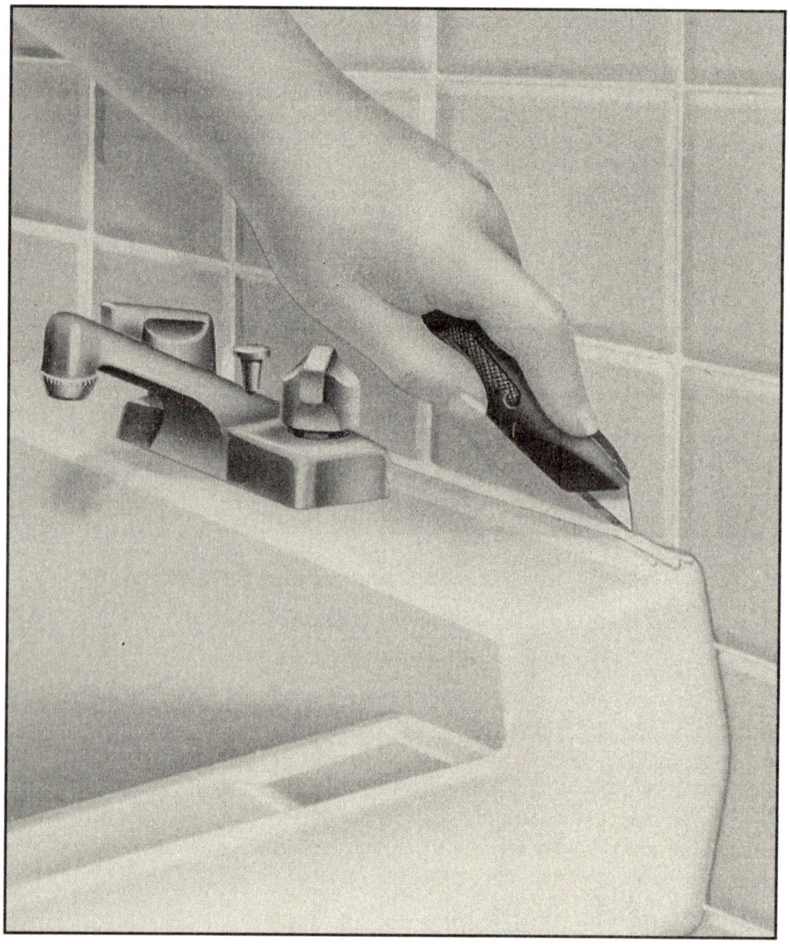

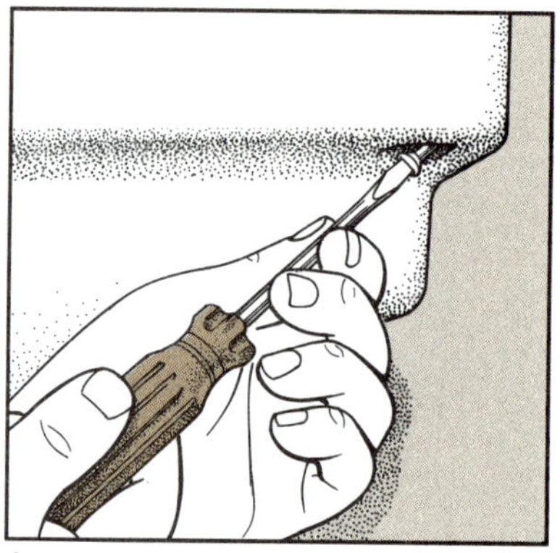

1 After the caulk at the top of the sink has been cut through, remove the screws that hold the sink to the wall.

2 Shut off the water below the sink, or in the basement, and loosen the compression nuts on the supply risers.

Sink/vanity retrofit

Sink/Vanity Retrofit was written by Merle Henkenius. Illustrations by George Retseck. Doors are available from Porta-Door Co. Inc., 65 Cogwheel Ln., Seymour, CT 06483. This company's wide product line includes cabinet drawers and hardware and other products you would find useful if you decide to go the custom vanity route.

One sure sign of an outdated bath is a wall-hung sink. Not only do these fixtures look low budget, they deny you the valuable storage space offered by a vanity cabinet. If your bathroom is cramped, as most are, then a vanity will add storage space. By concealing the sink's plumbing, it also will make the bathroom look a little less mechanical, and it does so without costing a fortune. Making the change is easier than it looks.

If adding storage space is not your top priority but fixing up an old bathroom is, then now also is the time to replace the sink, especially if its faucet set is worn out and dripping. It also makes sense to replace the sink if you are thinking of painting and freshening up the grout lines in the tilework.

Choosing a Vanity

The unit used here is a 24-in.-deep oak-front vanity with two drawers and a door to fit a limited space. The vanity top is a plastic composition material with a basin molded in. Finally, a Moen single-control faucet was chosen. The combined cost of these items was just over $200. If you have the patience to wait for specials and closeouts, you might well trim $50 from that figure. On the other hand, if you're so inclined, you could spend $1500 for a long vanity and an expensive top, basin and faucet.

As for the style of the vanity, consider the position of the water and drain fittings in your bathroom's wall or floor. Don't buy a vanity with drawers that will obstruct these piping connections. As for the length, you'll find standard sizes to fit almost any space, from 18 in. to 6 ft. If your vanity wall will abut the toilet, most codes require that the countertop ends at least 15 in. from the center of the toilet.

Finally, if you don't care for molded tops you can build a custom top of high-density particleboard and plastic laminate or tile. You would then cut a hole in the top for a porcelain, plastic or china basin.

You can shoot for an entirely custom installation by building the vanity cabinet as well. The cabinet is simply a box with a space for a toe-kick beneath it. The cabinet can be built out of high-density particleboard and covered with the same plastic laminate used on the top, or you can build it out of lumber. You can make the doors yourself or buy doors from a supplier.

Removing the Old Sink

To remove the old wall-hung sink, start by shutting off the water at the meter or beneath the sink. Then, cut through the caulk seam between the sink and the wall.

Change the blade in your utility knife if it isn't sharp. Often the bead of caulk at this joint has hardened, and it is difficult to remove. Cut through the caulk as completely as possible to reduce wall damage when you lift the sink off its support bracket. Next, check the lower sides of the unit for fastening screws. Not all sinks will have these screws, but if yours does, remove them (Fig. 1).

Loosen the compression nuts where the supply riser joins the compression adapters (Fig. 2). In this installation, the supply valves to the sink are located in the basement—a common arrangement in older homes. Your sink may have supply valves located on the risers below the sink, however. The process to remove these is basically the same. Loosen the compression nut at the top of the supply valve. If you want the extra convenience of having the supply valves located directly under the sink, now's the time to add them.

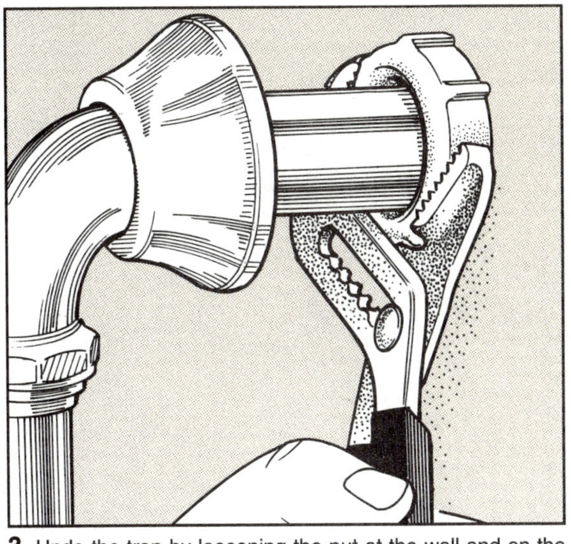

3 Undo the trap by loosening the nut at the wall and on the drain's tailpiece. Tongue-and-groove pliers work well here.

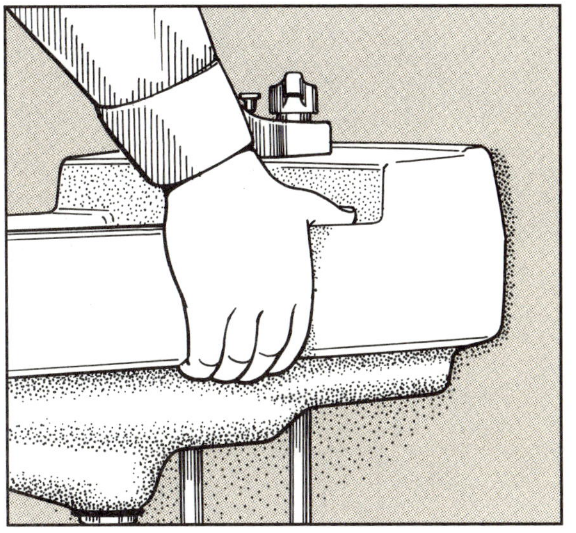

4 With all the plumbing connections undone, lift the sink from its sides and pull it clear of its wall brackets.

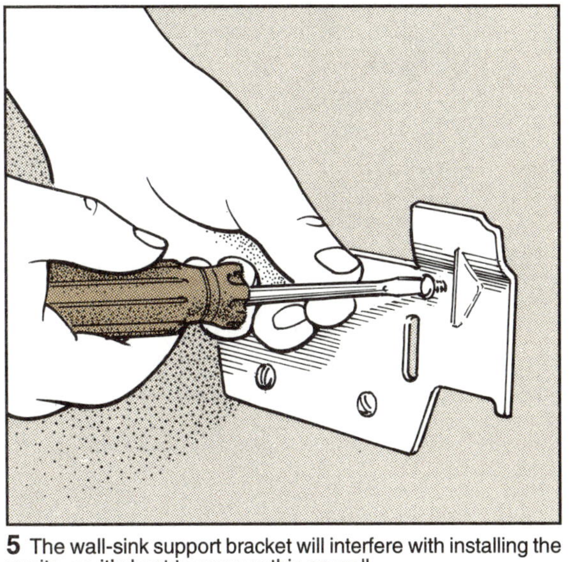

5 The wall-sink support bracket will interfere with installing the vanity, so it's best to remove this as well.

6 If the vanity cabinet tips away from the wall, shim the base with some pieces of scrap or cedar shingles.

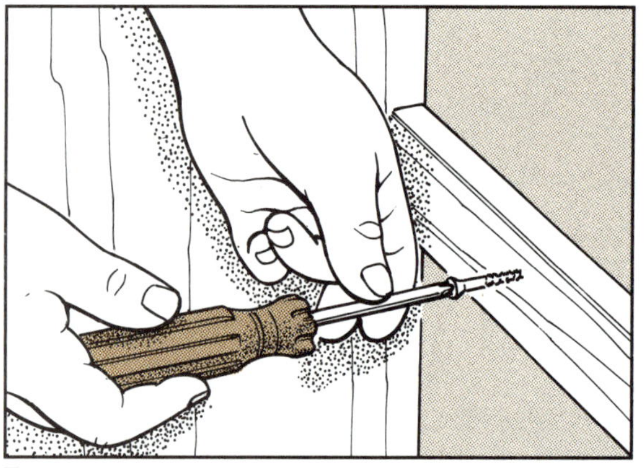

7 Locate the wall studs, bore the pilot holes and drive two screws through the vanity's back brace into the studs.

8 Press plumber's putty around the drain flange. Thread the drain into the flange from the underside of the basin.

Remove the trap, and lift the sink up and out until it breaks free (Figs. 3 and 4). Next, remove the metal support bracket (Fig. 5).

Wall Repair

Some older wall-hung sinks, especially those with front-mounted faucets, have extra-high decks. These will leave some wall damage exposed above the new vanity top. It's usually easier to make these repairs before installing the countertop. Mostly, it's simply a matter of patching the rough areas with drywall compound.

You might find it easier to paint the wall before installing the vanity. This way, you won't have to cover the vanity with a dropcloth or neatly cut in around it when painting.

Installing the Vanity Cabinet

To install the vanity, pry the baseboard and shoe molding from the vanity wall using a flat bar. Use a block of wood behind the flat bar to prevent it from breaking through the drywall. If the nails holding the trim in place are visible, then it may be easier to punch them through the trim using a nailset, rather than trying to pry away the trim and nails at one time.

Slide the vanity against the wall in a position that allows for easy access to the permanent plumbing. If your plumbing pipes enter through the floor, you need to bore holes in the cabinet floor. Measure carefully and use a holesaw to make these holes. If the permanent drain ends at the floor level, install a 6-in.-long plastic tailpiece extension with a compression fitting to raise the drain opening. Then, lift the vanity onto the pipes. If the pipes enter from the wall, as most do, the open back of the cabinet will accommodate the plumbing connections.

A common problem associated with any cabinet installation is a sloping floor or out-of-plumb wall. As such, a cabinet may fit against the wall at the floor, but at the same time, may gap away from the wall near the top. To correct this problem, shim the base until the cabinet fits flush with the wall (Fig. 6). With minor shimming, silicone or latex tub-and-tile caulk will hide the shim. Extreme gaps can be concealed with lengths of cove molding, which are stained or painted to match the bathroom's woodwork.

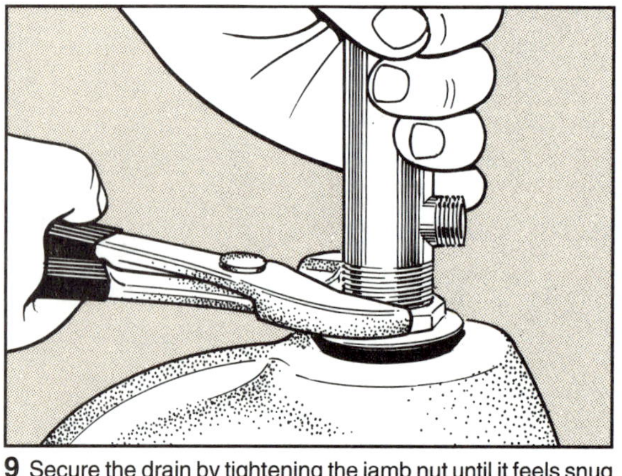

9 Secure the drain by tightening the jamb nut until it feels snug and most of the putty is squeezed from the flange.

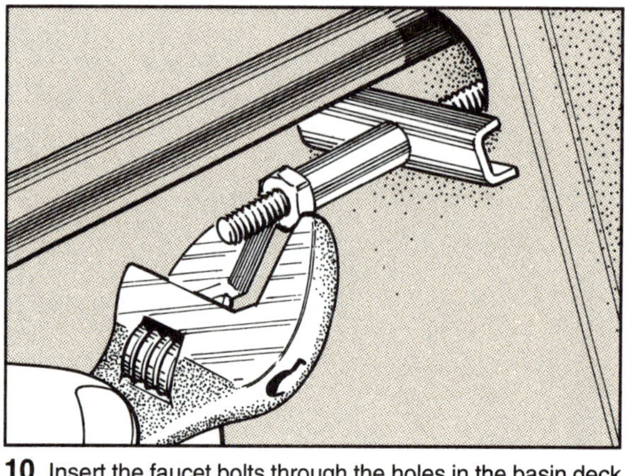

10 Insert the faucet bolts through the holes in the basin deck (the top of the vanity). Tighten the nuts.

In any case, position the vanity against the wall and locate the wall studs behind it. Bore pilot holes through the vanity's back support and into the studs. Screw the cabinet to the studs (Fig. 7).

Plumbing the Vanity Basin

Before installing the vanity top, mount the faucet and drain assembly in the basin. Begin by pressing a 1/4-in.-dia. roll of plumber's putty onto the underside of the drain flange (Fig. 8). Insert the drain through the bottom of the basin and turn it into the flange threads. Then, tighten the jam nut on the drain until its rubber washer seats against the drain spud and most of the putty is squeezed from the flange (Fig. 9). Don't overtighten this nut. Stop when it feels snug.

Next, slide the base gasket over the faucet bolts, and insert the bolts through the sink's deck holes. Thread the jamb nuts onto the bolts and tighten one side of the faucet. Pivot the other side of the faucet until it's aligned properly on the deck, and tighten the second nut (Fig. 10).

With the faucet and drain mounted in the basin, install the pop-up assembly. Start by inserting the pop-up drain plug into the drain. Skewer the pop up with the lift lever. Then, tighten the ring surrounding the lift lever until it feels snug.

Next, feed the lift rod through its hole in the top of the faucet and slide the adjustable clevis onto the rod. Push the lift lever down as far as it will go (thus raising the pop-up plug in the basin), and connect the clevis clip and the clevis to the lever. The lift lever should pass through the second hole from the bottom on the clevis. Tighten the clevis setscrew against the lift rod (Fig. 11).

Chosen here was a faucet that came with supply risers permanently attached. If yours has threaded shanks, attach 18-in. ball-head risers to the shanks before mounting the basin or top. A vanity offers little working room, and making these connections in advance will save you the bodily contortions required to connect them later, after the vanity is installed, using a basin wrench.

12 Apply adhesive caulk to the top of the vanity cabinet. Put a dot at each corner and at several places in between.

13 Place the vanity top on the base and push it against the wall. Wipe off any adhesive that oozes from under the top.

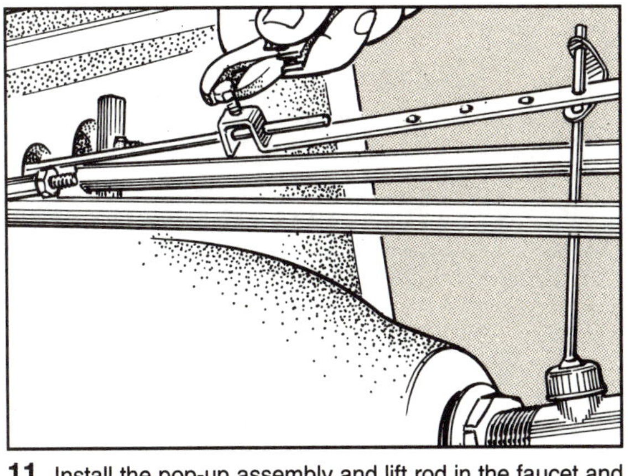

11 Install the pop-up assembly and lift rod in the faucet and basin. Tighten the setscrew against the lift rod.

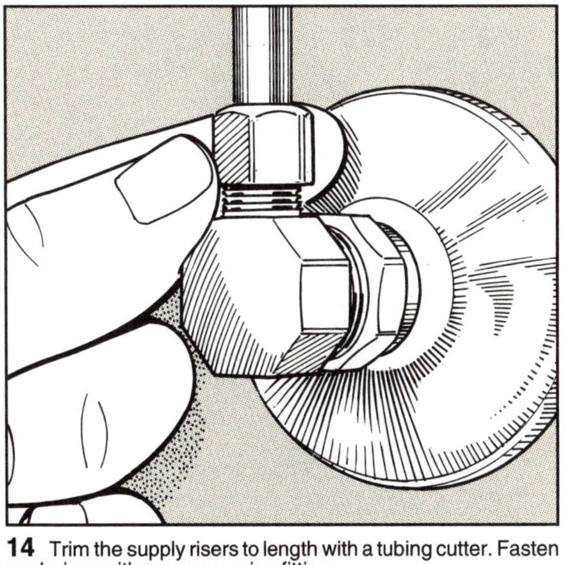

14 Trim the supply risers to length with a tubing cutter. Fasten each riser with a compression fitting.

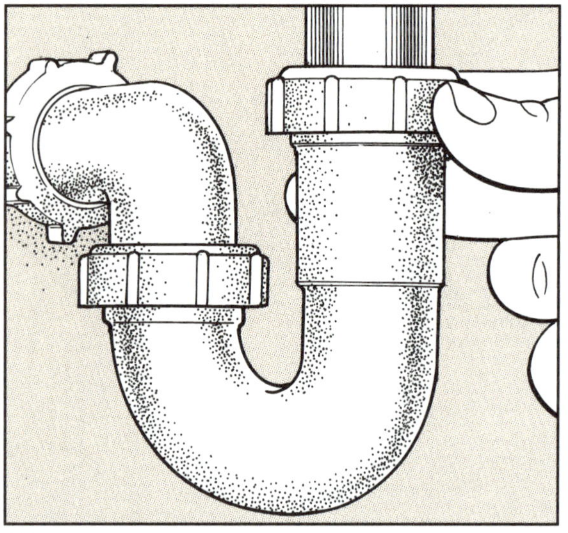

15 Use a plastic trap for the new drain connection. Hand tighten the nuts on the trap—do not use a wrench.

16 Seal the vanity top where it meets the wall with latex tub-and-tile caulk. Smooth the bead with your finger.

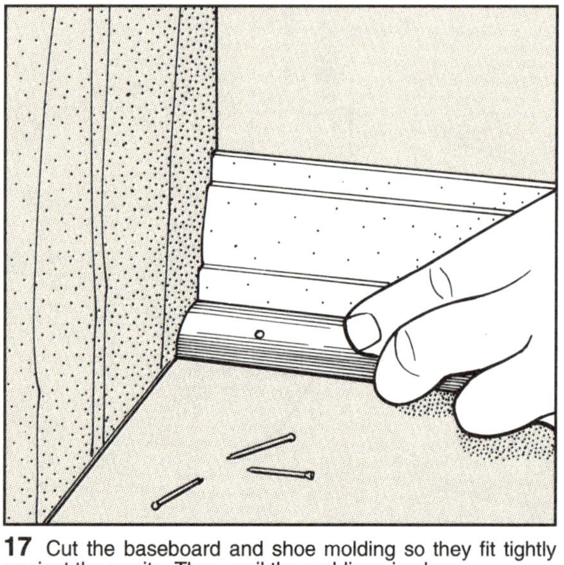

17 Cut the baseboard and shoe molding so they fit tightly against the vanity. Then, nail the moldings in place.

Setting the Countertop

If your countertop is made of wood, you could screw it to the vanity from below, through the cabinets' corner brackets. But with a molded top, it's best to cement it to the cabinet and the wall. Construction adhesive works well and so does silicone caulk. Just squirt a small amount of caulk on the top of the cabinet in a half-dozen places. Then, lift the counter onto the vanity, so that the back splash rests flush against the wall (Figs. 12 and 13). Before caulking the backsplash, however, make the plumbing connections.

To connect the supply risers, bend them to meet the compression adapters head on. This is usually a compound bend, requiring a little care to avoid kinking the risers. Don't bend the riser near the adapter or the compression nut and ring won't fit. With the risers aligned, mark them with a pencil and cut them to length with a tubing cutter. Finally, slide a compression nut and ring onto each riser and tighten it into the adapter (Fig. 14). Avoid overtightening. Finger-tight, plus two full-rounds, will be sufficient.

You may be able to reuse the old chrome trap from the wall-hung sink. If so, it's a good idea to replace the friction washers. If the old trap has seen better days, the best replacement is a plastic-tube trap, which has beveled compression washers. These traps are inexpensive, rust-free and the nuts don't require wrenching. Hand tighten the nuts on the new trap (Fig. 15).

Finishing Touches

With the vanity and top installed, caulk the backsplash and replace the baseboard and shoe molding. The best caulk to seal the vanity backsplash is a latex tub-and-tile variety (Fig. 16). Just wet the seam between the backsplash and the wall, and lay a bead of caulk in the joint. Work the caulk into the joint with your finger, and wipe away all excess caulk with a damp rag. As the caulk cures, it will shrink slightly, yielding a watertight seam that is nearly invisible.

As for replacing the woodwork, if you can, reuse the base and shoe molding. Crosscut them to length, and fasten them with finish nails (Fig. 17). Countersink the nailheads and cover the nail holes with color-matched putty.

Don't forget to check for leaks. Turn on the water to the faucet, either in the basement or vanity cabinet. Run both hot and cold water through the faucet to check for leaks at the compression adapter or at the supply valve. Let the water drain to check for a leak at the trap. With any luck, your installation will be good and dry, and offer years of trouble-free service.

Installing a Floodlight was written and photographed by Merle Henkenius. The light shown was made by GAMPAK (475 Bloy St., Hillside, NJ 07205), accommodates two 150-watt, weatherproof floodlamps. The fixture comes with its own weatherproof surface-mount box.

Installing a floodlight

■ There's no better way to extend a day than with a house- or garage-mounted floodlight. If this idea doesn't appeal to you, rest assured that it will appeal to the youngsters around the house. Besides offering a measure of added security (and safety), a floodlight can improve a range of outdoor activities, from backyard barbecues to driveway basketball. To top it all off, floodlights are relatively easy to install.

Variations on a Theme

Floodlights take a variety of forms and are installed in a variety of ways. A quick trip to your local home center will reveal several design options. You'll see the traditional fixture—like the one shown here—but you'll also see rectangular quartz-halogen lamps. Both are available in 1- and 2-lamp kits. Quartz lights are more efficient, but also more costly.

Of course, you'll find some designed for wall installations (like the one shown), and others for soffit installation. The primary difference is that wall installations are weatherproof. Soffit lights, because they enjoy eaves protection, are less so. Some will have motion-sensing ON/OFF switches, and some will have light-sensing photocells. Still others can only be switched manually.

When it comes to wiring a floodlight, you'll have several options. You can fish cable into finished walls, thereby providing indoor switch control, or you can surface-wire with conduit, placing the switch on an

1 To access power from an existing ceiling box, first use a screwdriver to punch a new box hole for the supply cable.

2 Staple the new cable alongside the ceiling joist within 8 in. of the ceiling box and every 4 ft. thereafter.

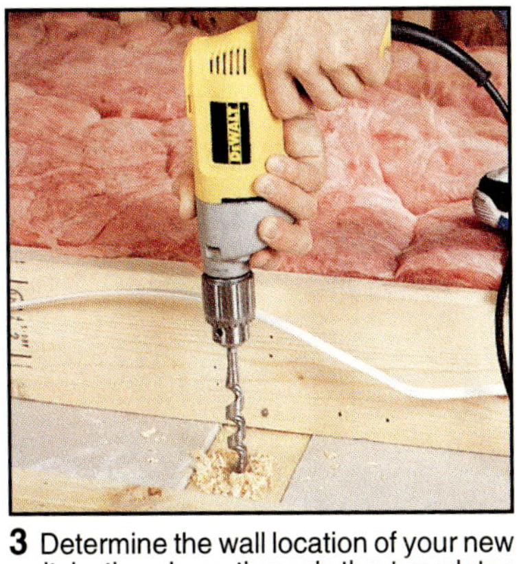

3 Determine the wall location of your new switch, then bore through the top plates of the same wall from above.

exterior wall or post. Another option is to surface-wire some of the installation and fish the rest. If you opt for surface-wiring, all boxes and connectors will need to be weatherproof. Where allowed, plastic boxes and conduit make these installations quick and easy.

As for the installation shown, a standard 2-lamp fixture with a light-sensing photocell was used. When the switch is left in the ON position, the light comes on automatically when it gets dark. This feature does offer some security when no one is home.

Electrical Access

Sometimes, the easiest access to existing power is through the garage. Unfinished garages make wiring easy, especially if you don't mind having the switch in the garage as well.

This light was installed on a gable end of a house, accessing power in the attic (from an overhead hallway light below). It was also desired to have the switch inside, near the back door. This required a little more work, but not much more.

The hallway light had its power originating at a ceiling box, with a 2-wire switch loop running down to a wall switch on the main floor. This configuration, which is very common in newer homes, is required if you hope to pull power from a ceiling box. Had the power originated at the switch box, with only a switch loop extending to the ceiling, a different power source would have had to be found.

Begin by shutting off power to the circuit in question and removing the ceiling fixture. This done, go to the attic and use a screwdriver to punch through an unused knockout in the existing ceiling box (Fig. 1). After feeding 14/2 (with ground) cable into the ceiling box, staple the cable next to the box and every 4 ft. alongside the ceiling joists (Fig. 2).

After reaching the top plate of the wall that will hold your new switch, bore down through the top plate (Fig. 3) and feed two cables into the wall cavity (Fig. 4). One of these cables extends power to the switch from the existing ceiling box, while the other will carry power from the switch to the new floodlight. Be sure to push through enough cable to reach well past the switch location in one direction and the floodlight location in the other.

If your cable needs to travel across several ceiling joists to reach the floodlight location, bore through each joist and pull the cable through these holes (Fig. 5).

After pulling cable to the gable wall of the attic, staple it several times more on its way to the fixture location (Fig. 6). Codes require a staple within 8 in. of the fixture box. Finish running the cable by bringing it through a 1⅛-in.-dia. hole bored through the outside wall where you want the light to be.

4 Feed two cables—one for the switch, and one for the floodlight—through the switchbox hole and into the wall cavity.

5 When crossing ceiling joists, bore a cable hole through the center of the joists and pull the cable through.

6 Bring cable up the attic or the gable wall that will support the floodlight and staple it alongside a convenient stud.

7 Turn a nipple or threaded adapter into the back of the box and feed the new cable through this extension.

8 After installing a lamp holder on each end of the box, mount the box on the outside wall with two wood screws.

9 Join all white wires together and all ground wires together. Then hook the black (hot) wires to the photocell.

Installing the Fixture

The fixture shown has a weatherproof metallic box, two adjustable lamp holders, a rubber weather gasket and a cover plate, which contains the photocell. To keep water from entering the box through the cable opening, it's a good idea to install a nipple in the rear opening of the box. A threaded-steel nipple will work here, but you also can opt for a plastic conduit adapter. After wrapping Teflon tape around the threads, tighten the adapter into the box opening (Fig. 7).

Thread the two lamp holders into the sides of the box. Again, use Teflon tape to seal the threads. The lamp-holder fittings come with locknuts, like those used on box connectors, which lock in the angles of the holders. With the adapter and lamp holders in place, pull the switch cable through the adapter and screw the box to the house siding (Fig. 8).

To wire the fixture, begin by joining the cable's bare-wire ground to the fixture's grounding lead wire, and to an insulated grounding pigtail. Then bond the pigtail to a screwhole at the back of the box. Next, join all white (neutral) wires in a twist connector. To power the fixture, join the circuit's black wire to the black wire of the photocell, and the photocell's red wire to the black wires from the lamp holders (Fig. 9). Finally, install the cover plate, making sure that the edges of the box are covered on all sides by the fixture's rubber weather gasket (Fig. 10).

Installing the Switch Box

To install a new switch and switch box, begin by identifying the stud space that contained the cables pushed down from the attic. Because a cut-in box needs to be held several inches away from a stud, choose a spot in the center of a stud space and 42 in. above the floor, as measured from the bottom of the box. Hold the cut-in box against the wall, face forward, then trace around it with a pencil (Fig. 11), and cut along the traced lines with a drywall saw (Fig. 12).

With the box opening cut, reach into the stud space to retrieve the cables. After trimming them to length, feed each cable through its own box opening and press the box into the wall (Fig. 13).

Finally, tighten the screw that draws the support bracket against the drywall, and strip the cables of their sheathing within the box. At this point, you also can strip ½ in. of insulation from all black and white wires.

To wire the switch, join the white wires in one twist connector, the ground wires in another one and press the two black wires into their stab-in slots in the back of the switch. After screwing the switch yoke to the box, install the cover plate (Fig. 14).

10 Push the sensor into the box, then press the fixture's rubber weather gasket in place. Tighten the cover securely.

11 Determine the precise location of your switch box, then hold a cut-in box in this spot and trace around it.

12 Use a drywall saw or a sabre saw to cut the opening for the new box. Be sure to cut right on the line for the best fit.

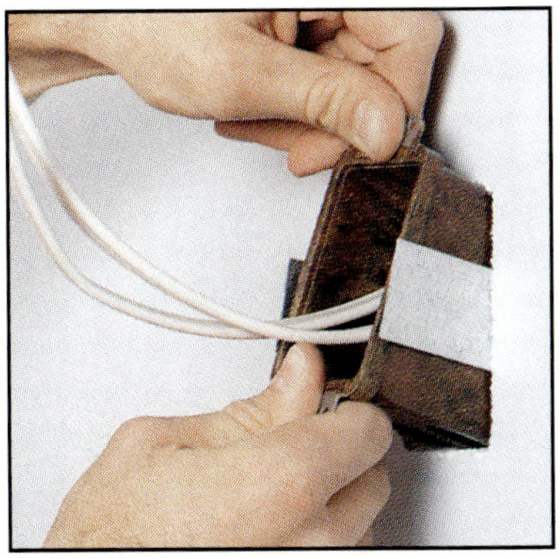

13 Pull the cables into the cut-in box and press the box into the wall. Then tighten the bracket screw securely.

14 Join both white wires together and all ground wires together. Then attach both black wires to the switch.

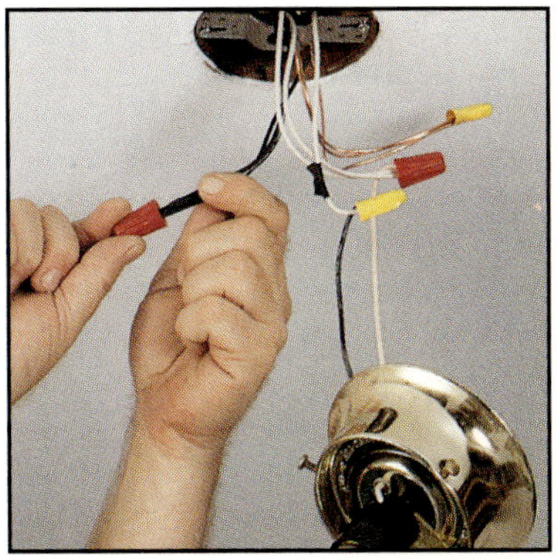

15 To access power, join all white wires, black and ground wires. Then join the black fixture wire to the white switch wire.

Installing a garage door opener

■ What's new in garage door openers? Safety. Redundant safety. Since the early 1980s, manufacturers have built auto-reversing mechanisms into their power units. As soon as the door hits anything above floor level, the motor automatically reverses itself. While this was a welcome improvement, safety officials wanted more. As a result, every opener manufactured after January 1, 1993 must have a backup, or redundant, auto-reverse mechanism located at the door.

Manufacturers responded to this requirement by providing infrared sender/receiver units, which are installed just inside the doorway, several inches off the floor. The moment the infrared bean is interrupted by an object or person, the descending door stops and reverses.

Preliminary Considerations

With redundant safety mechanisms built in, there's little chance that a door opener will cause serious injury or damage. This is good news. The bad news is that equipment designed to be this sensitive requires careful adjustment and a host door that works perfectly. If your overhead door will not stay put when opened halfway, if its tension springs are adjusted unequally, if one side binds or drags when used manually, a safety-sensitive electric opener will sense a hazard and refuse to cooperate.

If your garage door could use some adjustment, consider calling a professional before installing the new opener. Door adjustments are not as easy as they appear, and the tension springs and related hardware are often under extreme pressure.

While manufactured safety is mandated by federal agencies, installations will be regulated at the local level, through building and safety-code statutes. Check with your local codes office for permit and inspection requirements.

Your installation also will require electrical power, in the form of a permanently installed receptacle, located within reach of the unit's power cord. Don't be tempted to run an extension cord from a wall outlet to the power unit. The resulting voltage drop could shorten the life of the motor.

In some cases, the garage is wired for an opener when it was built. If yours wasn't, you'll need to bring power from an existing circuit.

Finally, you'll need overhead ceiling joists to support a site-built support hanger. Because few openers come with their own hanger assemblies, you'll need 6 to 8 ft. of angle-iron, bolts, lock washers and lagscrews.

Installing a Garage Door Opener was written by Merle Henkenius. Photos by Merle Henkenius. For more information about Stanley garage door openers, write to Stanley Home Automation, 800 S. High St., Covington, OH 45318.

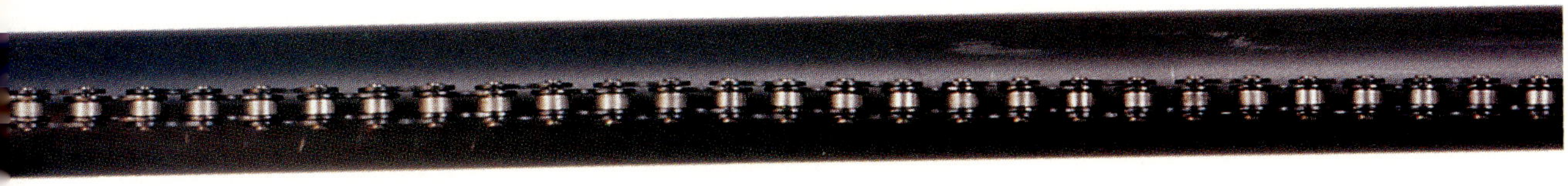

Putting it All Together

A Stanley garage door opener with infrared sensors was chosen for this installation. Stanley makes a variety of openers and you can expect to pay about $140 for a standard 1/2-hp Stanley opener, and close to $300 for the professional model.

The first step is to insert the endcap in the pipe or tube that spans the gap between the power unit and door header. The cap goes into the power-unit end of the pipe (Fig. 1).

Next, install the traveler, which is the tube-mounted bracket that joins the two ends of the drive chain (Fig. 2). It travels forward and back along the tube when the door is opened or closed. It also provides a manual disconnect latch, if you ever want to bypass the power unit. The traveler simply slides onto the tube, but its positioning is critical. You'll find the word "Door" stamped into one end of the traveler. This end must face the door. With a track-mounted door, the traveler should be positioned 39 to 41 in. from the power unit.

With the traveler in place, install the idler assembly (Fig. 3). The idler assembly is a sprocket-fitted length of square tubing that connects the tube to the door-header bracket. After placing the idler assembly on the door end of the tube, insert the remaining end into its support fitting on the power unit (Fig. 4).

Next, attach one end of the drive chain to the traveler (Fig. 5). This connection is made with a 2-piece repair link, similar to that of a bicycle chain. This link is secured by a slotted key, which must be installed face-up. Once the link is in place, feed the chain out a little at a time until it reaches the power unit. At this point, bring the chain around the drive sprocket on the unit (Fig. 6), and pull out more chain toward the idler assembly.

At the idler assembly, remove the remaining chain from the spool and feed it through the sprocket (Fig. 7), pulling out most of the slack between the sprocket and the traveler. Connect this end of the chain to the traveler as well, using a second repair link. Then take all but ½ in. of sag from the chain by rotating the adjustment bolt on the power unit (Fig. 8).

1 Lay out all parts on the floor, then slide the cap onto the power-unit end of the tube until it hits the retaining flange.

2 Slide the traveler assembly onto the end of the track tube and position it 39 to 41 in. from the power unit.

3 Slide the idler assembly onto the door end of the tube. The idler will later fit into a header bracket.

4 Carefully slide the capped end of the track tube into the bracket that's mounted on top of the power unit.

5 Attach the drive chain to the traveler with a repair link supplied in the kit. The retainer clip must face up.

6 Bring the chain around the drive sprockets on the power unit, making sure all the links are completely engaged.

Installing the Unit

The first step in the mounting process is to establish the exact center of the door opening. Simply measure the opening, divide by two and mark dead center on the header above the door. To establish the correct bracket height above the floor, you must first determine the maximum height of the door as it arches over its curved track. To do this, raise the door until the top panel rolls to its highest point on the track, just before it turns horizontal. Then prop the door open at this height and measure from the top of the door to the floor. Add 2 in. to this height to clear the door, which yields a workable bracket height.

In the installation shown, the bracket height fell above the structural header, so a 2×4 brace was nailed above the header to support the bracket. After marking the bracket height on the 2×4, use a level to extend the center-of-door mark up to the brace (Fig. 9).

With the bracket marked for position, anchor it to the 2×4 support, using lagbolts and a socket wrench. Then lift the idler assembly end of the tube up to the bracket and lock it in place with its pin (Fig. 10).

With the idler arm locked into the bracket, lift the power unit and rest it atop a stepladder. Then open the door completely. The door in the overhead position gives you the required height for the power unit. While the tube does not need to be level, it does need several inches of clearance above the door. You can opt for a position about 3 in. higher than the door, this time taking your measurement off the ceiling.

This distance tells how long to cut the angle-iron for the support hanger. While building the support, close the door and return the power unit to the floor.

While there are any number of reasonable support designs, you can secure yours to a 2×4 brace (Fig. 11), which is anchored to the ceiling joist with 4-in.-long screws. Once your brace is firmly attached, measure from a common wall to establish the center point, and attach two support legs to the brace, using ¼-in. lagbolts. After lifting the power unit in place, attach it to the hangers, using bolts provided in the kit. To keep the power unit from twisting the hangers sideways, bolt a length of angle-iron diagonally across the vertical hanger supports (Fig. 12).

Make the door-to-traveler connection with a 2-piece L-shaped bracket, known as a bar link. Attach this at top and bottom with keyed pins. Then bolt the two halves of the bracket together, using the bolts provided in the kit (Fig. 13).

Installing the Redundant Sensors

Because direct sunlight striking an infrared receiving unit can trigger a default, the first order of business is to determine which side of the door opening will get the

7 At the idler assembly, remove all remaining chain from the spool and feed it through the return sprocket.

8 After connecting the return end to the traveler, tighten the chain by adjusting the bolt on the power unit.

9 Establish and mark the centerline of the door, then transfer this mark to the bracket support board above the door.

10 Attach the support bracket to the brace with lagscrews and lock the idler into the bracket with a keyed pin.

11 Attach a 2x4 cleat to the ceiling where the joists fall. Then lag a piece of angle-iron to the side of the cleat.

12 To control side-to-side movement, bolt a third piece of angle-iron diagonally between the two vertical hangers.

most sun. With this in mind, install the sending unit on the sunny side and the receiving unit on the shady side.

The binding terminals on these units are recessed and surprisingly small, so be sure to wire the units before installing them (Fig. 14). The kit comes with two low-voltage, 2-wire cables.

Wiring configurations will vary, but the Stanley unit shown required that the cable with the pin connector be attached to two terminals on the receiving unit. The remaining 2-wire cable is then joined to the receiver and sender.

To install the infrared units, begin by establishing a common height above the floor and then screw the L-brackets to jack studs on both sides of the door. Then bolt the sender/receiver units to the remaining two brackets (Fig. 15), and bolt these brackets to those mounted on the jack studs. (Adjustment can be made by rotating the sensors or brackets.) Bring the low-voltage cable along the walls and across the ceiling, securing it with shielded staples. Finally, plug the pin connector into the back of the power unit (Fig. 16), and install a 60-watt bulb behind the unit's light diffuser.

Wiring the Control Switch

When shopping for a garage door opener, you'll find a few options you may not have known about. In addition to operating the power unit and light, both manually and remotely, some systems allow you to hard-wire a passage door so that the light comes on for 5 minutes after it's opened. You also can use your remote control to turn on an entry light or porch light. The hard-wired control switch also may allow you to lock the overhead door or use the power unit's light without the power unit.

While simple open-and-shut systems will require only a doorbell switch with only two terminals, more complicated controls will require four or five wires and more connections. For the sake of this illustration, the multifunction control offered with Stanley's professional series is shown. Because the prewired cable had only two wires, a new cable run along the surface of the drywall was used, secured with staples every few feet.

Hookup was still easy, as all wires are color coded and all terminals are color labeled. It's a simple, like-color to like-color arrangement (Fig. 17).

Final Adjustments

These units require a bit of fine tuning. For the unit shown, the first attempt yielded a fault, as indicated by a flashing light. The problem was that the unit was calibrated to carry less of a load than the door required. By adjusting a screw at the back of the unit, the problem was corrected. This is done incrementally, to avoid setting more load capacity than is needed.

It was then found that the door would travel 2 or 3 ft., stopping neither fully closed nor fully open. This problem was corrected by advancing one of two adjustment screws on the bottom of the unit (Fig. 18).

13 Attach the bar link to the door and traveler with keyed pins. Then bolt the two halves of the link together.

14 Insert the low-voltage wires into the receiver/sender terminal slots and tighten with a small screwdriver.

15 Install the L-brackets on the jack studs for the door opening. Then, attach the infrared sensors to the brackets.

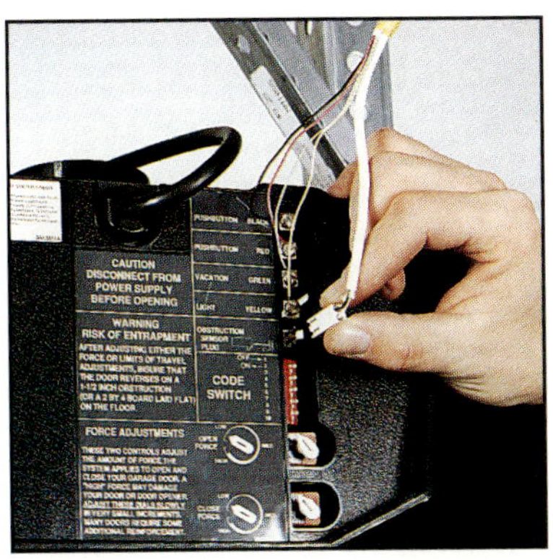

16 Attach the low-voltage receiver cable to the back of the power unit. The cable has a 2-pin stab connector on the end.

17 Screw the base of the control to a garage wall and tighten each color-coded wire to the control's terminal block.

18 Make the necessary performance adjustments by turning the screws located at the back and bottom of the power unit.

Installing under-cabinet lights

When building a new home, it's not easy to anticipate all the spots where task-lighting will be needed. After a few months, however, sins of omission become painfully obvious. One such area is the kitchen counter, where upper cabinets tend to block the light from overhead fixtures. Given the amount of work done on kitchen counters—and all of it food related—under-cabinet lighting can prove especially useful. Luckily, these fixtures are not that difficult to install even after the house is finished.

The fixtures in the installation shown were 18 in. long, $4\frac{1}{2}$-in. wide and $1\frac{1}{4}$-in. deep. This shallow depth allowed the fixture to be concealed behind each cabinet's lower front rail. Viewed head-on, neither fixture is visible.

Text and photos for *Installing Under-Cabinet Lights* by Merle Henkenius. Fixtures used here were made by Seagul Lighting (P.O. Box 329, Riverside, NJ 08075). Each fixture requires a single 15-watt fluorescent lamp which is sold separately.

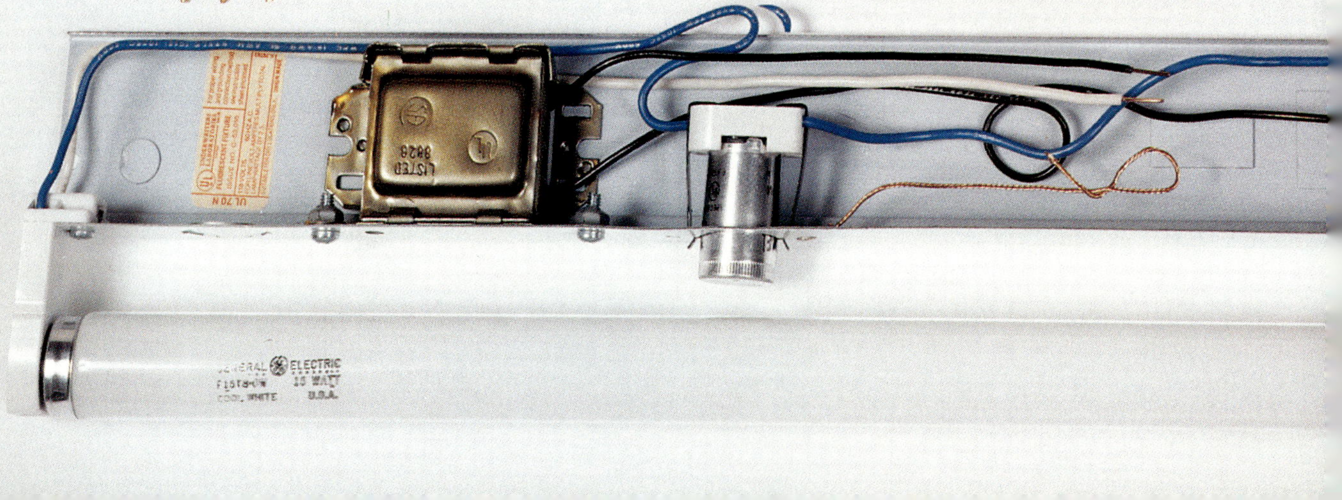

The fixtures came with their own switches, which are designed to be installed in one of several channel knockouts. These were not used in this installation. Instead, both fixtures were wired to a new single-pole switch mounted in the wall below the cabinets. Both fixtures are controlled by this switch.

Electrical Access

The first order of business is to determine where you'll gain access to electricity. Because electrical codes prohibit tapping into kitchen receptacles dedicated to small appliances, your best bet is to access an existing general-lighting circuit.

To find a circuit with the capacity for expansion, use this simple rule of thumb: Assign 1.5 amps to each light and receptacle on a circuit. At this rate, a 15-amp breaker would accommodate 10 devices (light fixtures, receptacles), and a 20-amp breaker, 13 devices. To determine the number of devices on a circuit, shut off the power and count all the dead light fixtures and receptacles.

In the installation shown, the easiest point of access was an unfinished area of the basement, just below the kitchen. Because the basement lighting circuit was underrated, it was possible to tap into an existing porcelain fixture with a pull-string switch.

1 Locate the best position for the electrical cable, then bore a hole through the rear cabinet rail and into the wall.

2 If necessary, bore a hole through the side partitions of adjoining cabinets so the fixtures can be joined with conduit.

3 Position a cut-in switch at the same height as other switch boxes in the room. Then, trace around the box.

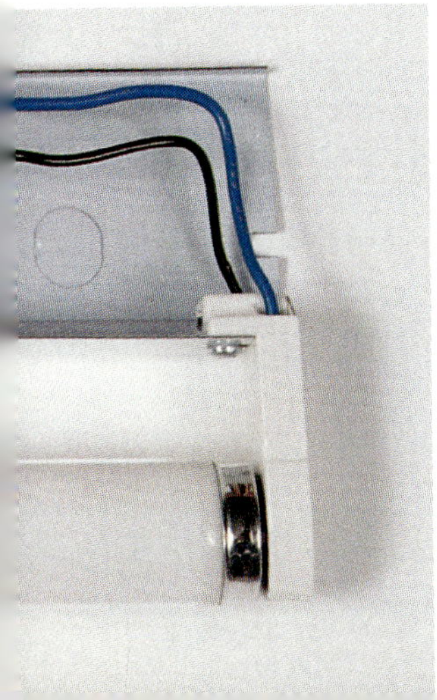

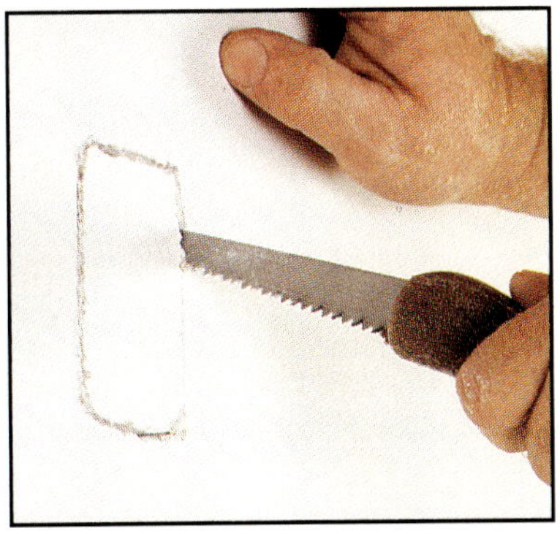

4 Use a drywall saw to cut along the traced line. Work close to the line to eliminate any patching required later.

5 Feed a fish tape into the box hole from the basement. Then, attach the cable to the end and tape the connection.

6 Using the fish tape, gently pull the cable into the basement. Avoid cutting or abrading the cable insulation.

7 To get power from a ceiling fixture, join the like-colored wires from the new cable to those of the power feed in the box.

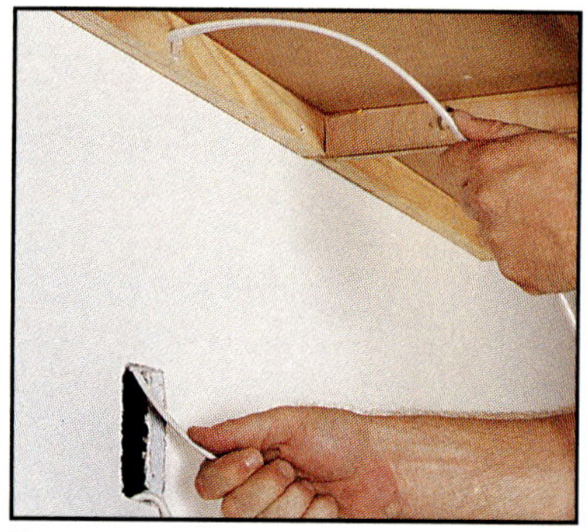

8 To run the cable between the fixture and the switch, feed the cable through the cabinet hole, down to the opening.

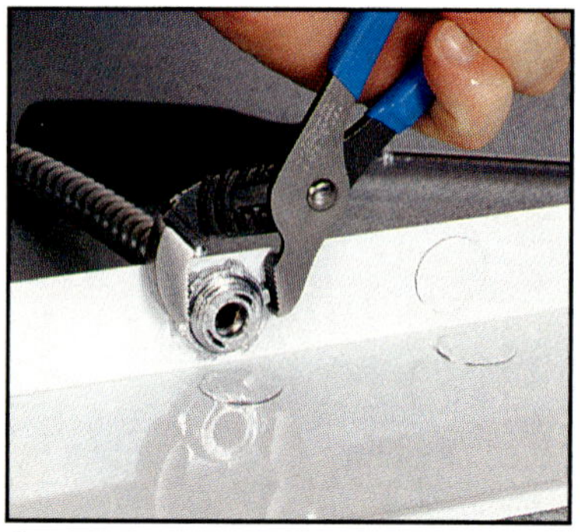

9 Protect exposed cable lengths with flexible conduit. Join the conduit to the fixtures with box connectors.

10 Once the cable is fed through the conduit, attach the fixture channels directly to the bottom of the cabinet.

11 Install flexible conduit between fixtures, too. Use box connectors to secure it, then run wires through it.

Where to Begin

Begin by locating an open stud space between the overhead cabinets and the countertop. Your goal is to keep all supply wiring, plus the new switch box and cabinet-access hole, within this stud space. An electronic stud sensor can help pinpoint the best box location. Tapping on the wall and listening for a change of sound as you move across the studs also will work.

Once you've settled on a location, bore a hole through the rear cabinet rail at this point (Fig. 1). This is also a good time to bore a hole through the adjoining cabinet sides (Fig. 2). This hole allows joining two fixtures with flexible conduit.

Next, locate the switch box, using the height of the other switches in the room as a guide. Plan on using a non-metallic cut-in box for this job. Simply press the box against the wall and trace around its perimeter (Fig. 3). Then cut out the hole using a drywall saw along the traced line (Fig. 4).

Installing Cable

With the opening for the cut-in switch box made, go into the basement and bore a hole into the stud space from below. To make sure the hole falls in the correct stud space, measure from a feature common to both sides of the floor, such as a plumbing drain.

Use an inexpensive fish tape to pull new cable between the new box opening and the basement. Feed the tape up from the basement, while a helper pulls it through the cut-in opening. With the fish tape through the box opening, fasten 14/2 (with ground) cable to the tape's hooked end, and tape the cable securely in place (Fig. 5). Then, pull the fish tape and cable into the basement (Fig. 6).

Once in the basement, pull the cable to your target ceiling box. When moving across joists, bore holes through the middle of the joists and pull the cable through. When running along a joist, staple the cable along the side of the joist every 4 ft. and within 8 in. of the box.

To wire the circuit extension, first shut off the power to the circuit at the service panel. Then remove the existing fixture and drive a screwdriver through an unused knockout in the box. Feed the new cable into the box and strip the sheathing from the cable, leaving at least 8 in. of wire exposed below the box.

Then strip ½ in. of insulation from each new wire, and cut three insulated pigtails—one white, one black and one green. Next, fasten one end of each pigtail to its terminal screw on the fixture, and join all like-colored wires with wire connectors (Fig. 7). As always, the brass terminal gets the black wire; the silver terminal, the white wire; and the green terminal, the green wire. With all connections made, replace the fixture and move upstairs. Complete the rough wiring by pulling a short length of cable between the cabinet and the switch box opening (Fig. 8).

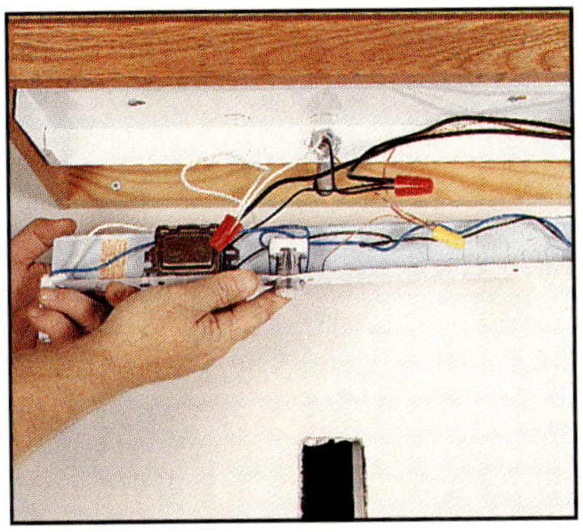

12 Using wire connectors, join the like-colored switch and fixture wires with those going to the other fixture.

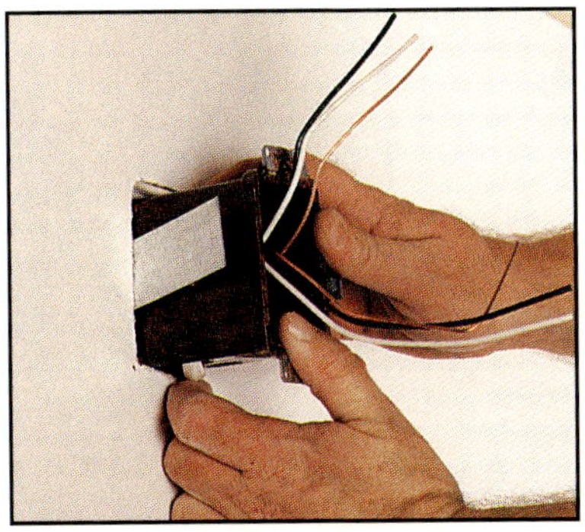

13 After pulling both cables into the cut-in box, press the box into its opening. Then, tighten the support bracket.

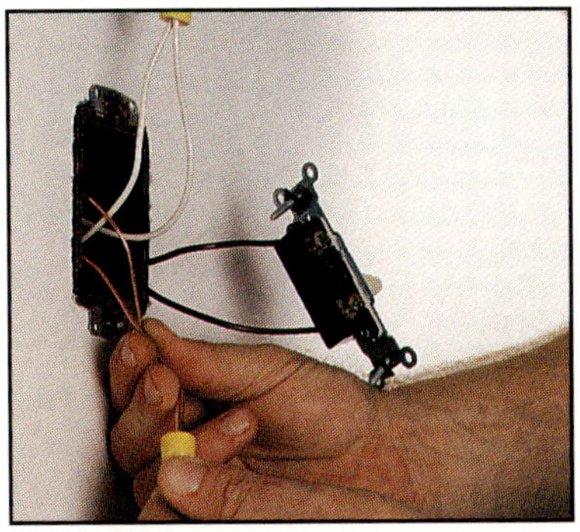

14 Join the wires to the back of the switch, then press the switch into the box. Install a cover plate and test.

Installing the Fixtures

Most electrical codes require exposed lengths of wiring to be encased in conduit. In this case it meant two short pieces of conduit, one between the fixture and the wall, and the other between the two fixtures. Begin by cutting a 6-in. length of ½-in. flexible conduit and fastening it to a standard cable connector. Then remove the appropriate knockout plug from the first fixture, slide the connector into this hole and tighten it in place (Fig. 9).

Also remove a knockout from one end of each fixture and install cable connectors in these openings. These connectors are later joined by a short length of conduit.

Under-cabinet fixtures are designed to be screwed directly to the bottom of a cabinet. While this is easily done, beware of a common pitfall. With some factory-made cabinets, the floor of the cabinet is made of thin composition board. If your cabinet is made this way, an alternate fastening method is in order. You might drill the cabinet floor and use machine screws with the nuts concealed inside the fixture channel. Or, you can beef up the floor with a piece of plywood, stained or painted to match the cabinet.

In the installation shown, short screws were used and each fixture was tightened directly to the bottom of the cabinet, approximately 4 in. from the wall (Fig. 10).

With the fixtures mounted and cable fed through the flexible conduit at the rear of the first fixture, join the two fixtures with a second length of conduit. Then feed individual jumper wires through this conduit, so that the two fixtures can be wired together (Fig. 11).

Because fixture ballasts are heat producing, use high-temperature wire—available at hardware stores—for these jumpers. You can use bare wire to join the grounding pigtails that are attached to each fixture channel.

To wire the two fixtures, use wire connectors to join the black and white switch wires to the black and white lead wires from the first fixture, and to the jumper wires for the second fixture. Tie all blacks together in one wire connector and whites in another (Fig. 12). Then join the black and white leads from the second fixture to the jumper wires, and finally join all the grounding wires.

Wiring the Switch

To complete the wiring, pull both cables in the box opening into a new cut-in box. After stripping the sheathing from the cables, press the box into the opening (Fig. 13) and tighten the screw that binds the support clamp to the wall.

As always, only the hot (black) side of the circuit is switched. Join both neutral (white) wires with one connector and both ground wires with another connector. Then press the black wires into their stab-in slots in the back of the switch (Fig. 14). To finish the job, install the switch and cover plate, then put a lamp in each fixture and snap the light diffusers in place. Turn on the circuit power and make sure everything works.

Installing surface wiring

Much of the dread of making an electrical upgrade is based on the need for cutting into finished walls and ceilings. Fishing wire through closed spaces is always a gamble as hidden structural components can foil the entire effort. Then, of course, there's the problem of wiring along brick or masonry walls.

One solution to these problems is decorative surface wiring. While not the most desirable option under ideal conditions, the system can be a real problem solver in the right places.

Surface wiring is not a new concept; it's been seen in old schools and commercial buildings. The difference today is that modern surface wiring components are not only attractive, but also come in a range of colors and profiles. Some are also made of plastic, which eliminates the need for redundant grounding.

Installing Surface Wiring was written and photographed by Merle Henkenius. Surface wiring components shown here were made by Wiremold Co.

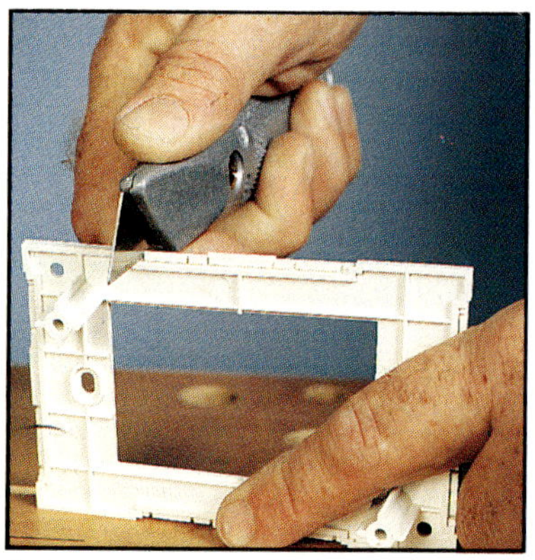

1 Before installing each box baseplate, use a utility knife to cut the ends of the knockouts, and snap them off with pliers.

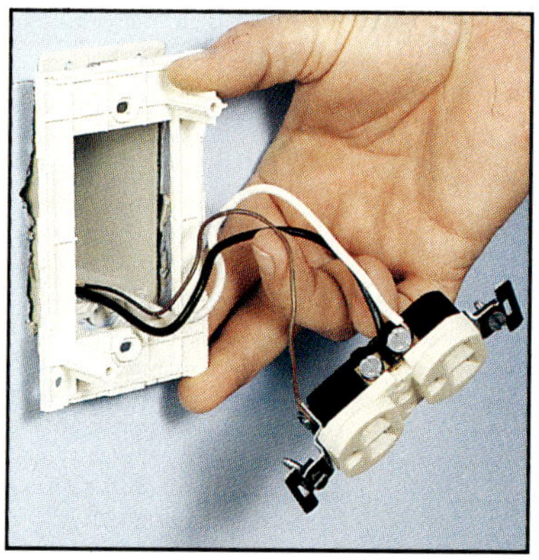

2 After unscrewing the receptacle from the power-source box, slip on the new baseplate and secure with anchors.

Choosing Components

A typical installation of one new receptacle and a switched ceiling light requires enough channel to reach the new box locations, three box extensions, a T connector to branch to the switch, an inside corner connector to carry the channel across the ceiling and a round ceiling fixture box. You also need a few accessory packets that include an assortment of wire clips, track connectors, screws and plastic anchors, wire connectors, a standard single-pole switch, a receptacle, a ceiling light and No. 14 insulated wires. You need one black, one white and one green wire for each device that is to be wired.

3 Use tin snips or a hacksaw to cut the base channel to length. Use a hacksaw only when cutting the trim channel.

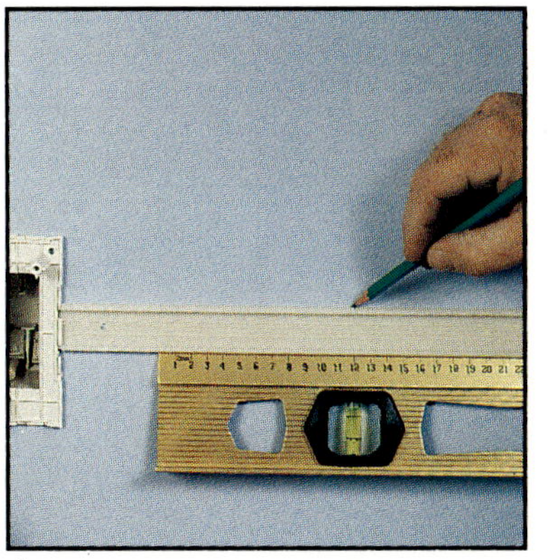

4 After boring holes through the channel on 18-in. centers, level the channel and mark the hole locations on the wall.

Code Considerations

Several electrical code requirements will rule your installation. To determine whether your circuit has enough capacity for the new component, assign 1.5 amps to each existing outlet. At this rate, a 15-amp circuit will handle 10 outlets, and a 20-amp circuit will handle 13 outlets. Shut off your circuit and use a lamp to verify which outlets are without power. Then, add up the number of dead outlets to determine how many new fixtures can be added.

Each receptacle and fixture also needs to be grounded, as does any metallic box you use as a starting point. All ground connections should be made with insulated wire, and all wires should be the same size as those used in the existing circuit.

Check with local codes for the number of wires allowed per box. You are allowed to count all ground wires as one and each device as one. Generally speaking, you are allowed six wires per track and box.

Getting Started

This system has wire channels, channel connectors, box extensions and box baseplates. The 2-piece channels are composed of a base channel that's screwed to the wall and a trim channel that covers the wires. The wires are held in place with thin plastic clips that attach to the base channel, and snap-on connectors to conceal the joints between connecting channels.

Each baseplate and box has knockouts, so that the base channel will extend slightly into the box baseplate and the trim channel will extend into the box extension. Choose the knockouts that will provide the best entry point for each receptacle or switch. Make the knockout cuts with a sharp utility knife and break off the tabs with pliers (Fig. 1)

Next, determine the outlet to use as the power source. Shut off the power at the panel, remove the cover plate from that box and pull out the receptacle. Then, slide the baseplate over the existing box (Fig. 2), and screw it to the wall with the anchors provided in the accessory kit.

5 Secure the channel with drywall anchors and screws. At a **T** connection, break away the edge to make room for the wires.

6 Use an awl to punch anchor holes through the baseplates and wall. Then, attach with drywall anchors and screws.

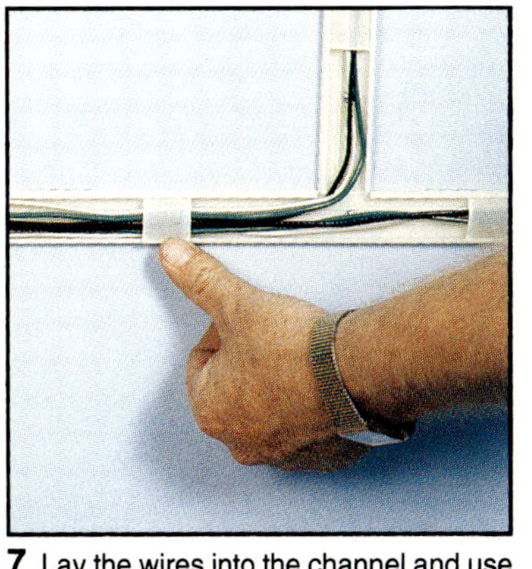

7 Lay the wires into the channel and use wire clips to hold them in place. Use wires of the same size as the original circuit.

8 With wires in place, measure the trim channels exactly and snap them in place over the base channels to conceal wiring.

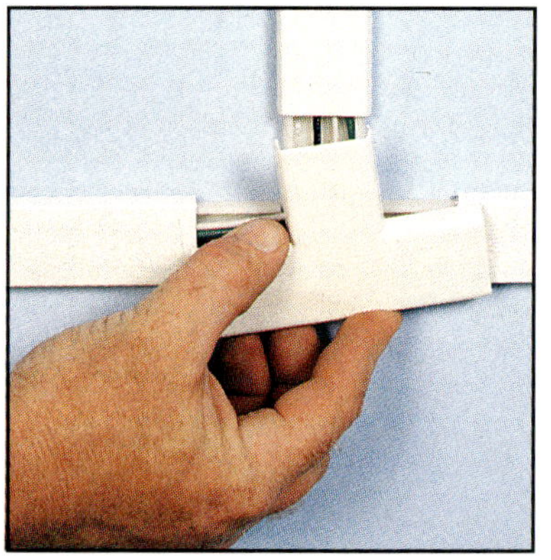

9 Snap connectors over the trim channels at T and L branches. Trim channels extend under connectors about $\frac{1}{4}$ inch.

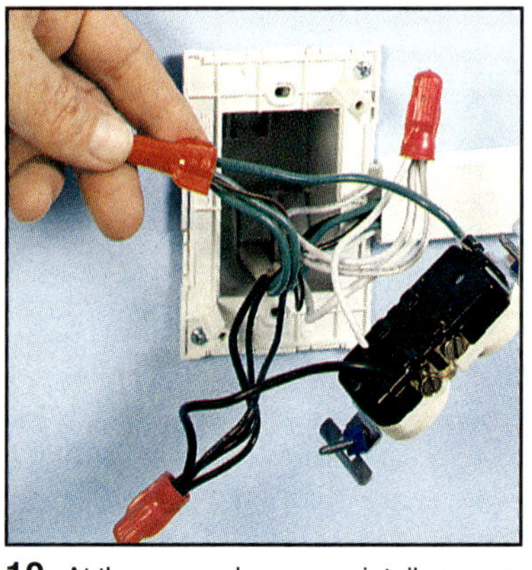

10 At the source box, use pigtail connections to attach receptacle and new wiring. Join together all the same-color wires.

11 Use a utility knife to cut the ends of the knockouts in the extension boxes. Then break away the knockouts with pliers.

Installing the Channels

After the baseplate at the power-source outlet is in place, it's time to cut and position the first length of base channel. When bringing the channel to a new outlet box, first cut the base channel to length with a pair of tin snips or a hacksaw (Fig. 3) and bore screwholes every 18 in. Insert one end of the base channel into the power-source baseplate knockout and use a level to align the piece accurately so that it is parallel to the floor (Fig. 4).

While holding the channel level, mark each drywall anchor-hole location on the wall. Then, use an awl to punch the anchor holes into the drywall. Use a hammer to tap the anchors into place, and screw the base channel to the wall.

To run wires to a switch box or a ceiling fixture, add a vertical section of base channel to create a T joint. At the T, break a section from the edge of the continuous horizontal channel to make a space to run the wires. Then, mark and punch the anchor-hole locations and fasten the adjoining base channel in place with screws (Fig. 5).

After fastening each length of base channel that will join a box baseplate, secure the baseplates to the wall with the knockouts removed (Fig. 6). Continue adding base channel and box bases in the same manner until you've completed your circuit extension layout.

With the channel and box layout completed, lay the wires into the base channel and snap wire clips over them to hold them in place (Fig. 7). In the installation shown, two sets of three wires were run from the existing receptacle—one to a new receptacle box and one branching off to a new switch and ceiling box.

When measuring and cutting the trim channels that cover the wires, it's best to hold the extension boxes and connectors in place to determine the exact length of trim channel that's needed. Inline, corner and T connectors have built-in stops that require an exact fit. Only about $\frac{1}{4}$ in. of channel is actually covered by each end of the connector or the extension box. While holding each extension box or connector in place, mark the exact trim channel cutoff location on the base channel.

Then, hold the trim channels in place and mark the cutlines as indicated on the base channel. After cutting each length of trim channel with a hacksaw (don't use snips for the trim channel), snap it in place over its base channel, again, using the pencil marks as a guide (Fig. 8). Then, install the connectors where required to conceal the wires (Fig. 9).

Wiring the New Devices

After the base channels, trim channels, connectors and box baseplates are in place, it's time to connect the wires and install the extension boxes and cover plates. Before installing the boxes, connect the new wiring to the power-source receptacle and wire each new receptacle.

To connect the wires at the power-source receptacle, first remove the receptacle and install insulated pigtail wires to its hot, neutral and ground terminals. The brass-color terminal gets a black wire, the silver-color terminal gets a white wire and the green terminal, a green wire. Use twist connectors to join all like-color wires in the box with those of the receptacle (Fig. 10).

Wire the remaining receptacles with pigtails, and the last receptacle without pigtails. To mount the extension boxes, use a utility knife to cut the ends of the knockouts (Fig. 11), and snap off the knockouts with pliers. Mount the boxes to the baseplates with screws (Fig. 12). With the boxes in place, simply secure the receptacles to the boxes in the usual manner (Fig. 13). Finally, install the receptacle cover plates.

Wiring Switch and Ceiling Light

If you've laid out your channels and box bases for a new ceiling light and wall switch, these components should already be in place, with the wire, channel trim and connectors installed. The vertical channel shown was connected to the receptacle channel with a T joint, and, after joining the switch baseplate, the channel was carried around the ceiling corner with an L connection.

Wiring the switch is really a snap, because only the hot (black) wire is diverted through it. Cut the black wire and connect the ends to the two switch terminals, leaving the white and green wires intact (Fig. 14). After mounting the switch, install the switch cover plate (Fig. 15) and move on to the ceiling light. First, install the ceiling box and pull the wires down through it (Fig. 16). Use twist connectors to join the fixture leads to the circuit wires (Fig. 17). Mount the fixture, install bulbs and attach the globe or diffuser.

12 To mount the extension boxes, simply screw them to the baseplates. Pigtails are not required at the end of the circuit.

13 Finally, install the receptacles in the extension boxes just as you would in an ordinary in-wall receptacle box.

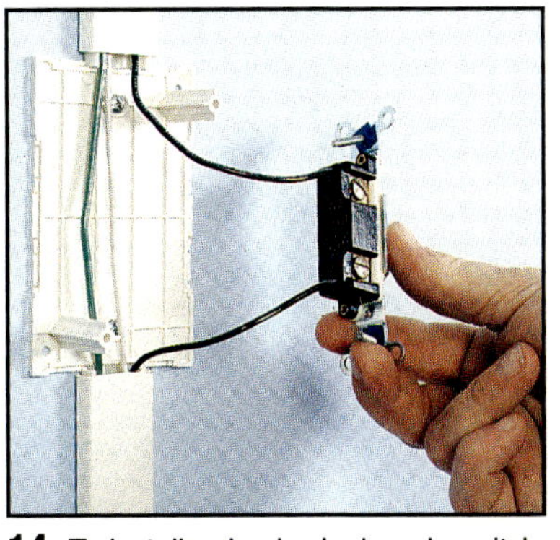

14 To install a simple single-pole switch, connect the black wire only. Leave the white and green wires intact.

15 After the switch is wired, secure it to the extension box with screws and attach the switch cover plate.

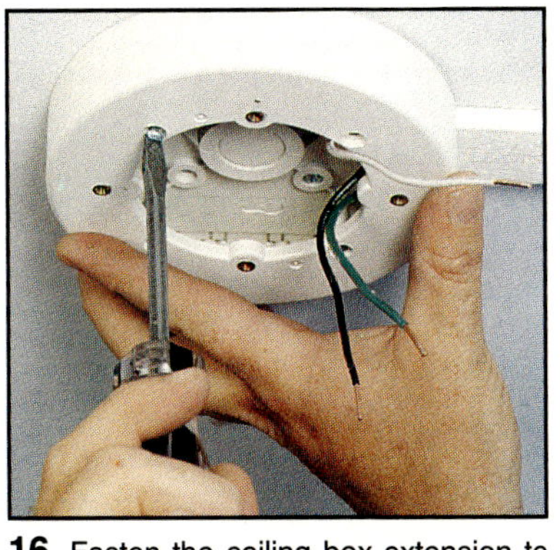

16 Fasten the ceiling box extension to its baseplate with screws before connecting the wires to the ceiling fixture.

17 To wire the ceiling fixture, join all like-color wires with twist connectors. Then, install the bulb and diffuser.

1 Locate the hole template on the edge of the door between 6 and 8 in. above the lockset. Mark the hole locations.

2 Use a holesaw to bore a hole for the lock mechanism. Stop when the pilot bit breaks through the other side.

3 Remove the holesaw and slide it into the pilot hole on the other side of the door. Finish the cut from this side.

4 Bore the hole in the edge of the door, making sure the bit is perpendicular to the door in both directions.

5 Slide the bolt assembly completely into its hole, then scribe around the bolt plate with a sharp utility knife.

6 Remove the bolt assembly, then chisel out the stock below the plate (about $\frac{1}{8}$ in.) so the bolt plate fits flush.

Installing a deadbolt lock

Text and photographs for *Installing a Deadbolt Lock* by Merle Henkenius. The lock shown is a double-cylinder deadbolt with a 1-in throw and a saw-resistant bolt made by Weiser Lock (6660 S. Broadmoor Rd., Tucson, AZ 85746). The strike plate was made by M.A.G. Engineering & Manufacturing (15261 Transistor Ln., Huntington Beach, CA 92469).

■ Most thieves are opportunists, so much so that mere inconvenience is often a substantial deterrent. A deadbolt lock, for example, can make an otherwise easy break-in a lot less appealing. It's not that doors with deadbolts can't be forced or picked, it's that deadbolts increase the amount of noise and time needed for a break-in. This increases the likelihood of being caught. When other common-sense precautions are also used, such as outdoor lighting and heavy-duty window latches, most thieves would rather take their business elsewhere.

Using deadbolt locks is unquestionably a good idea. But the type of deadbolt you choose is a bit more complicated, especially if your door has glass window lights or glass side lights. Should you install a single-cylinder deadbolt, which can be operated from the inside with a knob, or a double-cylinder lock, which must be keyed from both sides?

The problem with a single-cylinder lock is fairly obvious. To get in, an intruder merely needs to break the glass, reach in and turn the knob. For this reason, many sources advocate a double-cylinder deadbolt, which can only be thrown with a key, from both the outside and the inside.

The problem here is that you not only make it harder for a keyless intruder to get in, but for keyless family members to get out in a hurry, especially in the event of a fire. As such, many building and safety codes prohibit the use of double-cylinder deadbolts on residential entry doors. Their argument is bolstered by the fact that glass can make a lot of noise when broken, and the last thing an intruder wants is a lot of noise.

7 Slide the bolt assembly into place again. Then bore pilot holes and attach the assembly with the screws provided.

8 Slide one side of the lock mechanism through the slot in the bolt assembly. Then slide the other side into place.

9 Securely join the two sides of the lock mechanism by driving two screws through the inside lock mechanism.

10 Mark the face of the deadbolt with a grease pencil. Then throw the bolt against the jamb to mark the jamb hole.

11 Locate the centerpoint of the marks left on the jamb. Then bore the jamb hole to the proper depth.

12 After testing the operation of the lock, secure the jamb plate by driving long screws into the jack studs.

Seen in this light, a single-cylinder deadbolt, which is keyed only from the outside, offers nearly as much real-world deterrence as a double-cylinder lock, without the fire-safety hazard.

In the installation shown, an architectural-grade, double-cylinder deadbolt with a 1-in. throw and a saw-resistant bolt was chosen. The strikeplate was replaced with an oversize, heavier version. The new plate is nearly 8 in. long and includes six mounting screws, four of which are 3 in. long. These screws are long enough to pass through the jamb and into the jack stud of the wall framing. The advantage is greater strength, spread over a larger area.

Boring the Door Holes

Every deadbolt and lockset comes with a paper template that will help you spot the locations of the edge and side holes in the door. In most cases, the template offers two or more setback depths and two edge widths. The lock shown required a 2¾-in. setback, and the steel-clad door was 1¾ in. thick. The deadbolt was positioned 8 in. up from the lockset, to accommodate the oversize strike plate. If you use a smaller plate, you can lower the lock mechanism an inch or two.

Begin by folding the template along its dotted line and taping it to the door. Then use a pencil to mark the two hole locations (Fig. 1). After removing the template, use a holesaw to bore through one side of the door (Fig. 2). As soon as the pilot bit pierces the opposite side of the door, remove the saw and complete the hole from the other side (Fig. 3). Working in from both sides of the door is important. In the case of a wooden door, boring completely through can splinter the opposite side. In the case of a steel-clad door, the lightweight steel skin can tear away as the saw teeth poke through.

To bore the edge hole, which will accept the lock bolt, use a Forstner bit or a spade bit (Fig. 4). The trick here is to bore the hole as straight as possible. While you'll be able to sight along the top of the drill, correcting any side-to-side error, it pays to have a helper sight the vertical orientation. In any case, bore through the edge of the door until the bit enters the lock hole.

Installing the Bolt Plate

Lock-blot slides come in two forms: those with faceplates that must be mortised into the edge of the door, and those that have no plates and are simply driven into the bolt hole.

The bolt shown came with a plate, so the next step was to chisel out a recess in the edge of the door to accept the plate. Begin by inserting the bolt into its hole and marking the door edge around the perimeter of the plate. Because pencil lines can be too wide for close work, use a utility knife to mark the perimeter (Fig. 5). Then use a 1-in. chisel to remove enough stock so the bolt plate will fit flush with the door edge (Fig. 6).

As always, the danger is that you'll overcut, so work carefully, shaving out thin ribbons of wood with each pass of the chisel. If your chisel is sharp, hand pressure will be enough.

Assembling the Lock

With both holes bored and the edge of the door recessed for the bolt plate, slide the bolt into its hole and press the plate into the recess. Bore two screw pilot holes through the bolt plate and into the edge of the door. Then attach the bolt assembly by driving screws into the door edge (Fig. 7).

Next, install the two lock cylinders. Begin by feeding the inside cylinder through its slot in the bolt assembly. (The inside cylinder has screwholes, the outside cylinder does not.) Then tip the outside cylinder into the slot next to the inside cylinder, and press both cylinders against the door (Fig. 8).

The lock shown came with three long bolts that join the two cylinder halves. Two of these bolts have standard Phillips-heads, but the third has a nonremovable slotted head. This bolt lacks the slot surfaces needed to back it out from the lock with a screwdriver. Use the two Phillips-head bolts to join the two halves of the lock (Fig. 9) until the entire installation is completed and tested. Only then can you back out one of the Phillips-head bolts and replace it with the nonremovable bolt.

Setting the Strike Plate

Strike plates, especially oversize ones, need not be mortised in when there is adequate space between the door and jamb. Because there was plenty of clearance, it was decided to surface mount the plate.

If you'd prefer to mortise in your strike plate, simply proceed as shown here to determine the proper position of the bolt hole. Then center your plate over this hole and trace its perimeter on the jamb. Remove the waste with a sharp chisel.

The most critical aspect of setting a strike plate lies in pinpointing exactly where to bore the doorjamb. You can do a good job with careful measuring, but an easier method is to let the bolt tell you where to bore. Mark the four corners of the bolt face with a grease pencil (Fig. 10). A crayon or lipstick also will work.

Begin by withdrawing the bolt and closing the door. Make sure the lockset is engaged. Then use a key to throw the bolt hard against the doorjamb several times. The bolt will transfer the grease-pencil marks to the jamb. Then simply bore the jamb at the centerpoint of the marks (Fig. 11). Because the bolt's throw is longer than the jamb's width, drill completely through the jamb and into the wall framing slightly.

Finally, close the door and throw the bolt into the jamb hole. Then position the oversize strike plate and bore holes in the jamb to accept the plate's 1¼-in. screws. Make sure that the plate is oriented so the two shorter screws are near the inside edge of the jamb, and the 3-in. screws are nearer the doorstop, in line with the wall studs.

With the strike plate secured by the two shorter screws only, open and close the door several times, locking and unlocking the bolt each time. When you're satisfied that the lock works smoothly, bore the remaining pilot holes and drive the 3-in. screws through the strike plate and jamb, and into the jack studs (Fig. 12).

Installing an in-ground sprinkler system

If you were to make a list of the most approachable do-it-yourself home-improvement projects, installing an in-ground sprinkler system probably would not top the list. Start thinking about it and the problems of layout and machinery seem to get in the way. It all seems a bit overwhelming.

Some manufacturers are trying to make the idea much more appealing. Not only will you find all the components for the job at your local home-improvement center, but for the price of a stamp you'll get professional help in laying out the system. If you still have questions, there's often a toll-free phone number to help you along the way.

The installation is a lot of work. When it's done, however, you'll have saved more than 50% when compared with a professional installation.

System Considerations

Not every property will accommodate a sprinkler system. If the waterline from the street to the meter is smaller than ⅝ in. (because of mineral deposits), or if your water pressure is down in the 20-psi range, your options are extremely limited. A heavily landscaped yard, or one with a good deal of concrete or hefty tree roots, also will limit your options and make the job more difficult.

To determine water pressure, you can call your local water company. A more precise method is to measure the pressure at an outside faucet. Use a water-pressure

1 To test your water pressure at a sillcock, use a pressure gauge and an adapter that connects the gauge to the threaded spout.

Text and photos for *Installing an In-Ground Sprinkler System* by Merle Henkenius. The installation shown here has the Lawn Genie trademark, which is a division of Hardie Irrigation, makers of the Rain Jet commercial line. The firm also puts out the worksheet with a formula to determine how much water you system delivers in gallons per minute.

gauge attached with a hose-thread adapter (Fig. 1). To help you judge the capacity of your water supply, one manufacturer offers a worksheet that includes a formula to determine how much water your system delivers in gallons per minute.

No matter what your delivery capacity at the meter, however, it is important to know that friction will reduce the output somewhat. Every fitting, turn and length of pipe will subtract from the raw total and you may have to upsize the piping that supplies the sprinkler system to achieve appropriate flow rates.

Plan your sprinkler system to begin inside the house, as near the water meter as possible, and exit the house through the rim joist directly above a basement wall. Just outside, you need a code-approved vacuum breaker to protect the potable water system from contaminants.

From the vacuum breaker, plan a single underground line that connects your water system with the sprinkler system zone valves. Each zone valve feeds a separate piping run and the sprinkler heads attached to it. The size of the yard and the water delivery rate dictate the number of zones needed. The zone valves are connected, via low-voltage wire, to a central control panel. At the panel, you can program the zones to cycle separately and sequentially. The control panel used here has a battery backup that saves the program during power outages. If you're on a tight budget, manual shut-off valves can be substituted for electronic valves.

Sprinkler heads are available in several spray patterns. Some will broadcast 360° arcs others only 180°, 90° or 45° arcs. Also available are drip heads designed for gardens.

To ensure proper flow at the sprinkler heads and uniform coverage, you can send your layout worksheet and a scaled drawing of your yard—with house, driveway, sidewalks, trees and other significant landscape features—to the sprinkler system manufacturer. You'll receive a detailed layout including pipe sizing, head types and locations, the number of zones and zone valves, and the best piping routes to take.

Use PVC piping; it's familiar and universally available. With this aterial, the joints are either threaded or glued. Before cementing PVC components together, paint the mating surfaces with a solvent/primer to remove the glaze. To keep pipes from freezing, you need a few pressure-activated brass drain valves. When the water is shut off, the valves open and the lines drain.

2 Begin the trenches by using a spade to slice out sod in squares. Set the sod on a tarp and dig the trenches 10 in. deep.

3 Splice tees into the sprinkler head supply pipes at head locations. Use joint primer and PVC cement to connect the tees.

4 Dry-connect sprinkler heads to nipples and tees and compare height with grade. If necessary, try a longer or shorter nipple.

5 Make final threaded connections with Teflon tape to ensure leakproof joints. Be sure to orient directional heads correctly.

6 Thread pressure-activated brass drain fittings into horizontal drain tees. Use Teflon tape to seal threads and tighten securely.

7 Place coarse gravel under drain fittings to help keep soil from clogging fittings. When backfilling, also add gravel on top.

Outdoor Work

Use spray paint to mark each head location on the lawn. Then, pick the most convenient locations for the zone valve groupings. Begin the pipe trenches by using a spade to slide out the sod in small squares (Fig. 2). Set the squares aside on a plastic tarp and dig the trenches 10 in. deep.

Lay out the piping and splice in tee fittings at each sprinkler head location (Fig. 3). Where water will be trapped, and at the end of each piping run, splice a threaded tee on its side for a pressure-activated brass drain fitting. Under each drain tee, dig the trench several inches deeper.

With the zone piping in place, connect each sprinkler head to its tee with a plastic threaded nipple. Using nipples ranging from 1 to 3 in. long, test assemble each sprinkler head, nipple and tee, and check that the head is at the correct height in relation to the grade (Fig. 4). With all the heads at the right height, disassemble and reconnect the components, using Teflon tape to ensure leakproof joints. Make sure that any directional heads are turned in the appropriate direction (Fig. 5). Then, thread on the brass drain fittings using Teflon tape to seal the threads (Fig. 6), and fill the recess under the drains with gravel (Fig. 7).

To connect to the zone valves, first place threaded tees in each pipe near the valves and install brass drain fittings. Then lay the PVC supply pipe in its trench and place an additional drain at the end near the valves. Thread PVC adapters to the valve ports, and glue the piping to the adapters (Fig. 8).

While in the area, make the low-voltage wiring connections. From low-voltage cable running in the trench containing the water supply line, join the white wire to the stranded lead from each of the zone valves using a wire connector (Fig. 9). Then, join each valve's remaining lead to its own colored wire from the cable. Color coding is important here, as each color will be fastened to a unique terminal in the panel and each valve will be controlled by it. With the zone valve connections made, cover the valves with the access box (Fig. 10).

Before backfilling, add gravel to cover each drain fitting. Then, fill and level the trenches a few inches at a time. Tamp each layer firmly in place before adding more soil to minimize settling. Finally, replace the sod.

8 Use threaded male adapters and glue to join the piping to the zone-control valves. Each valve controls one sprinkler branch.

9 Attach white wire from control panel with the white wires from valves. Colored panel leads go to remaining valve leads.

10 Cover the zone valve grouping with an access box and backfill the hole. The top of the box offers access to control valves.

11 Bore a hole for pipe and low-voltage cable. If your home has a brick facade, start with a hammer drill and masonry bit.

12 After assembling vacuum breaker with pipe and fittings, slide assembly through hole. Vacuum breaker remains vertical.

Connecting To The House

Begin by boring a hole through a rim joist large enough to accommodate the low-voltage cable and copper supply line that will enter the house (Fig. 11) Then, build the vacuum breaker and copper pipe assembly. This assembly extends up from the pipe exit hole to the breaker and then down to the PVC supply pipe in the trench. To keep from scorching the vacuum breaker, solder the copper fittings before connecting them to the vacuum breaker.

Assemble the components so that the vacuum breaker will be in a vertical position when the assembly is installed. Feed the piping through the rim joist opening (Fig. 12), and attach the other end to the PVC supply pipe with a threaded adapter and 90° fitting (Fig. 13).

On a ¾-in. line near the meter, splice in a ¾-in. copper tee. Immediately increase the pipe size, if necessary, and route the copper piping into the appropriate joist space. Install a full-flow ball valve and extend the pipe toward the incoming pipe from the vacuum breaker (Fig. 14).

Just before connecting the pipes, install a reducing tee. Connect a threaded adapter to the reduced piping and connect a boiler drain to it. This assembly will allow you to drain the system before winter (Fig. 15).

Screw the control panel box to the wall near a 120-volt receptacle. Join the white wires from the low-voltage cable to the two common screws in the panel. Then, bind each colored wire under its own terminal (Fig. 16). Finally, install the backup battery (Fig. 17), plug in the unit (Fig. 18) and program the panel according to the manufacturer's directions.

13 After gluing a PVC threaded adapter to 90° fitting, connect to copper feed line. Then, glue PVC supply pipe to fitting.

14 Splice a tee into a ¾-in. cold-water line to supply sprinkler system. Increase pipe diameter and add a full-flow ball valve.

15 Before connecting inside piping to outside piping, install a reducing tee and boiler drain so the pipes can be drained.

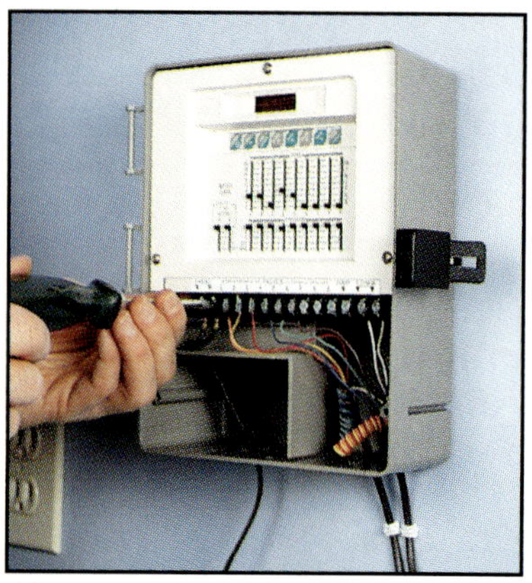

16 Mount the electronic control panel and connect the cable wires from the zone valves to the terminals in the panel.

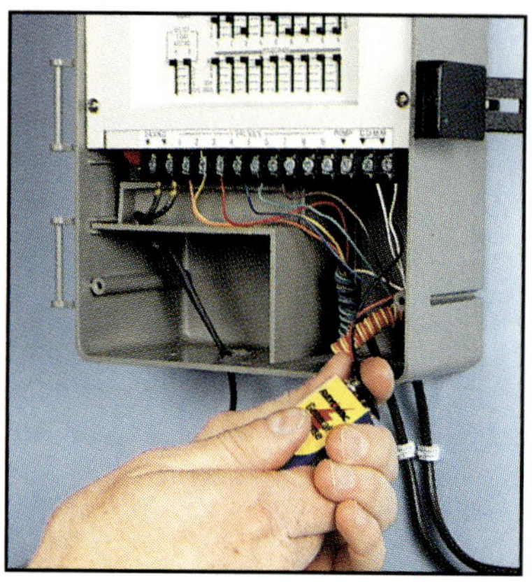

17 Attach a 9-volt battery to its harness inside the control panel. The battery saves the program during power outages.

18 Finally, plug the transformer into the nearest power receptacle and program the control panel according to instructions.

1 Dig the hole slightly larger and deeper than the nursery pot and check all measurements with a tape measure.

2 Measure liquid fertilizer in the proper amount and pour into a watering can. Dry fertilizers can also be used.

3 Pour 1 gallon of fertilizer solution into the hole, making sure that the sides of the hole are also treated.

Planting trees and shrubs

The nice thing about building a home in a new development is that everything is new and clean and uncluttered. Unfortunately, these are also the primary disadvantages. Without well-established trees and the sense of permanence they confer, that spanking-new home can appear misplaced—even foreign to its environment.

Of course, after the down payment, and after that breathtaking cash drain known as "new-house incidentals," there's often precious little left for landscaping. It's all compounded by the nagging realization that trees take a long, long time to mature.

A $300 Compromise Solution

For about $300 you can buy a few trees and shrubs. But this is a good and reasonable start. By planting a few trees now, they'll have several years of growth while you work on the finishing touches. In this sense, trees and shrubs are more timely investments than perennials along the walkway.

This is compromise thinking, of course, and compromises are best measured against the all-or-nothing alternatives. In the ALL corner are those who advocate rolling the cost of plantings into the mortgage. But do you really want to pay interest on those plants every month for the next 20 or 30 years? If you do, expect them to cost up to three times their purchase price.

In the NOTHING corner, of course, are those dear and sensible souls who don't mind living on a moonscape until they've saved the money to do it all at once. Each theory has merit, but in the end, compromises aren't so bad.

Inexpensive Professional Help

The first suggestion is to have an architectural landscape plan drawn up. Not only will this give you some professional help in designing an attractive yard, but it will help focus priorities. It's a simple matter of scale. One look at a blueprint and you'll know which plantings should come first, second and so on, as finances allow.

A professional landscape plan need not be expensive, and shouldn't be, when expense is the primary incentive for doing your own work. Many nurseries and garden centers have certified landscape architects on staff or on retainer, and they also make good use of university students majoring in this field.

For $50 to $150, you'll get a workable plan, and often this fee will be refunded with the purchase of a given amount of merchandise.

Timing Your Plantings

The best times to transplant trees and shrubs are early spring and fall. While summer plantings are common, owing mostly to mortgage company closing dates, summer heat can take its toll. Even if you were to water religiously, and at the same time not overwater, a summer-planted tree is going to just hold its own. It probably won't grow, but will hunker down and use all its reserves to stay alive. In that sense, a tree planted in July has little growth advantage over one planted in September.

Planting Trees and Shrubs was written by Merle Henkenius. Photos by Merle Henkenius.

4 With a helper holding the pot, raise the bush by its stem until the root ball is completely free from the pot.

5 Lower the root ball into the hole and center it from side to side. Make sure the stem is as straight and plumb as possible.

6 Small, irregular branches may be trimmed at planting, but most shaping should wait at least one growing season.

7 Determine the best location for the plant. Then using a spade, cut the sod and lift it out for use elsewhere.

8 Excavate the soil for larger trees using a shovel or spade. Keep this sod on hand for future gardening needs.

9 Pour liquid fertilizer on both the root ball and around the inside of the hole to encourage new root growth.

Planting Bushes

The plan shown began with a black haw bush (*Viburnum prunifolium*) near the front corner of the house. The first step was to scale off the blueprint to determine its exact placement. A quick check with a ruler will get you pretty close.

If you'll be planting without the aid of a scaled plan, try to avoid the common pitfalls of scale. When determining placement, remember how big your tree or bush will be when fully mature. A bush that will spread to 8 ft., for example, should not be planted 3 ft. from the house.

After pinpointing your preferred location, measure the depth and diameter of the temporary planting pot, and dig a hole to match this size. Then over-excavate the diameter by several inches and recheck all dimensions with a tape measure (Fig. 1). The slight over-excavation provides room for a layer of uncompacted soil next to the root system.

To feed the plant, mix liquid starter fertilizer in a watering can (Fig. 2) and pour the mixture onto the sides and into the bottom of the whole (Fig. 3). The recommended volume is about 1 gallon. Lacking a specialized starter fertilizer, you can use any blend that has a high phosphorous content, such as 5-10-5 (the middle number denotes the phosphorous percentage). When using granulated fertilizer, 1 to 2 tablespoons sprinkled into the hole will be adequate.

With a helper holding the pot, lift the bush by its stem (Fig. 4) and separate the root ball from the pot. Then lower the ball into its hole (Fig. 5) and pack the area around the root ball with soil. Water the area generously. Finally, to slow evaporation and to make mowing a little easier, cover the excavated area with wood-chip mulch.

Traditionally, the over-excavation gap has been packed with peat moss, to encourage root growth and to hold moisture. But these days, most experts recommend packing this gap with some of the soil that was taken from the hole. The thinking here is that the plant needs to make its way in real soil eventually, and that prolonging an artificial, potted-plant environment does more harm than good.

Finish by using pruning shears to remove any small, irregular branches that may have sprouted below the primary branches on the bush (Fig. 6). More of the lower branches will need to come off eventually, but it's a good idea to allow a full season of growth before doing any real shaping.

Planting Potted Trees

Consider some river birch trees (*Betula nigra*) to plant on an open area of the lawn. Begin by establishing the best locations, and then cut through and remove the sod in these places with a spade (Fig. 7).

10 Use a 2x2 to tamp the soil firmly around the sides of the root ball. This reduces the need for support stakes.

11 Use wood-chip mulch to help hold in moisture. Cypress mulch is good because it's long-lasting and rot-resistant.

12 With ball and burlap plantings, make sure to wet the ball thoroughly before planting. A garden hose works best.

13 Once the ball is lowered into place, use a utility knife to cut off all the burlap from the top of the root ball.

14 To help support the tree, drive a 2x2 stake—diagonally across the trunk—at least 16 in. into the ground.

15 Wrap the trunk a couple of times with a strip of sturdy cloth. Then, loosely tie the trunk to the stake.

The river birches came in larger pots than the black haw bush and required larger holes. As with bush planting, use the dimensions of the pot to determine the size and shape of the hole. Shovel all excavated soil into a wheelbarrow, and save it for elsewhere on your lawn or in your garden (Fig. 8).

Because of the larger root mass of these trees, pour some liquid fertilizer directly onto the root ball (Fig. 9). After placing the tree in its hole, use a length of 2×2 lumber to tamp down the soil around the root ball (Fig. 10). Because trees are naturally taller, and therefore more susceptible to wind, a loose soil pack can allow too much movement at the root level. Once all the soil is packed in, water the root system and cover the area with cypress mulch to slow evaporation (Fig. 11).

Planting Ball and Burlap Trees

The last tree planted was a large autumn purple ash (*Fraxinus americana*) with a large burlap-covered ball that was far too heavy for much movement. When dealing with such a large tree, be sure to measure the ball carefully then dig a hole to match its dimensions, including several extra inches around the perimeter to allow for easier alignment.

Typically, the burlap is left in place; so after rolling the ball to the edge of the hole, wet it thoroughly with a garden hose (Fig. 12). Then sprinkle it with fertilizer solution. Also fertilize the sides and bottom of the hole, then roll the ball into place and straighten the trunk.

Use a utility knife to trim all burlap from the top of the ball (Fig. 13). Then tamp soil around the edges and over the top, and finish by covering the excavated area with cypress mulch.

Many people believe that all large trees should be staked. But the verdict is still out on this practice. Your choice most clearly depends on the size and shape of the tree. Evergreen trees should be staked, because their needle-laden branches offer greater resistance to wind. A strong, bracing gust could conceivably lever them right out of the ground. But other trees are less likely to need additional support, at least for long periods. If pushing and pulling on the trunk produces much movement in the hole, go ahead and stake the tree. But if it doesn't, leave it alone.

When staking evergreens, drive three stakes—about 120° apart—several feet from the tree and run wire or rope supports to the trunk. To keep the supports from cutting into the trunk, pad the wire or rope with short lengths of garden hose. When staking trees like the autumn ash, drive a 2×2 stake diagonally across the trunk (Fig. 14), then tie the tree to the stake with a length of sturdy cloth. Protect the trunk to keep the stake from damaging the tree. You can either wrap the trunk in cloth before tying the two together or you can wrap the trunk to the stake with several figure-eight twists, making sure plenty of cloth separates the two (Fig. 15).

Garden cart

Any gardener knows what a chore it can be to haul materials around the yard. Whether you're moving plants, bags of fertilizer and seed, or tools, it is a relief to have a convenient way to move all this stuff, namely a sturdy garden cart.

In designing this cart, utility was combined with good looks. It was built out of mahogany marine plywood finished with a tough exterior polyurethane so it will resist moisture. Plywood panels were fastened using aluminum channel, so it would be reasonably lightweight. The cart rides on 20-in.-dia. wheels and a ¾-in.-dia. solid-steel axle. In other words, it's built to take it. To make the cart convenient to use, the front panel slides in and out of its aluminum channel.

The cart's woodworking is not difficult. The wooden parts are cut to size and then fastened with aluminum angle stock. The metalwork is also straightforward. Since you probably don't own the die and die stock to thread the axle, you might be able to rent one or ask a student in an industrial-arts class to cut the threads. A machine shop should also be able to do the work inexpensively.

Garden Cart was written and photographed by Neal Barrett. Lead photo by John Griebsch. Technical art by Eugene Thompson. A supplier of marine plywood is M.L. Condon Co., 246 Ferris Ave., White Plains, NY 10603. The heavy-duty spoked wheels shown were manufactured by Martin Wheel Co. Inc., 342 West Ave., P.O. Box 157, Tallmadge, OH 44278.

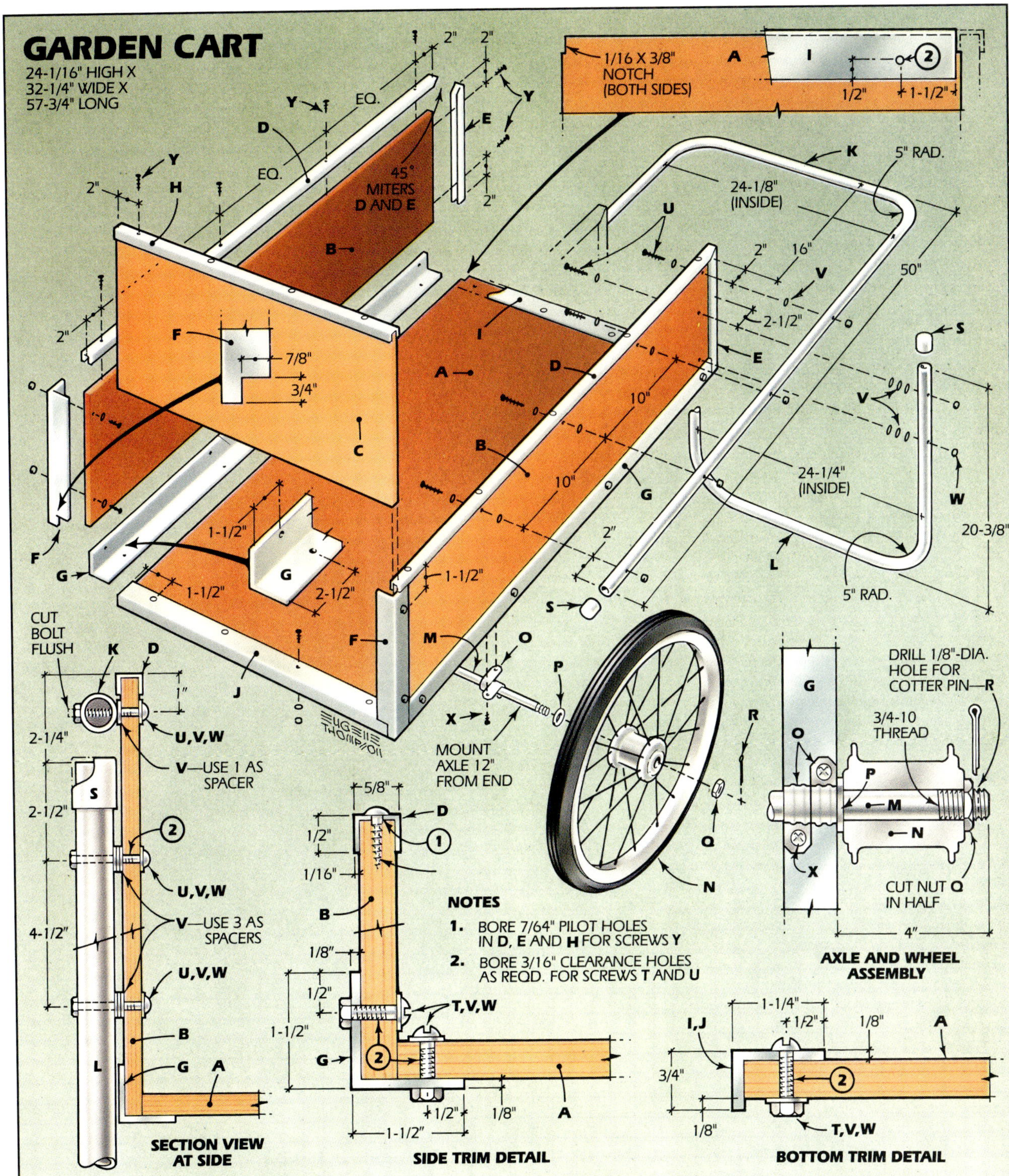

MATERIALS LIST—GARDEN CART

Key	No.	Size and Description (use)
A	1	½ x 23 x 41½" mahogany plywood (bottom)
B	2	½ x 12 x 41 1/16" mahogany plywood (side)
C	1	½ x 13½ x 23 15/16" mahogany plywood (end)
D	2	½ x 41⅛" aluminum channel (side top trim)
E	2	½ x 12 13/16" aluminum channel (side end trim)
F	2	1½ x 1½ x 11 11/16" aluminum angle (corner trim)
G	2	1½ x 1½ x 39¾" aluminum angle (side bottom trim)
H	1	½ x 23 15/16" aluminum channel (end trim)
I	1	¾ x 1¼ x 22⅞" aluminum angle (bottom trim)
J	1	¾ x 1¼ x 23" aluminum angle (bottom trim)
K	1	¾-in.-dia. x 10-ft. electro metallic tubing (handle)
L	1	¾-in.-dia. x 10-ft. electro metallic tubing (leg)
M	1	¾-in.-dia. x 32¼" cold-rolled steel bar stock (axle)
N	2	1¾ x 20-in.-dia. (wheel)
O	4	1-in.-dia. conduit strap
P	2	¾-in.-inside-dia. washer
Q	2	¾"-10 hexnut
R	2	⅛ x 1¼" cotter pin
S	4	1-in.-inside-dia. plastic cap
T	28	¾" x 10-32 rh machine screws
U	12	2" x 10-32 rh machine screws
V	60	No. 10 washers
W	40	No. 10-32 hexnuts
X	4	½" No. 8 self-tapping screw
Y	16	¾" No. 6 self-tapping screw

Building the Cart Body

Although the cart body was built from mahogany marine plywood, you can use marine fir plywood or pressure-treated plywood.

Begin construction by laying out the cart pieces on the plywood sheet. Support the plywood on a sawhorse, and clamp a straightedge to the panel to guide the saw when cutting the panels to size (Fig. 1).

Next, smooth the ends of the plywood panels using a belt sander or a hand-sanding block and 120- and 220-grit sandpaper.

Apply the finish to the plywood panels before the cart is assembled. By doing so, even the areas covered by the aluminum channel and angle stock will be protected by the finish. Drive finish nails into the panel ends and suspend the panels between sawhorses (Fig. 2). Apply the finish.

Next, cut the $1\frac{1}{2} \times 1\frac{1}{2}$-in. angle stock. Since it's hard to see a layout mark on the aluminum surface, put a piece of masking tape over the angle stock and mark your cutlines on the tape with a pen. Clamp the angle firmly in a vise, and make the cut (Fig. 3). Cut just to the waste side of the line, and then remove burrs and square the cut if necessary using a file. Cut the notches in the front piece of the angle stock.

Put another piece of tape along the angle stock, and mark for the pilot holes along the length of the workpiece. Bolt a fence to the drill-press table, and then clamp the angle stock to the fence to support it while drilling the holes (Fig. 4).

Cut the $\frac{1}{2}$-in. channel stock to length for the top and edge of the side panels. Next, cut the miters on the pieces by laying them in a miterbox supported on a piece of $\frac{1}{2}$-in.-thick scrap (Fig. 5). File off any burrs after the miters are cut.

Drill the pilot holes in the $\frac{1}{2}$-in. channel stock the same way as with the angle stock.

Next, install the channel stock on the top and back edges of the side panels. Bore $\frac{7}{64}$-in.-dia. holes into the panel before driving the screws (Fig. 6). Fasten the channel to the panel using $\frac{3}{4}$-in. No.6 round head self-tapping screws (Fig. 7). Remove the sharp corner where the channel is mitered using a file (Fig. 8), If you lack a fine file, use a sanding block and fine abrasive paper.

Place a bottom angle in position on a side panel, and clamp it in place with a small scrap block behind it. Use the angle as a template to bore pilot holes in the panel (Fig. 9). Fasten the angle stock to the panel using machine screws, so the screwheads are on the panel's inside (Fig. 10).

1 Cut the plywood panels to size using a circular saw. Clamp a guide to the panel and run the saw along it.

2 Suspend the panels from between sawhorses. Apply the exterior polyurethane finish on the panels' faces and edges.

3 Apply tape to the angle stock, and mark the cutline on the tape. Clamp the angle stock firmly while cutting it.

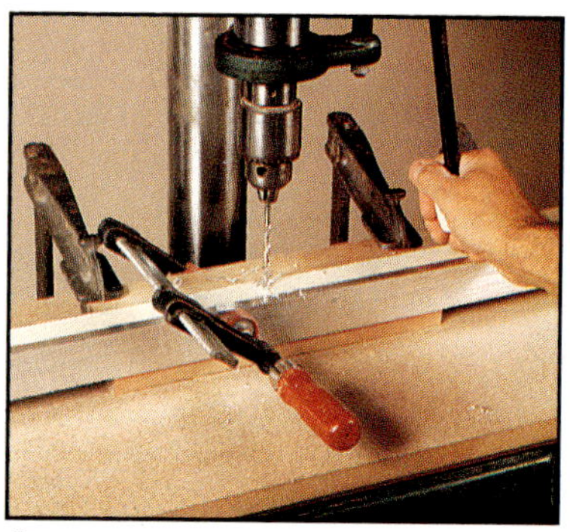

4 Clamp a fence to the drill-press table. Clamp the angle stock to the fence to support the stock while drilling.

5 Cut miters on the ends of the channel stock in a miterbox. Support the channel walls with a scrap block.

6 Place the channels on the panel edges. Bore the pilot holes for the screws that hold the channels in place.

7 Screw the channels in place using self-tapping round head screws. These screws hold firmly in marine plywood.

8 File a small bevel on the miter corners where channels meet. If you lack a fine file, use a sanding block.

9 Clamp a scrap block and an angle to a side panel. Bore pilot holes through the panel, the angle stock and the channel.

10 Attach the angle stock to both sides and the bottom with machine screws. The screwheads go inside the cart.

11 Lay the bottom panel upside down on the bench. Position the side panels and bore the pilot holes.

12 Test fit the sliding panel. If it sticks a little, apply lubricant to the panel edges and to the channels.

Cut a piece of $3/4 \times 1\,1/4$-in. angle stock to length for the front end of the cart bottom. Drill the pilot holes through both the angle and bottom panel, and install it with the screwheads on the inside of the panel and the washers and nuts on the bottom.

Lay the bottom panel upside down on the workbench, and place one of the sides in position (Fig. 11). Bore plot holes through the bottom. Again, use a backer block to prevent splitting out the veneer where the bit exits the hole. Screw the bottom and side together.

Cut the remaining piece of $3/4 \times 1\,1/4$-in. angle stock to length for the open side of the cart. Drill the pilot holes through it, and fasten it in place. Test fit the sliding panel (Fig. 12). If the panel binds slightly, apply a bit of wax or Teflon spray to both panel end and the angle stock that forms the track. Cut and apply the 1/2-in. channel stock along the top edge of the sliding panel.

Wheels, Axle, Handle and Stand

The axle is made from a piece of 3/4-in.-dia. cold-rolled bar steel. You can cut it to length with a hacksaw, but it's easier to specify the length and have the material supplier cut it.

Cut the threads on the axle using a 3/4-in.-10 die (3/4 in. dia., 10 threads per inch) held in a die stock. Clamp the axle upright in a vise and position the die over the end of the axle. Apply some cutting oil to the bar, and slowly advance the die about one-eighth of a turn. Then, reverse direction to clear the chips from the die's cutting edges. Proceed until you have threaded 1 in. of the axle (Fig. 13). Repeat the procedure on the other end.

Position the axle on the cart bottom, and fasten it in place using two conduit straps at each end of the axle. Drill pilot holes through the angle stock, and attach the straps using 1/2-in. No.8 screws (Fig. 14).

The wheels are stock and a pair cost about $116.

Slide a 3/4-in. washer over each end of the axle (Fig. 15), and slide the wheel against the washer. The wheels are held in place by a 3/4-in. nut, but since the nut is too thick for this application, you must cut it in half.

Clamp the nut in a vise, and cut it in half with a hacksaw (Fig. 16). Use a file to clean up the cut surface and remove any rough edges. Tighten the nut until the wheel is held in place without any side-to-side play.

Next, install a cotter pin through the axle to hold the nut in place. To mark the pin hole, dimple the axle with a centerpunch (Fig. 17).

Remove the nuts, wheels and axle. Place the axle on a support block. This block is just a piece of scrap with a shallow 3/4-in.-wide channel cut into it. Clamp the

13 Cut the threads on the axle. Take small turns, back off, and then cut some more. Use plenty of cutting oil.

14 Attach the axle to the cart bottom using electrical conduit straps and screws. Use two straps at each axle end.

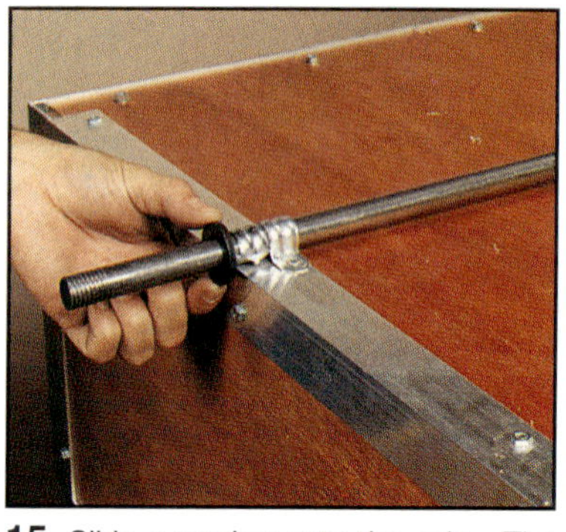

15 Slide a washer onto the axle. The washer acts as a bearing surface between the wheel hub and cart.

16 Clamp the nut in a vise and then saw it in half. Clean up the saw marks with a fine file or sanding block.

17 Temporarily install the wheels and nuts. Dimple the axle, using a centerpunch to mark the cotter pin hole.

18 Clamp the axle and support block to the drill-press table. Use cutting oil when drilling the cotter pin hole.

block and the axle to the drill-press table. Set the drill press to its slowest speed, apply plenty of machine oil to the bar stock and drill the hole (Fig. 18).

The drill bit will probably leave a burr when it exits the bar stock. Do not use a file to remove this burr as it will damage the axle threads. Instead, clamp the axle in a vise and use the die, with plenty of cutting oil, to remove the burrs.

Reinstall the axle on the cart. Install the cotter pins through the axle. Bend the legs of the cotter pin to the side with a pair of pliers (Fig. 19).

Make the leg and handle from ¾-in. electrical conduit. This material is easier to bend without kinks than aluminum tubing. The conduit is bent using a jig made from scrap plywood. You can also rent a conduit bender to do the job.

To make the jig, trace the desired radius on two pieces of panel stock. Cut the radius using a sabre saw, then use a router to cut a ½-in.-rad. cove along the shaped edge. Screw the two pieces of panel stock together so that the coves oppose each other. This makes a bending form with a 1-in.-dia. cove along its edge

19 Clean off the burrs on the axle made from drilling the cotter pin hole. Install the axle, washer, wheel, nut and pin.

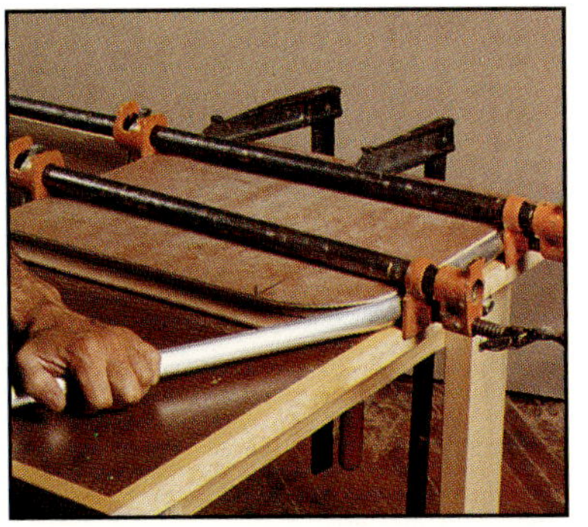

20 Align the marks on the tubing with those on the jig and clamp the bending jig securely to the workbench.

21 Press the tubing caps on the handle and leg. Soften them, if necessary, in hot water or use a heat gun or blow dryer.

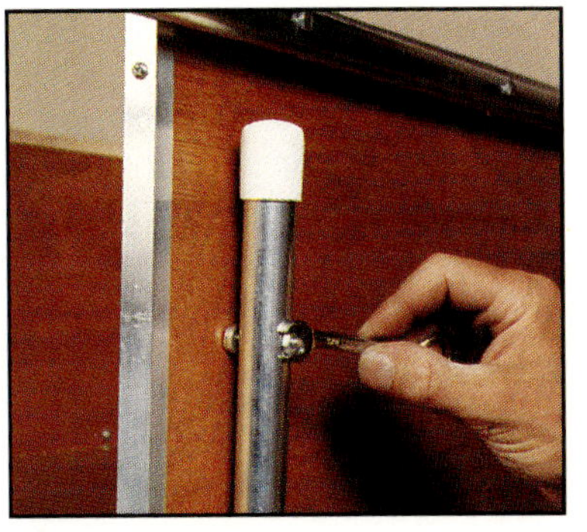

22 Use three washers between the leg and the sides. Cut off the excess screw shaft and file it smooth.

Mark the beginning and end of the bend on the form. Use the marks and the dimensions in the plan to make the bend in the tubing at the correct place. Mark the tubing with a pencil, and align the tubing with the marks on the form. In bending the handle, the entire 10-ft. length of tubing is used. The leg, however, is bent to shape and the excess material is cut off. You should bend the leg and then cut it to length. Bending the tubing at full length allows you to take advantage of the leverage the tubing provides (Fig. 20). With both the leg and the handle, the form is clamped securely to the bench and the tubing is clamped to the form.

Press the plastic furniture caps on the ends of the leg and the handle (Fig. 21). You can buy these caps at a local hardware store. If the caps are difficult to press into place, soak them in hot water for a few minutes to soften and expand them.

Next, drill pilot holes through the leg and handle for mounting screws. Clamp them on the cart and use the holes in the leg and handle as a guide when boring the pilot holes into the cart body. Use scrap blocks to prevent the drill bit from splintering the plywood as it exits.

Use 2-in. No.10-32 screws (32 threads per inch) to install the legs and handle on the cart (Fig. 22). Use three washers between the leg and cart sides, and use one washer between the handle and cart side to maintain proper spacing. The 2-in. screws are longer than necessary for this job, so cut off the excess screw with a hacksaw. Use a file to smooth the cut end of each screw.

Natural lawn care

If you've been using synthetic chemical—and chemicals alone—to improve your lawn, you're missing alternative strategies that will not only help you reach your goal, but are kinder to the environment, as well. While synthetic chemicals can be effective, most sources agree that we've been relying on them too heavily. It may take a season or two, and setbacks are to be expected, but a less-toxic approach is workable. Alternate methods abound, though adopting the right combination of measures takes some education.

Prior to the wide use of chemicals, beginning in the 1960s, people had reasonably attractive and functional lawns. They were not the vast manicured stretches of blue-green perfection occasionally glimpsed today. They were a little spotty in places and generally included a mixture of turf grasses, low-growing clover and a few weeds. In other words, they were a lot like many chemically treated lawns seen today.

Which brings us to an important element in enlightened lawn care—altered expectations. As it turns out, perfection is a costly concept both environmentally and financially. By slightly diminishing your expectations, your lawn can become a self-sustaining pleasure, and not a hole into which you pour money and energy.

One problem with chemical pesticides and herbicides is that they offer only a temporary solution. Over the long term, weeds, diseases and insects still enjoy the upper hand. For example, if you apply a selective crabgrass herbicide, with luck, you'll kill the current stand of crabgrass. The problem is that thousands of crabgrass seeds lie ready to start the cycle anew. A similar conundrum exists with insects. Insects are best controlled by other insects. But when we kill the nuisance bugs, we also kill their natural enemies. A new batch also can drift over from your neighbor's lawn.

Another problem is that many of us have never figured out exactly which chemicals to use, or how and when to apply them. We might apply a pesticide for the grubs we find in June not knowing that grubs don't feed until the third week in July. All we end up killing are beneficial insects and birds.

Old Grasses

Here's the most important thing to know about lawns: if you establish a disease- and draft-resistant grass, many of your lawn problems will go away. Often the best way to reduce water and chemical usage is to till up that beloved, old-generation bluegrass.

The problem is that traditional bluegrass has a very shallow root structure, with nearly all of its roots within 5 in. of the surface. When surface moisture is depleted

Natural Lawn Care was written by Merle Henkenius. Illustrations by George Retseck. An enzyme-activated soil conditioner is Nitron Formula A-35 from Nitron Industries, P.O. Box 1447, Fayetteville, AR 72702. Insecticidal soap is made by Ringer Crop., 9959 Valley View Rd., Eden Prairie, MN 55364. Ringer markets the Safer line.

quickly, as it is in many parts of the country, the grass becomes distressed and susceptible to disease. The more constant subsoil moisture that rests only a few inches farther down remains out of reach. Lacking sufficient moisture, traditional bluegrass will also revert to its thinned-out, conservation mode, which is an open invitation to deep-rooted weeds to fill the gaps. Add to this the fact that traditional bluegrass has little shade tolerance, becomes thatch bound annually and is genetically vulnerable to several kinds of blight and a host of insects, and pretty soon other grass varieties begin to have real appeal.

Consider an equally traditional, though hardier, competitor: tall fescue, or K-31 fescue. Its roots are long enough to reach the more constant subsoil moisture. What this means to you is a tremendous water savings. It is also genetically more resistant to fungal and bacterial leaf blight, and grubs find its roots much less appealing than bluegrass roots. When well established, it can actually choke out some weeds, and as a clump grass, it won't invade the neighbor's yard or your flower garden. Finally, it won't commit suicide with a dense layer of thatch.

Improved Turf Grasses

If tall fescue (with its coarse leaves and rapid top growth) is not for you, then you might consider red fescue or one of the new, fine-blade dwarf fescues. Some varieties have roots that reach down a foot or more and are poisonous to some insects.

Certain grasses have always harbored microorganisms (fungi) called *endophytes*, which produce alkaloids that are poisonous to sod webworms, cutworms, aphids and chinch bugs. The new blends contain enough of these toxins to make a difference.

If you can't bear to part with bluegrass, you might try overseeding with one of the newer, hardier bluegrass varieties. Overseeding is understandably slower than starting from scratch, but several years of overseeding with an improved variety will greatly improve your lawn. In three to five years, the new variety should overtake the old.

Overseeding can be done in the spring or fall, though fall is better. When overseeding bluegrass, it's best to use another bluegrass variety. Assuming an autumn seeding, start by dethatching and removing the debris. Then overseed and rake it in so that the seeds are partially covered. Finally, water deeply, then wet the soil daily for several weeks.

Traditional warm-season grasses, also have been improved. The newer zoysia grasses (such as Meyer Z-52) are less cold-sensitive and therefore stay green longer and can be successful farther north. To further green-up your zoysia grass, you might overseed with a fescue. In fact, many turfs can benefit from a judicious overseeding with complementary varieties. Perennial rye grasses are popular overseeding choices.

CHEMICALLY TREATED BLUEGRASS LAWN

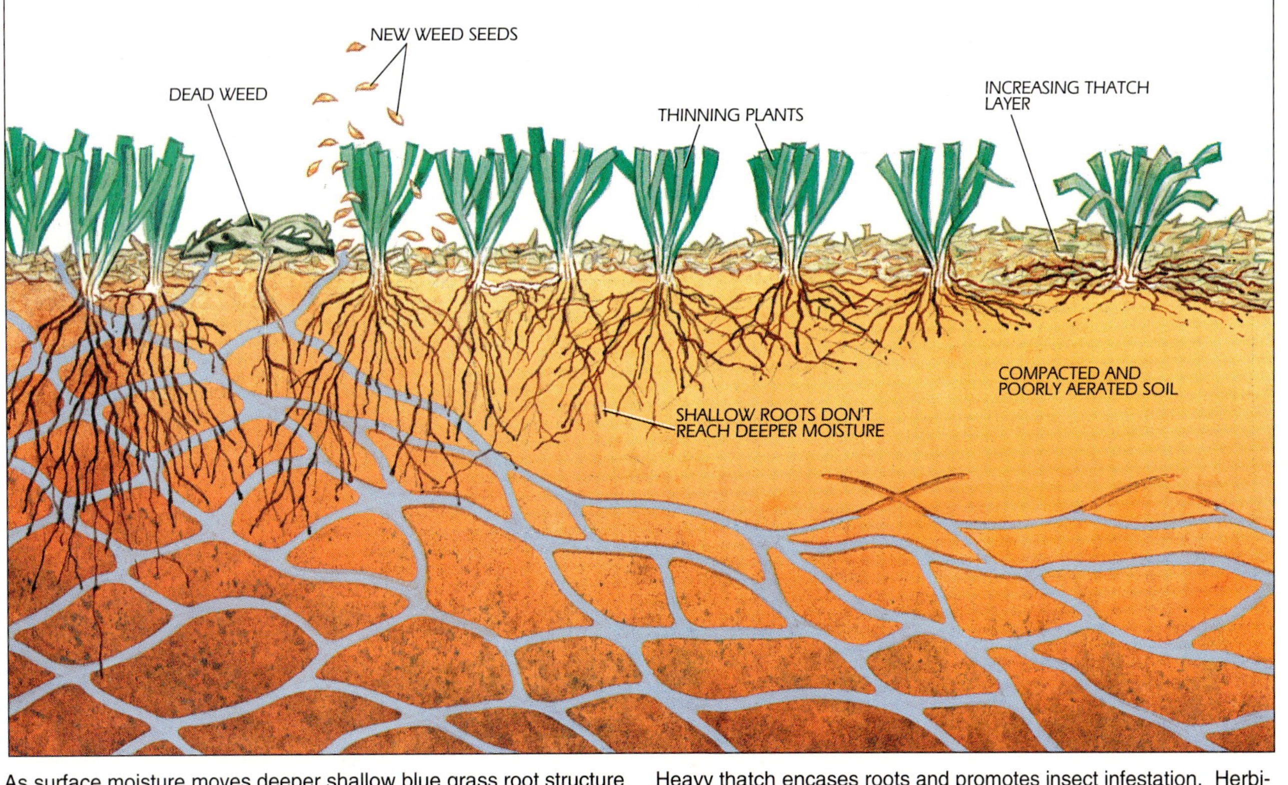

As surface moisture moves deeper,shallow blue grass root structure can't reach water. Pesticides eliminate earthworms, which create nonaerated, compacted soil. Thinning and shallower roots follow. Heavy thatch encases roots and promotes insect infestation. Herbicide treatments kill weeds while new airborne weed seeds start growth again.

Because no single grass is right for all situations, a blend of grasses will often prove more durable. Most lawn centers can custom blend grasses to your specifications. Check with your county extension agent for the best mixes for your area.

Turf Management

Thatch accumulation is an almost universal trouble source which is encouraged by heavy doses of fertilizer. Thatch is a dense matting of plant matter that accumulates at ground level. Where thatch is dense, grass populations thin out. Thatch harbors and encourages insects and shields the root structure from moisture and nutrients. It also renders the chemical treatment of subsurface pests ineffective. Virtually all Southern grasses, plus bluegrass, rye grass and the fine-leaf fescues need mechanical dethatching at least once a year.

A condition most problem lawns have in common is compacted soil. Turf grasses need an aerated soil to thrive, while most weeds favor compacted soil. Soil-aeration machines cut plugs from the top layer of soil, leaving holes that help alleviate compaction. The plugs then break down and are assimilated into the topsoil layer. While you should aerate each spring, the best nature aerators are earthworms and ants, which ironically, are the first victims of pesticides and quick-release fertilizers.

In fact, without these two aerators, and the millions of microorganisms that follow, it's doubtful that any lawn could be sustained in good condition for long. The thousands of tunnels they create keep the soil loose and provide direct downward pathways for moisture and nutrients.

As an added bonus, earthworms consume thatch and convert it to plant food. The earthen castings left by earthworms, for example, are up to seven times richer in nitrogen than normal soil. As for microbes, they are indispensable, as they render nitrogen extracted from a wide range of organic substances. They are what separates active soil from inert dirt.

Besides dethatching and aerating, use a mulching mower with a sharp blade to return nutrients to the soil. Contrary to popular belief, grass clippings do not contribute to thatch buildup—the clippings are 90% water and they decompose quickly.

Synthetic Fertilizers

While you might not want to eliminate synthetic fertilizers entirely, you can often cut back to fertilizing once a season, or less, by keeping your turf aerated and dethatched and by using a mulching mower.

Choose a slow-release fertilizer and water it in deeply. Too much applied too often merely burns the grass, reduces the earthworm population (and nitrogen-converting microorganisms), simulate top growth and encourages thatch accumulations. The best time to fertilize cool-season grasses is after the peak growing period, in late fall. Warm-season grasses should be fertilized before the peak growing season.

Natural Fertilizers

Natural fertilizers, made of bone meal, blood meal, feathers, seaweed, fish byproducts, bat droppings, ash from sunflower-seed hulls and a variety of other substances are becoming increasingly popular. Most of these packaged fertilizers also include nitrogen-converting microbes. The primary difference between conventional, inorganic fertilizers and organic fertilizers is that inorganics exist in a ready nitrate state. The moment you add water, the nutrients can be absorbed by plant roots.

Organic fertilizer, in contrast, first must be converted by microbes in the soil from an organic to an inorganic state. The microbes actually produce the nitrates. As this process takes place deeper in the soil, the nitrates are not as exposed to surface runoff. This is not to say that nitrates from organic material cannot be eroded from the soil, or leached downward through sandy soil, but that the problem is a lesser one. Because nutrients are released slowly, organics can be applied at any time throughout the year.

The one disadvantage is that organics are generally more expensive. You may be able to beat the system, however, by buying the ingredients in bulk (less microbes) and mixing your own. Look to blood meal for nitrogen, bone meal for phosphorus, and sunflower-seed ash for potassium. (If this option is available at your local gardening supply outlet, it should be able to suggest a proper mix for your area.)

Improving Soil Structure and pH

Don't automatically assume that a thin, pale turf needs fertilizing. It well may, but often the soil structure or soil pH is the problem. Grasses grow best in at least 6 in. of topsoil. By digging down a foot or so, you'll be able to see how much topsoil you have, as evidenced by its darker color. Composted manure, which is odorless, also can be added to the surface a little at a time as can peat moss and gypsum pellets.

Another option is to treat your lawn with an enzyme-activated soil conditioner. Research indicates that by increasing certain enzymes in the soil, water-tension factors are altered and the soil is made more water permeable and absorbent. As such, water-borne nutrients are more easy accessed by plant roots and soil compaction is reduced.

The only way to check for proper pH is with a soil test. You can call a professional or take a soil sample into your local lab, extension office or university. Home testing kits are also available through catalogs and garden centers. An alkaline soil will need an application of sulfur or gypsum, while acidic soils will benefit from a sprinkling of lime. Turf grasses do best within a pH range of 5.6 to 7, and your extension agent or dealer will know which plan is best for your lawn.

As for watering, it's always best to water more deeply and less often. To hold down fungi-related leaf blight, water in the morning so that the grass dries quickly. Avoid evening waterings.

Weed, Pest and Disease Control

When it comes to weed control, a healthy, well aerated, dethatched and nutrient-rich turf will choke out all but the most stubborn invaders. The rest can often be managed by hand weeding and mowing.

Pest management, on the other hand, is really a matter of numbers. A few pests won't make that big a difference, and may even signal a healthy lawn. When your lawn is naturally disease and insect resistant, and is kept healthy using the methods described above, the degree of damage is often acceptable.

The natural approach pays the biggest dividends in the area of insect and blight control. Natural insect control takes two primary forms. You can use natural substances that attack the body of the insect directly or release disease-causing microorganisms (fungi, nematodes), which burrow into the target insect, killing it in the process.

A word of caution is in order, however. Insecticides, of any kind, should be used sparingly and only as a last resort. Some beneficial insects will be killed in the process, no matter what you use.

One of the most effective, broad-spectrum insecticides is extracted from the seeds of African and Southeast-Asian neem trees. The active ingredient, azadirachtin, is a growth regulator, which is to say that it causes death. It's effective on a variety of pests, including aphids, gypsy moths and webworms.

Though it has a very low toxicity, it does have a 2-to-7-day residual period, during which it remains effective. Because of this, its use in a vegetable garden is certainly inappropriate.

Insecticidal soap is another proven insect killer. It's made from fatty-acid salts derived from animal fat and plant oils. When sprayed on soft-bodied insects, it kills them by breaking down their cell-wall membranes. Insecticidal soap works well on sod webworms.

For effective control of hard-bodied insects, such as june bugs and Japanese beetles, pyrethrum, an extract from the chrysanthemum flower, works well To treat infestations of subsurface grubs, you might try mail-order nematodes, which kill grubs from within, or milky-spore disease (bacillus popillae), which is a fungus that attacks grubs and other soft-bodied subsurface pests. Once established, milky spore disease remains effective for years.

For treatment of bill-bug larvae, diatomaceous earth works. Diatomaceous earth is a sediment taken from the seafloor and is made up of millions of dead, single-cell creatures that dehydrate soft-bodied insects on contact.

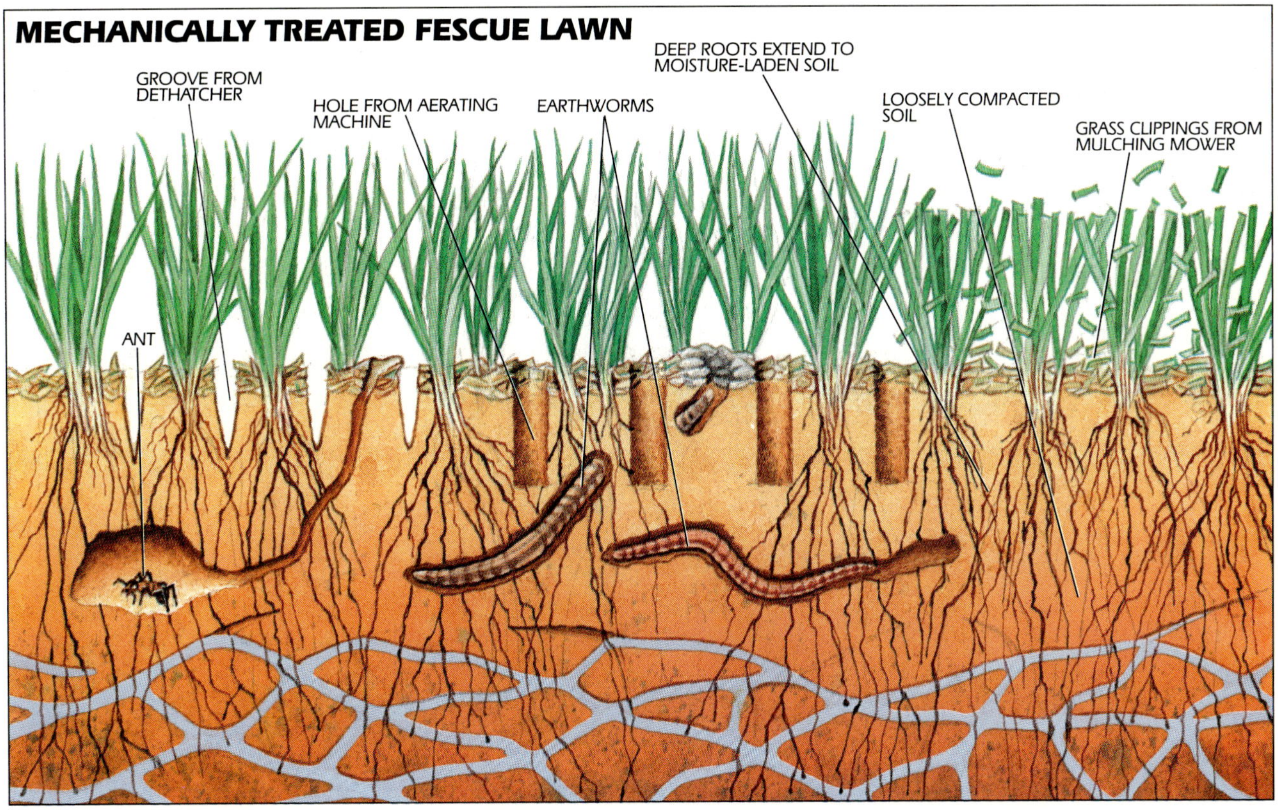

Deep-rooted fescue variety reaches moisture up to 10 in. deep. Earthworms and ants aerate soil through tunneling, and earthworms contribute nutrients. Thatch layer is kept in check through dethatching and a mechanical aerator further loosens soil. Grass clippings from frequent cutting with a mulching mower decompose and provide nutrients.

Sealing concrete floors

At first glance, painting a garage floor—or any concrete floor—may seem simple enough. You just scrub the floor as best you can, buy a few gallons of enamel porch paint and roll it on. While this is exactly the way it has been done for years, the results often have been disappointing. New EPA limits on paint solvents have not been a big help. These limits have driven some of the most rugged paints from the consumer marketplace.

Environmentally friendly, water-based epoxy enamels do work reasonably well when applied to concrete floors in basements or in workshops. They are well worth considering for these areas if you want a pigmented surface. But when automobiles enter the picture, the slab in your garage becomes a different beast than the concrete floor in your basement.

Vehicles have a tendency to leak fluids and, on hot summer days, they often arrive with sizzling hot tires. The first problem is that no conventional paint will stand up to oil, gasoline, brake fluid, transmission fluid or any of the petroleum-based lubricants needed to keep the family car on the road. A few drops on a painted floor will cause the paint to blister, and once blistered, no amount of cursing or coaxing will make a second coat adhere any better.

The second problem is that conventional paints are thermo-plastic, which means they soften with heat. Park a vehicle with hot tires on this paint, and the paint will soften, in some cases enough to stick to the tires. Each time you back away, a patch of garage floor paint can go with you, leaving an unsightly blotch.

To avoid this problem, you need a paint that is thermo-setting—in other words, it cures with heat. These specialty paints have been used at the commercial level for years, and work well when installed properly.

The problem with thermo-setting paints is that they really aren't made for homeowners. They are generally 2-part epoxies, which must be mixed on-site and applied very quickly, often in less than 30 minutes. Moreover, while many such paints may now meet VOC (volatile organic compound) limits, depending on your state's regulations, they still require extreme caution. You need plenty of ventilation, protective clothing and a good respirator to apply these paints safely. In other words, you need professional equipment and expertise. Expect to see "Not For Residential Use" printed on each can.

Liability has a lot to do with manufacturer reluctance to sell these products to consumers, but warranties are also at issue. As it turns out, no matter how good the paint, surface preparation is critical. As such, most sources recommend sandblasting or acid-washing a concrete floor before painting. With sandblasting and two coats of paint, a typical garage floor job could easily cost more than $500.

A Safe, Easy Alternative

In the search to find something that would repel oils and road salts and still be easy to clean, you can use Enviroseal Surface Guard. It is a clear latex that repels oils, antifreeze and road salts. These materials simply bead up, and can be swept or wiped away. It goes down thin and milky but cures clear in 3 to 4 hours. Best of all, it is not hazardous to breathe, and all tools can be cleaned with water.

Unfortunately, it's a little pricey. Coverage ranges from 150 to 200 sq. ft. per gallon, depending on surface roughness, and costs about $65 per gallon. Moreover, as present, the smallest available container holds 5 gallons. As such, you may want to split the cost with a neighbor. Or, as this sealant contains a UV stabilizer, you might want to use the remainder to treat your driveway.

Text and photos for *Sealing Concrete Floors* by Merle Henkenius. Paint used here can be obtained from Hydrozo Inc., 1001 Y St., P.O. Box 80879, Lincoln, NE 68501. The concrete cleaner used was Sure-Fix, manufactured by W.R. Bonsal Co. (P.O. Box 241148, Charlotte, NC 28224).

1 Use a putty knife to scrape any paint splatters, construction adhesive or other debris from the surface of the floor.

2 Be sure to vacuum any loose debris from control joints. Any material left behind will be trapped permanently.

3 Use a stiff brush and a strong degreaser or concrete cleaner to remove oil spots and tire grime from the surface.

Application

The 24×24-ft. garage floor shown was less than a year old, but it still required a good cleaning. Had it been treated with a curing agent when poured, the curing agent would have to have been stripped with a power washer. The first step is to sweep the entire floor, then scrape up any paint drips and other debris left behind during construction (Fig. 1).

Next, vacuum the entire floor, including the control joints (Fig. 2). Then wash all soiled areas and oil spots with a commercial concrete cleaner (Fig. 3). A solvent degreaser or even an oil-lifting dish detergent can also work. The trick is to keep scrubbing until only the faintest trace of a spot remains. If oil spots are fresh, cat litter or portland cement scrubbed in with a standard masonry brick can save a good deal of time. When finished, hose down the entire area with water and let it dry for 24 hours.

Because sealants will separate in storage, use a drill-driven paint mixer to blend the solution. Pour a quart or so of the sealant into a paint bucket and then about 2 gallons into your garden sprayer (Fig. 4).

Working from the bucket, use a 3-in. brush to cut in a 6-in.-wide path around the walls (Fig. 5). Also carefully cut in along the expansion joint between the garage floor and driveway, and around all permanent floor features such as the overhead door tracks (Fig. 6).

With the perimeter cut in, use the tank sprayer to apply a fairly thick layer of sealant to an area about 10×10 ft. (Fig. 7). Before moving on, allow each area to saturate for 5 minutes, then work the sealer in with a medium-bristle push broom (Fig. 8). Sweeping increases penetration and also eliminates any voids caused by air bubbles. By working backward, and by pulling any excess sealant into the dry areas, you can keep the sealer from puddling.

If puddling occurs that can't be removed with the push broom—in control joints for example—simply sweep out these areas with your cut-in brush (Fig. 9).

Plan your work so you won't be crossing over the newly coated areas when they are still wet. You can begin in a back corner of the garage and move toward the garage door opening in sections that are about 10 ft. square. Then, return to the back of the garage and begin another strip, continuing in this way until the floor is done.

Of course, working in the confines of a full basement can be quite a bit harder. Just plan your escape route beforehand and never apply sealer to an area larger than can be easily reached with your broom.

4 Pour sealant into a paint bucket for cutting-in purposes, then fill a low-pressure sprayer for the larger areas.

5 Begin applying the sealer by cutting in the entire perimeter of the floor. Be sure to use a stiff-bristle paintbrush.

6 Take extra pains to apply sealer around areas that are open to the weather, like this garage door opening.

7 Using a standard garden sprayer, start in one corner of the floor and begin applying sealant in manageable segments.

8 After allowing the sealant to penetrate for about 5 minutes, use a push broom to even out the coverage.

9 Any excess puddling of sealant in control joints or other depressions should be swept away with a brush.

Decorative concrete

Most people see concrete without noticing it. To them, it's ubiquitous and, worse yet, boring. They couldn't care less about its looks because it's not supposed to look good. Architects, engineers and homeowners choose it for its strength and durability. It's the material of choice for highways, dams, sidewalks and sky scrapers. It's a municipal and handy material, but many people who are not familiar with its possibilities think it lacks grace and presence.

At first, it's hard to believe that concrete *can* be elegant. That's a lot to ask—that something works just as well in the Hoover Dam as it does underfoot at an outdoor cocktail party. Where building materials are concerned, however, it's true—concrete has grace under pressure.

Worked by skilled hands, it can be finished in a variety of patterns, colors and textures, even to the point of looking like something else, including flagstone, brick and slate. This versatility expands anyone's design options for that pool deck, patio or walkway.

Why not use brick, stone or slate? Each of these is a fine material, but natural materials (and to a lesser extent, brick) dictate the color and shape you must work with, and not all options are available in all areas.

Concrete is generally less expensive than quarried materials, which often must be shipped over long distances. Decorative concrete is more expensive than regular concrete, of course, and its cost varies greatly by location and even among contractors in the area.

Concrete can look like stone, slate or brick. At this house, it was finished to look like the stone on the drive and brick on the walkway. Even the "wooden beam" risers are really concrete.

Remember, get several bids and avoid those that seem drastically low. For instance, regular concrete may cost $2.50 per sq. ft. in the Northeastern states, with decorative concrete costing from $4.50 to $8 per sq. ft.

Decorative Concrete was written by Roy Berendsohn. Photos by Merle Henkenius and Portland Cement Association. Illustrations by George Retseck.

Concrete Basics

To understand what makes concrete beautiful, you have to understand what it's made of and how it works.

Concrete consists of portland cement mixed with sand and gravel or crushed stone. Portland cement, as its name implies, cements the sand and gravel or crushed stone together. The cement is made of calcium (usually finely ground limestone) silica (sand), aluminum, iron ore and small amounts of other materials (sometimes fly ash, for instance). These materials are quarried, crushed, ground and blended. Then they are fired in a kiln with an average temperature of about 2700°F—hot enough to melt steel. The material emerges from the kiln as marble-size pellets known as clinkers. These are ground into a fine powder, and this is bagged or delivered in bulk as portland cement.

The beauty of portland cement is that, to form a rock-like mass, all you do is mix it with sand, gravel or crushed stone and then add some water. The chemical properties of portland cement are such that it reacts with the water in a process known as *hydration*.

Here's how hydration works: Water and cement particles form a solution. To the naked eye, this solution appears as a paste that coats each grain of sand and each piece of gravel or stone.

If you could see the paste at a molecular level, you would notice that water molecules arrange themselves around each particle of cement (each particle is about 1/100 of a millimeter in diameter).

In the process, heat is generated as the molecules rub against each other and arrange themselves. Excess water molecules make their way to the slab surface and evaporate off into the atmosphere. Other water molecules are locked out of the hydration process by the bonds formed by the hydrating cement particles. It takes decades for this water to escape, and this is why concrete gets harder as it gets older.

The water that was involved in the hydration process remains behind indefinitely as a crystal known as water of hydration. Under ideal circumstances, concrete takes its time arranging these cement/water-of-hydration particles. When the hydration process is essentially complete (it takes several weeks), you have a well-organized mass of sand and stone bonded in a matrix of cement/water-of-hydration particles. Because this bonding takes place at a molecular level, it's extremely thorough and very strong.

The unique characteristics of concrete make it a formable and formidable pavement that you can color and shape to look like brick, stone, or slate. As an added bonus, the pavement grows stronger with age.

Faux Slate, Stone and Brick

Finishing concrete to make it look like brick, slate or stone is not a typical do-it-yourself project. You would have to invest in the tools and finish quite a bit of experimental concrete before you pour the main pavement. It takes experience and the right tools to make concrete look like something it's not, so it makes more sense to hire a masonry contractor for the job.

The basic process, however, it not complicated.

Masons pour and place the concrete like they would for regular concrete, using a 3000-pound to 4000-pound psi mix, the typical concrete for outdoor pavements.

At this point, there are several methods that cement masons use to shape the concrete to look like brick, stone or slate.

In one method, they press strips of building paper or a paper stencil into the wet concrete using a float (Fig. 1). For faux stone, the masons cut strips of building paper. For a brick pattern, they buy a ready-made paper stencil.

Next, the masons spread colored granules over the concrete to give it the desired shade of brick or stone (Fig. 2). They work the granules, known as dry-shake compound, into the concrete, again using floats. Incidentally, dry-shake compound also increases the surface hardness of the concrete.

In the case of paper strips, the granules are carefully scraped off before the strips are lifted from the concrete. With paper lattice, the surface area is too large to do this, so the lattice is carefully peeled from the concrete after the dry-shake compound has been floated (Fig. 3). The area underneath the paper appears as mortar joints,

These faux granite cobblestones are finished with a sealer to give them a soft sheen and better resistance to stains.

This walk is textured and colored to look like dry-laid red flagstone. The pattern choice in this paving system is unlimited. The stone can be all the same size, interlocked shapes, laid in rows or completely random in shape and pattern.

1 A stencil is laid on the wet concrete and then pressed into the surface with a magnesium hand float.

2 Colored granules, known as dry-shake compound, are spread over the stencil. The compound is worked in with a float.

3 The stencil is peeled off, and the concrete is left to cure. The area beneath the stencil appears as mortar joints.

while the area between the strips is colored to look like slate, stone or brick.

To achieve the faux finish of dry-laid stone (without contrasting-color mortar joints), the masons use stamps, rollers and mats to press a shape into the concrete. In this case, a sheet of 2-mil polyethylene plastic is spread over the concrete. This prevents the concrete from sticking to the stamp or roller. It also gives nicely rounded edges to each stamped shape.

To achieve the faux mortar joints with this method, the masons spread mortar over the slab and scrape off the excess, so it fills in the joints between the stamped patterns. Afterward, they use a rotary floor polisher to remove mortar residue from the slab's face.

Finishing Up

The rest of the job is straightforward, and homeowners may elect to do some of it themselves. Soil is raked up to and nearly leveled with the concrete—remember, in most cases the concrete's color and shape are limited to its surface. If the homeowner wants it, the masons can return and apply a sealer to the concrete to give it a slightly glossy appearance. This sealer helps protect the concrete against weathering and from stains such as those caused by the tannic acid that leaches from leaves. It also helps bring out the slab's color.

Now that the concrete has been given a little personality, it's not surprising that people will comment on how nice all that brick, stone or slate looks. Whether you set them straight or not is up to you.

Faux-finished concrete is a good choice for a pool deck, since it wraps nearly around any shape. The pavement, including the faux mortar joints, can be colored to match or offset the pool itself and its surroundings.

Concrete patterns and colors can be intermingled. Faux tile is surrounded by concrete finished with a porous texture.

Paving brick driveway

Paving Brick Driveway was written by Cliff Gromer. Photo by Roy Attaway; how-to photos by Cliff Gromer. Pavers: Spring Hue and Chambersburg Repressed Chamfered Pavers by Glen-Gery Brick, Wyomissing, PA 19610; Retaining wall blocks: Keystone Blocks, Anchor Concrete Products, Brick, NJ 08724; Installation: Lombardi Paving, Matawan, NJ 07747. Glen-Gery has many different styles and colors of pavers, as well as other types of bricks, to satisfy the requirements of any landscape or paving job.

■ If your driveway looks like a jigsaw puzzle marred by cracks and make-do patch jobs, consider redoing this drab and boring surface with handset driveway pavers. They are available in a wide range of materials including concrete, asphalt and brick and in an even wider range of colors, textures and patterns.

Perhaps its greatest asset, however, is the paver's flexibility. While rigid concrete and asphalt surfaces can crack due to relentless freeze-thaw cycles, a mortarless, semirigid interlocking grid of pavers—set on a bed of sand—is designed to float with the ground movement and give with any stress. The pavers themselves can be laid relatively

quickly once the base is properly prepared. Once installed, pavers can be easily replaced if damaged or removed for access to underground utilities.

For the job shown, repressed chamfered brick pavers from Glen-Gery Brick were chosen. One color, Spring Hue, was used for the overall pattern, while another, Chambersburg, was used for occasional darker-colored accents. Also chosen was a herringbone installation pattern, but there are other options to suit different tastes. These should all be on view at your local brick dealer.

Before You Begin

Generally, there are five key steps to installing a paver drive: preparing the site, laying down a subbase, installing a sand bed, laying the pavers in place and installing edge restraints to keep the pavers from moving.

Depending on your experience, you can do all or part of this job yourself. For most of us, however, the best path would be to have the surface and subbase prepared by professionals, leaving the less complicated installation of the sand bed, brick pavers and edge restraints to fill our weekends.

This badly cracked and broken asphalt driveway was a perfect candidate for replacement. Brick pavers are a very durable and attractive alternative to asphalt and concrete.

1 Begin by breaking up old asphalt or concrete. Use an air hammer and a compressor or work with a pick and prybar.

2 Remove all the concrete or asphalt debris. Then, excavate to the proper depth to accommodate the subbase and the pavers.

3 Once the surface is prepared, lay down a 6-in.-thick layer of reprocessed concrete to establish the primary subbase.

4 Then, install the secondary subbase by spreading a blended layer of crushed concrete and ¾-in. crushed stone.

5 If you need a retaining wall, lay out the position of the wall using level mason's string, as shown.

6 Spread a base of the sand where the retaining wall will be, and then start installing the block. Level each in place.

Site Preparation

Begin by laying out the areas to be paved. Drive stakes into the ground at the corners, and run mason's string to establish reference points for the finished surface. For proper drainage, allow a minimum slope of 1 in. in 10 ft.

Take up your existing driveway material and determine the condition of the subgrade. A professional usually can tell if extensive subgrade preparation will be necessary by the age and condition of the existing surface. A relatively new surface with severe cracking usually indicates a problem. You can rent an air compressor and a jackhammer to break up concrete (Fig. 1), or use the old reliable pickax and prybar method. Once the surface is broken, remove all the debris. You can use the tried-and-true wheelbarrow-to-pickup-to-dump method, if this is allowed in your area, or simply arrange to have a dumpster on site and hire a professional with a backhoe or Bobcat to remove everything (Fig. 2).

If the existing subgrade and stone base are in good condition, you can finish grade and compact the base, lay down your sand bed and install the pavers. Problems such as a shifting or settling subbase, poor drainage and so forth, however, require taking up the subbase and excavating the soil—normally about 8 in.—until you hit firm, unmolested ground.

Since stabilizing the subbase is critical for the finished job, unstable ground should be looked at by a professional for specific recommendations. Very wet ground resulting from a high water table or an underground spring in the area usually requires additional drainage measures, such as running a drainpipe from the subbase to the street—if zoning regulations permit—or into a small dry well. In the installation shown, the soft clay soil was stabilized by cutting down the grade a total of 12 to 15 in. to accommodate a deeper stone subbase for support and drainage.

In stable soil conditions, lay a subbase of ¾-in. crushed stone in 4-in. layers, raking it flat and compact-

7 Stagger the courses of block as you go up. It's better to align the full blocks first, and then cut the half blocks to fit.

8 Measure, mark and cut the blocks to size with a masonry saw or with a masonry blade installed in a circular saw.

9 As you stack the blocks, make sure to fully engage the retaining lip on the back of each with the course below.

10 Spread out the sand for the setting bed, and then compact it with a rented vibrator to a depth of about 1½ in.

11 Embed flat steel screeding bars in the sand bed. Adjust the height of the bars to match the bottom surface of the pavers.

12 Using a 2x6 board that spans the width of the bars, screed the sand base to a uniform height. Fill any gaps as you go.

ing it with a gas-powered vibrating machine. Use care around utilities to ensure uniform compacting. Under normal conditions, a crushed-stone subbase 4 to 6 in. deep is sufficient for a walk. Vehicle loads require 8 to 12 in. of crushed-stone subbase.

In soft-soil conditions, first lay down a 3-to-6-in. subbase of 3-in.-size stone in 3-in. layers. Recycled concrete, also called reprocessed concrete, is a less expensive alternative that works just as well (Fig. 3). Flatten and compact the subbase after each layer with the vibrator. Then spread two 3-in. layers of ¾-in. crushed stone or reprocessed concrete (Fig. 4). Vibrate to compact the surface after each layer. The final compacted surface will determine—in large part—the condition of the finished paved surface, so take extra care with this step.

Edge restraints are used around the drive to contain the pavers and to keep them from shifting. Various materials, including rot-resistant wood, metal or bricks set in concrete, can be used for restraints. On the job shown, a small retaining wall on one side and a simple concrete-filled trench on the other was used. No matter what edge-restraint system you use, establish the location of one side. Then lay out a sample of your paver pattern against this fixed edge for a trial fit. Keep in mind that adjusting the location of the opposite edge restraint a few inches can significantly reduce the number of cuts in the pavers that will be required to make the pattern fit in a balanced way. Once the location of both edge restraints is established, you can build the retaining wall.

Retaining Wall

To build the wall, lay out the position of the base course of blocks using stakes and string (Fig. 5). Lay down 1½ in. of sand for the setting bed. Smooth the sand and place the blocks down squarely on it.

Tap the blocks into position with a rubber mallet to set them to the correct height as determined by the mason's string. Butt the blocks along the string and, in

13 Set the bricks for the shoulder course on one side of the drive, and then start with the overall pattern in one corner.

14 When the pattern reaches the other side of the drive, stretch a string for the shoulder course and mark the bricks.

15 Pick up each brick from the pattern that needs cutting and number it in sequence so it can be replaced easily later.

16 Cut the bricks with a rented, water-cooled masonry saw. Cut each paver ¼ in. shorter than the mark.

17 Fit all cut pieces back into the pattern following the numbers. If a piece is a little too long, recut it.

18 Once all the cut pieces are in place, install the shoulder course, making sure each brick is flush.

the flat sections, check for level with a 4-ft. level (Fig. 6). Lay down the second course of blocks, staggering the joints over the base course. Measure for a half block (Fig. 7), then mark a whole block with a square and cut it with a masonry saw (Fig. 8).

A beveled lip at the rear of the block prevents it from shifting forward on the base course, so make sure this lip is pushed tight against the blocks below (Fig. 9). The weight of this upper course also prevents the base course from shifting.

Pavers

To lay the pavers, prepare the base by spreading the sand setting bed and compacting to a 1½-in. depth with the vibrator (Fig. 10). Then, screed the sand to a depth that will bring the pavers up to the desired finished height. Work from the top of the drive toward the street. First, lay down a pair of flat steel bars about 3 to 5 ft. apart. Then, adjust the height of the bars by placing a paver on each bar and running a mason's string between your reference strings on both sides of the driveway (Fig. 11). This string should just brush the top of the test pavers. Screed the sand by sliding a straightedged 2×4 or 2×6 down the length of the bars (Fig. 12).

Start laying the pavers by placing them squarely in the sand, one flush against the other. Don't slide them into position to avoid creating a ridge of sand against the paver. Start your pattern at one point—preferably a lower corner—and work outward from there. If you start your paving from different points, it's almost impossible to match up the areas where they meet. Select a starting point on the project that allows for continuous access, and set the pavers in the desired direction (Fig. 13).

In the project shown, a shoulder course of full straight pavers was used before starting the 45° herringbone pattern. A fixed edge reference was used on the left side of the drive—the retaining wall—but the right edge was let to float until the pattern covered the full drive area.

Fitting pavers around corners and other obstructions and against the shoulder course requires cuts. Several types of cutting devices are available, including masonry saws and mechanical and hydraulic guillotines. The saw is the most accurate tool and the best choice when you have many cuts to make.

Lay as many full pavers as possible in the pattern. To position the shoulder course on the right side of the drive, lay full pavers on top of the pattern and trace a line along the edge of the shoulder course to indicate the cuts needed in the pavers below. To set the left edge of the drive, run a string from the shoulder course at the retaining wall down to the sidewalk. Then scribe a line on the pavers for the required cuts (Fig. 14).

Remove the pavers to be cut. You can cut them one at a time, which can be time consuming, or use a numbering system to identify the position of each paver (Fig. 15) and cut them *en mass*. Mark the unit to be cut exactly at the edge line. Then cut 1/4 in. behind the line (Fig. 16). Never force a cut that doesn't fit. Fit the cut pieces back into the pattern (Fig. 17), and lay down the shoulder course—in this case, between the pattern and the retaining wall (Fig. 18).

Once all the pavers are laid into position, spread fine sand over the bricks and run a vibrator over the entire surface (Fig. 19). This further firms up the bedding sand and forces some sand into the joints between the blocks, which improves the interlock. Do not vibrate within 1 yard of an unrestrained edge of the paving. This will cause joints to open and force the surface to dip or bulge. Sweep loose sand into the joints to fill any voids completely, and continue sweeping to remove any surplus sand (Fig. 20). Finish the job by setting the right-side concrete edge restraint. Dig a trench 4 in. wide and 6 in. deep and trowel in some concrete (Fig. 21). Once the concrete has set (at least 24 hours), the drive is ready for service.

19 With all the pavers in place, spread a thin layer of sand over the surface and force it into the cracks with the vibrator.

20 Once all the cracks are filled with sand, sweep up any extra sand and rinse the entire surface with water.

21 Dig a 4-in.-wide x 6-in.-deep trench where the bricks meet the soil. Fill with concrete to keep the bricks from moving.

Introduction to siding

Siding is a big part of any house, usually occupying more square footage than anything else including roofing, windows and doors. In many ways, it's the face your house presents to your neighborhood and the community beyond. When the condition of your siding is combined with the appearance of your landscaping, you have a good visual definition of a great real-estate buzzword: curb appeal. The way your house looks from the street not only defines your pride in ownership but it also creates the first impression for potential buyers when it comes time to sell.

Cedar bevel siding *(left)* and shingles *(above)* are durable and attractive. Shingles are individually installed *(above)* or panelized *(left)*. Cedar siding is durable but requires paint, stain or sealer.

For most homeowners, good-looking siding is just a matter of periodic cleaning or painting. But for others, the chore of painting or the expense of having others do it makes them consider installing new siding, especially any of the maintenance-free versions. Some are just tired of their existing siding and want to change the whole appearance of their house. Still others are shopping for a new house and have the luxury of choosing any siding they want.

If you are in the market for new siding for any of these reasons, it's worth looking at this general introduction to siding. All the major material choices are covered and the quick-reference chart (page 147) will give you an idea of comparative installed costs. As always, make sure to check product warranties as well as up front costs. If you plan to hire contractors to install your siding, make sure to visit their projects where the siding has been in place for at least a year. A bad job doesn't show up immediately. It takes a little while.

EIFS Stucco

Once upon a time there was only portland cement stucco, but in the past 20 years, a synthetic stucco has come into wide use. Its formula replaces the portland cement with acrylic resins. It's known as Exterior Insulated Finish Systems (EIFS, pronounced eefs). The acrylic resins help to form a weatherproof surface. The material is troweled over insulated sheathing with mesh fastened to it.

EIFS combine durability with good thermal insulation. Their color is blended right into the finish coat, so you don't need to paint them.

Traditional Stucco

Traditional Stucco consists of three coats of a mix containing portland cement and sand (also called portland cement plaster). This is applied over wire mesh on sheathing, or the stucco is troweled over concrete block.

Properly installed stucco is incredibly durable, but details, such as coat thickness, have a major effect on its durability (the same is true of EIFS). While a small number of hairline cracks are considered inevitable, even on properly installed stucco, major cracking, flaking and delamination are not typical.

With either type of stucco, ask your contractor for references on jobs that were completed more than a year ago, to determine if the jobs have stood up well.

Redwood can be sealed, stained or painted. With maintenance, it is a durable and beautiful siding. The best type of redwood is clear all-heart grade. Less-expensive knotty grades are also available.

Vinyl siding is sold textured or smooth. The siding comes in 40-ft.-long pieces, eliminating lapping pieces. Window and corner trim can offset the main siding color or blend with it.

Brick

Brick is the most durable and the most expensive siding. It is considered to be maintenance-free, but sometimes it needs to have efflorescence (minerals that leach from the mortar and brick) cleaned from its surface.

Thin brick siding is made from full-width brick (not plastic or other materials) that is sliced into thin pieces. This system is useful for brick siding in remodeling jobs where installing regular brick presents structural problems. Thin brick is attached with adhesive and grout.

You have a right to demand good workmanship with any siding, but even more so with brick since it is unforgiving of sloppy installation. Ask your contractor for references where the brick was installed several years ago to determine how the installation has stood up.

Metal Siding

Metal siding is made from steel or aluminum sheet formed to look like wood siding. It receives a factory-applied coating, and the surface may be smooth or textured.

Aluminum siding is durable and if you don't like exterior painting, it will eliminate the need to paint for many years—20 years or longer depending on climate. Its color will fade as it ages, but modern siding has a more durable finish than that installed years ago.

It can be dented, however, by careless placement of ladders or bouncing hail stones. Aluminum siding also can buckle during heat waves if it's not properly installed.

Steel siding looks like aluminum siding, but it is more dent- and warp-resistant. It tends to be installed in the Midwest where violent hail-storms are common. A drawback is that it will rust if it is scratched to bare steel. These spots must be painted.

Plastic Siding

Plastic siding is molded with color throughout its thickness. This means that scratches are not obvious, and this siding is dent-resistant.

Plastic sidings come in two types: vinyl and polypropylene. Vinyl is the more widely used siding, and it can be smooth or textured to look like rough-sawn wood bevel siding. Polypropylene is only available molded to resemble cedar shingles, brick or stone.

Plastic siding has a reputation for good durability and color retention, and the modern versions of it have only improved characteristics. Any plastic siding, however, can buckle in hot weather if improperly installed.

If you like the way wood looks but don't want to paint, polypropylene plastic siding can be molded to look like cedar shingles. The molds for this siding were made from wood shingles. The siding is a panelized type with interlocking tabs.

SIDING CHOICES

The chart below represents premium grades in each category. Cost estimate includes building paper or similar covering below siding. Price does not include other building components, such as trim (prices as of March '94).

	COMMENTS	INSTALLED COST (per sq. ft.)
EIFS stucco:	Durable and more resistant to hairline cracking than traditional stucco. Has good insulating qualities and color retention.	**$4–5**
3-coat stucco:	A durable siding material, but may develop hairline cracks. Installation cost largely dependent on local labor market.	**$3–5**
Brick:	The most durable siding material. Sometimes develops efflorescence, which after several years needs to be cleaned.	**$5–8**
Thin brick:	Durable, but not widely used. Often employed in remodeling where full-width brick poses structural difficulties.	**$5–8**
Cedar shingles:	Durable, providing shingles are stained, sealed or painted at 3- to 7-year intervals.	**$2.50**
Panelized cedar shingles:	Same durability as cedar shingles, but more rapidly installed, making them a good choice for quick remodeling.	**$3**
6-in. cedar bevel siding:	Durable, providing that the siding is sealed, stained or painted at 3- to 7-year intervals.	**$2.50**
Redwood lap siding:	Equal durability to cedar, providing it is sealed, stained or painted at 3- to 7-year intervals.	**$2.50**
White pine siding:	Slightly less durable than cedar or redwood, but still provides good performance with paint or heavy-bodied stain applied at 3- to 7-year intervals.	**$1.90–2**
Southern yellow pine lap siding:	Good durability with paint or stain applied at 3- to 7-year intervals. Only rough-sawn variety holds paint well.	**$2.50**
Plywood panel:	Durability equal to pine siding when painted or stained at 3- to 7-year intervals. Easily and quickly installed.	**$2**
Hardboard:	To a greater extent than solid wood siding, durability is dependent on proper installation and control of moisture vapor inside the house. If it's not factory-coated, then it must be painted.	**$1.50–1.75**
Oriented strand board:	Same comments as hardboard siding, but it can be stained.	**$1.50–1.75**
Aluminum:	Durable, but can be dented. Requires no maintenance beyond cleaning once or twice a year.	**$3–4**
Steel:	Durable and more dent-resistant than aluminum. Scratches or dents that penetrate to bare steel should be painted. Needs periodic cleaning, like aluminum siding.	**$3–4**
Vinyl:	Durable and dent-resistant compared with aluminum. The most widely available siding. Should be cleaned once or twice a year.	**$3–4**
Polypropylene:	Durable and dent-resistant, like vinyl siding. Molded texture of cedar shingles or stone may require more careful cleaning than smooth-faced sidings.	**$3–4**

Hardboard siding comes in individual pieces or panels. It may be primed or have a factory-applied topcoat.

Modern acrylic stucco systems look like traditional portland cement versions, but better resist hairline cracking.

After 40 years, aluminum siding is still popular. Often it's installed with new aluminum gutters, soffits and trim.

This "masonry" siding is really polypropylene, molded to look like sandstone. It can also look like brick or limestome.

Plywood Siding

Plywood siding is the least complicated siding to install. It comes in 4×8-ft., 4×9-ft. and 4×10-ft. sheets and in several grades. The better grades have fewer patches, which replace knots, in the face veneer. The siding is grooved to look like vertically installed wood siding, and it is often used on houses with contemporary or modern architecture. Contractors often refer to all plywood siding as T-1-11 (a specific type of plywood siding by Georgia-Pacific Corp.) but there are several different models.

Plywood siding is applied vertically, and the horizontal seams where the panels meet are often covered with a piece of 1×4 wood trim. A piece of aluminum flashing is bent to step behind the upper piece and over the lower piece where the panels meet. The panels also can be installed so the top piece overlaps the piece below it, in which case the flashing is omitted.

Plywood siding, and its trim, is most durable if you protect it with a heavy-bodied stain or a paint.

To remain attractive, plywood siding needs to be fastened in an orderly way using corrosion-resistant nails.

Solid Wood

Wood siding is often the choice of traditionalists, and when properly cared for, it is extremely durable.

There are several types of wood used to make siding: redwood, cedar, southern yellow pine and white pine. While western timber harvests have been curtailed in recent years, driving up the cost of white pine and redwood, these sidings are still available, as is cedar, which mostly comes from Canada. Wood siding has rich colors, textures, and shadow lines. Cedar and redwood also have notable natural decay resistance.

These woods are available as horizontally applied bevel siding and in other patterns, such as with a cove-shaped edge. You also can apply square-edged lumber vertically with narrow wood battens to seal the joints between each piece. This is known as board-and-batten siding. Of all the wood sidings, only cedar is commonly sold as individual or panelized shingles.

Besides the style of siding, you also have several grades to choose from. The better grades have fewer knots and are more expensive. Also, the best grades of cedar and redwood can be ordered with edge or vertical grain. This orients the wood's growth rings perpendicularly to the siding face, improving paint-holding ability.

Maintenance intervals for wood siding may range from three years between touchup of stain or preservative to five to seven years between paint jobs or complete restaining.

Oriented Strand Board (OSB) and Hardboard

OSB siding is made from wood strands that are oriented in layers under heat and pressure. The top layer is resin impregnated or protected with a sheet of resin-impregnated paper. Also, some OSB sidings have factory-applied topcoat or primer.

Hardboard siding has wood fibers oriented at random. The wood fibers are molded with a resin under heat and pressure. The top of each piece is protected by resins and a factory-applied primer or topcoat.

Both OSB and hardboard sidings perform best when water vapor inside the house is controlled through venting and vapor barriers. They resist weather best when painted.

Like wood siding, these materials are unforgiving of sloppy installation. You should ask to see the manufacturer's installation requirements before your contractor applies the siding.

SOURCE LIST

Plywood and Hardboard:
- American Plywood Assn., P.O. Box 1170, Tacoma, WA 98411
- American Hardboard Assn., 1210 W. Northwest Hwy., Palatine, IL 60067

Aluminum Siding:
- American Architectural Manufacturers Assn., 1540 E. Dundee Rd., Suite 310, Palatine, IL 60067

Masonry:
- Portland Cement Assn., 5420 Old Orchard Rd., Skokie, IL 60077
- Brick Institute of America, 11490 Commerce Park Dr., Reston, VA 22091

Vinyl Siding:
- Vinyl Siding Institute, 355 Lexington Ave., New York, NY 10017

Wood Siding:
- California Redwood Assn., 405 Enfrente Dr., Suite 200, Novato, CA 94949
- Cedar Shake & Shingle Bureau, 515 116th Ave. N.E., Suite 275, Bellevue, WA 98004
- Southern Forest Products Assn., P.O. Box 641799, Kenner, LA 70064
- Western Wood Products Assn., Yeon Bldg., 522 S.W. Fifth Ave., Portland, OR 97204
- Western Red Cedar Lumber Assn., 1200-555 Burrard St., Vancouver, British Columbia V7X1S7

Introduction to Siding was written by Roy Berendsohn. Photos by Western Red Cedar Lumber Association, Cedar Shake & Shingle Bureau, California Redwood Association, Certainteed Corp., Wolverine Technologies, ABTCO, Inc., United States Gypsum Co., Nailite International and Alcoa Building Products.

Architectural asphalt shingles are thick and have shadow lines like red tile or slate (above). They come in a range of colors, including blue and green.

Cedar roofing is available as a rough, thick shake that gives a roof a rustic appearance, or as a shingle, a thinner and smoother product that appears more finished. Cedar roofing can be chemically treated to make it fire resistant.

Introduction to roofing

Most people give little thought to their roof until one of two events occurs: it starts to leak or it looks so shabby it needs to be replaced. There are more roofing materials than ever—you don't have to settle for simple black asphalt shingles. You have your choice of color, texture and, of course, price. Furthermore, there's no reason your roof can't be worry free. Today's roofing products combine durability with good looks.

Asphalt Roofing

Asphalt shingles are the most common roofing material, and they come in two broad categories—organic base and fiberglass. Organic base means that the shingles are made of a cellulose mat saturated with asphalt and covered with mineral granules. Fiberglass shingles have a mat of woven glass fiber saturated with asphalt and covered with mineral granules.

Organic-base shingles have a Class C (the lowest) fire rating, while fiberglass shingles have a Class A (the highest) rating.

Introduction to Roofing was written by Roy Berendoshn. Photographs by Certainteed Corp., Ludowici-Celadon, Inc., James Hardie Building Products, Vande Hey-Raleigh, Southern Forest Products Assn., Cedar Shake & Shingle Bureau, Alcoa Building Products, and Metal Building Components Inc. If you plan to have your roofing installed, contact National Roofing Contractors Association, 10255 W. Higgins Rd., Suite 600, Rosemont, IL 60018 for tips on choosing a good contractor.

An important difference between the two types of shingles is that organic types are more flexible in cold weather than fiberglass ones. A good deal of controversy surrounds the installation of fiberglass shingles in cold climates. Some roofers refuse to install them, while others just won't install them in cold weather. These roofers cite the shingles' premature failure caused by their stiffness. Manufacturers, however, say that a properly installed fiberglass shingle is as good as any.

The two most common types of asphalt shingles are 3-tab, also called a *strip shingle*, and architectural, also called a *laminate shingle*.

A 3-tab shingle is a rectangular mat with two slots cut in its front edge. An architectural shingle has a heavy base mat and another mat or sections of mat applied on top of it. Aside from making the shingle heavier and more durable, this construction gives the roof shadow lines and a character like a tile or wood roof.

A standard 3-tab shingle can be organic or fiberglass based. Most architectural shingles have a fiberglass mat, although some are organic.

Finally, there are regional and specialized forms of asphalt roofing, such as a highly wind-resistant shingle called a T-lock. This is slotted T-shaped shingle that locks to the shingle below and to the shingle above. Some manufacturers also offer asphalt shingles without any tab cutouts—appropriately called "no-cutout" types. Roofs with a shallow pitch are often covered with a continuous sheet of asphalt called *roll roofing*.

Cementitious Roofing

Cementitious roof tiles offer traditional looks combined with the benefit of modern materials. These products are made from steam-cured cellulose fiber-reinforced portland cement or concrete. They can be molded to look like wood shingles, barrel-shaped tiles or slate.

Barrel-top clay tile is among the oldest roofing products (*above*). These tiles are also available in blue and green. Lightweight flat clay tile achieves strength from molded ribs (*left*).

A relatively new product is southern yellow pine shakes (above and right). They are 3/4 in. thick and are chemically treated to make them decay and insect resistant.

The strong suit of cementitious roofing tiles is their durability. Because they are a masonry material, they resist weather, insects and fire. Their nearly impenetrable surface also resists the formation of fungus, and because they are heavy, they resist wind uplift.

Clay Roofing Tiles

Clay tile is among the oldest and most durable of roofing materials. It gains its weather-resistant, fireproof and insect proof qualities from being made out of kiln-fired clay. Most people think these tiles are limited to the barrel-shaped type common in the West, but clay tiles can be flat, and they may have a glossy surface. They are also available in blue and green, aside from reddish brown.

Your curiosity is justified if you're wondering how roofers attach what is essentially a ceramic product to the roof deck. Tiles are fastened with a variety of clips and fasteners, but among the most interesting methods is a tie-wire system in which the tiles literally hang from wires suspended from the ridge of the house.

Metal Roofing

Metal roofing is available in the widest range of materials, combination of materials and configurations. It is fastened in a variety of ways and it comes unpainted or factory finished with various coating systems.

The most common types of metal roofing are: steel panels with exposed fasteners, steel panels with hidden fasteners and rust-resistant aluminum panels that look like shakes, shingles or tiles. Less common types of metal roofing are copper and terne-coated stainless steel (terne is an alloy of lead and tin). There are also steel panels finished with stone granules that are resin-bonded to the panel surface.

Regarding rust, steel panels achieve corrosion resistance with a coating of zinc (galvanized) or a mixture of zinc and aluminum (known as *galvalume* or *galfan*). Top-quality steel panels have both zinc and a factory-applied coating.

Steel panels attached with exposed fasteners tend to be used on agricultural and utility buildings, but they

Fiber-cement tiles offer the look and color of slate while providing comparable durability and fire retardance.

Concrete roof tile looks like slate, and uses aggregate instead of fibers to add strength. It comes in a wide variety of patterns.

ROOFING CHOICES

The chart below represents premium grades in each category. Estimates include complete cost of installation per 100 sq. ft. (1 square). Wide price variations on some products indicate that labor costs mount drastically with complexity of installation.

	COMMENTS	INSTALLED COST (per 100 sq. ft.)
Asphalt 3-tab organic shingle:	Lifespan of 10 to 15 years depending on climate.	$50
Asphalt 3-tab fiberglass shingle:	Lifespan of 15 to 25 years. Shorter lifespan may occur in cold climates.	$50-85
Architectural asphalt shingle:	A heavy, laminated shingle with a 20- to 30-year lifespan.	$150-200
Aluminum shingle panels:	Lifespan of 30 to 40 years. Panels look like tile or wood shake.	$350-450
Galvanized, utility steel:	In relatively mild climates, roof has 20- to 25-year lifespan. Expect fewer years in coastal climates.	$200-250
Standing-seam steel, painted:	Factory-applied coatings extend lifespan to 30 to 50 years.	$600-700
Concrete tile:	Very long lasting, with lifespan expected to be 40 to 50 years.	$500-600
Fiber-cement tile:	Lifespan expected to be in the 30- to 50-year range. Some types cannot be used in cold climates.	$400-600
Slate:	Best grades of clear slate make a nearly permanent roof with a minimum expected lifespan of 50 years.	$600-1000
Cedar shake:	With maintenance, roof can last 30 years.	$215-255
Cedar shingle:	With maintenance, roof can last 30 years.	$225-265
Fire-retardant cedar shingle:	With maintenance, roof can last 30 years.	$335-375
Southern yellow pine shake:	Pressure treatment reduces maintenance. Its expected lifespan ranges from 20 to 30 years.	$330-350
Wood composite shingle:	A relatively new product that has been on the market for 15 years, so lifespan of product is not known.	$150-160
Glazed clay tile:	Very long-lasting roof with a vitreous surface. Its expected lifespan is at least 50 years.	$700-800

Standing-seam steel roofing is available in a range of colors, including gray, green, blue and red. It can be factory-coated so it won't need to be painted, or it can be unpainted.

Another option in metal roofing is aluminum shingle panels. These are formed to look like wood shakes.

are more widely used on houses. Panels with no exposed fasteners are known as *standing-seam* types. The panels are joined with crimped or snap-together seams that stand vertically from the roof.

Wood Roofing

In the old days, wood roofing came directly from the tree with no enhancements. Today's wood shingles and shakes are more sophisticated.

For example, cedar roofing can be factory treated with chemicals to boost its fire rating from unrated to Class A, B or C. Southern yellow pine shakes are pressure treated to help them resist rot and decay, and although these shakes have been on the market only five years, their manufacturers expect the product to have a 30-year lifespan. Likewise, a composite wood shingle has been on the market for 15 years, and its manufacturer says it has substantial weather resistance.

In case you are wondering about the difference between a shingle and a shake, shingles are smooth and uniformly shaped while most shakes have a rough, uneven texture. Shingles are ½ in. at the thick end, while shakes can be ½ in. to ¾ in. thick. To get maximum durability out of a cedar roof, roofing contractors recommend you clean it with a pressure washer once or twice a year to remove moisture-holding debris and apply preservatives to help it resist sun and weather.

Slate Roofing

Slate roofing comes in two types—premium clear pieces and ribbon slate. Ribbon slate is not as durable as the premium clear product. It is distinguished by the ribbons of light color that run across its surface. The ribbons are high-carbon-content areas. They are an impurity in the slate and are weaker than the dark areas.

Slate comes in gray, purple, green and red. Properly installed it has incredible durability. It doesn't require much maintenance, although an old slate roof might need a little tender loving care such as fixing the occasional cracked piece.

2 A Dremel tool can strip rust with a drum and an abrasive sleeve. Small parts can be held while the rust is removed.

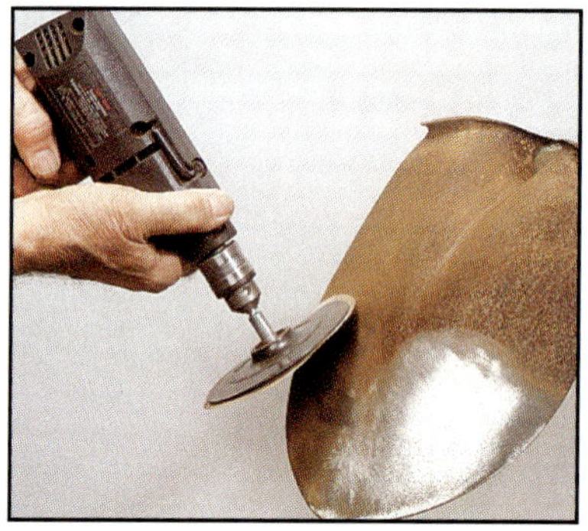

3 When using an electric drill, use the upper third of a disc sanding attachment to strip rust on curved surfaces.

1 A survey of rust-removal products (*clockwise from left*); abrasive stones in various shapes and abrasive sanding sleeves that chuck into a Dremel motor tool, sander belts, discs that chuck into a hand drill, abrasive strips and pads that you use by hand, wire brushes and chemical corrosion treatments. Don't forget to wear eye protection when using these tools.

Rust removal

Homeowners often deal with rust ineffectively. They often ignore it and paint over it, or they do a poor job of removing it. The result is a paint job that doesn't last. With a range of inexpensive tools and materials at their disposal, however, homeowners can fight rust and, in the bargain, produce well-protected metal that gives many years of service, even outdoors.

Text and photos for *Rust Removal* by Rosario Capotosto.

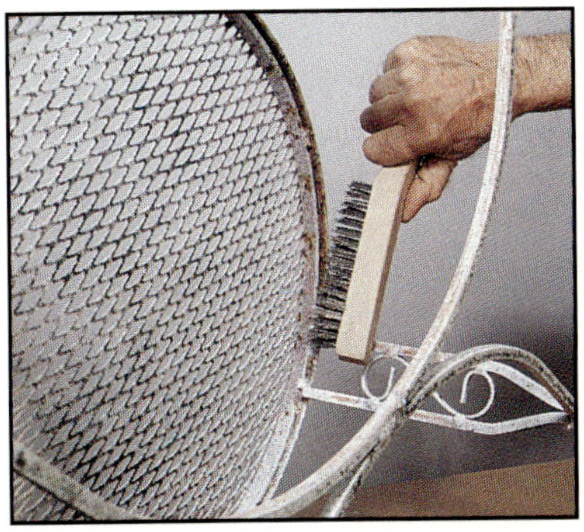

4 Use a hand wire brush to remove light rust from confined areas, such as the inside rim of a metal chair.

5 A belt sander is an effective rust stripping tool, especially on large flat workpieces clamped to a bench.

6 To stop saponification, use a specialty coating, like Gutter Shield, between the zinc primer and the topcoat.

7 Remove large pieces of loosened paint and loose rust using a wire wheel chucked into an electric drill.

8 Clean off remaining rust with an abrasive wheel. The 3M Paint and Rust Stripper was used with good results.

9 Seal a handrailing's post with a flexible exterior-grade caulk, such as silicone or acrylic latex.

10 Naval Jelly dissolves rust so it can be stripped *(left)*, while rust converters change it into a paintable oxide.

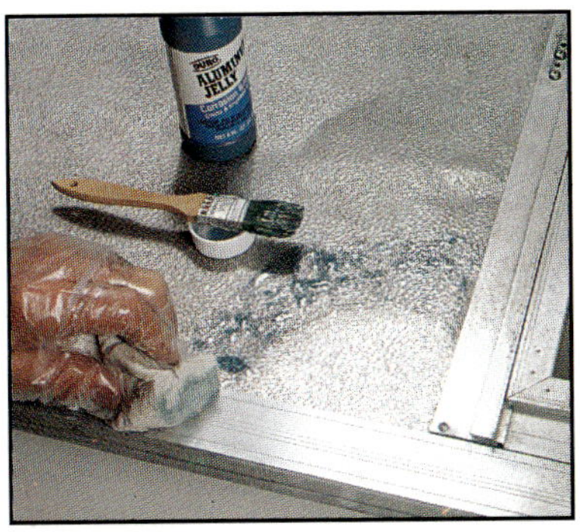

11 Remove corrosion on aluminum using Aluminum Jelly and a rag or plastic pad. Don't use steel wool on aluminum.

Rust Removal Basics

The rust-removal basics are simple. Paint manufacturers recommend that you first clean the surface thoroughly using detergent and water. Let it dry, then remove the rust and deteriorated paint. Finally, wipe off remaining dust with a clean dry rag and paint the metal. Some manufacturers recommend that you use a solvent to clean to bare metal. Check the directions on the can of paint you plan to use. The idea is to start with a clean surface so dirt and oil are not driven into the steel while removing the rust and paint. You should be left with a clean, well-abraded surface that forms a good foundation for the paint.

The most radical rust-removing tool, short of a sandblaster, is a small disc grinder. On the other end of the spectrum is the hand wire brush and attachments that chuck into an electric drill (Fig. 1). The abrasive wheels and cones produced by Dremel also work well. For example, you can hold a small workpiece in one hand and grind off the rust with a Dremel tool (Fig. 2) held in the other hand. If the rust is severe, clamp the workpiece in a vise.

The most versatile rust-fighting tool is an electric drill with a coarse abrasive disc. This is very handy for work on curved surfaces (Fig. 3). Often hand tools, such as a wire brush, are teamed with power tools to reach places an abrasive disc can't (Fig. 4).

Although not normally thought of as a rust fighter, the belt sander is effective on flat surfaces, especially if the workpiece can be secured to a workbench (Fig. 5).

Painting

The best foundation for a rust-resisting paint job is a primer that contains at least 84% zinc by weight.

There are two important things you should know about zinc-rich primers. First, they work best when the surface is well prepared. The zinc must make a good metal-to-metal (electrical) connection with the steel. The other point is that zinc reacts with paint resins, especially alkyds, and forms a crude soap. The process, called *saponification*, can cause the topcoat to peel away from the primer.

To prevent this, isolate the primer from the topcoat with an intermediate coat. Here, Rust-Oleum's Zinc-Sele Primer was used, followed by Gutter Shield as the intermediate coat and a gloss black alkyd topcoat (Fig. 6).

Rusty Handrails

Remove the loosest layer of rust and deteriorated paint from a handrail using a wire wheel chucked into a drill (Fig. 7). Next, use a stripper to remove as much of the remaining rust and paint as you can (Fig. 8). Work into tight areas with abrasive strips and pads.

After the railing is painted, caulk where the handrail is let into the masonry stoop (Fig. 9). This joint is vulnerable to corrosion. De-icing salts attack the base of the post, especially where the paint has been nicked by snow shovels.

Chemical Treatments

Rust-treating chemicals don't work well for large and heavy rust-removal jobs, but they're fine on small jobs.

The most common rust-fighting chemical is phosphoric acid Naval Jelly. It is shown here on a sample steel bar that was stripped using the jelly and an abrasive pad (Fig. 10). The bar next to it was treated with rust converter. To use this, you scrub off loose rust and apply the converter. It turns the rust into a paint-ready zinc-oxide film.

To clean corrosion off old-fashioned bushed-aluminum doors and windows, use Aluminum Jelly. Whatever you do, however, don't use a steel-wool pad in this process. Steel-wool particles will embed themselves in the aluminum and form corrosion in their own right. Instead, use a cloth or plastic scrubbing pad (Fig. 11).

Rust prevention

Rust Prevention was written by Roy Berendsohn. Photo by Rosario Capotosto, illustrations by George Retseck. For more information on corrosion, write to: NACE International, Technical Activities Group, P.O. Box 218340, Houston, TX 77218-8340; American Galvanizers Association, 12200 E. Iliff Ave., Suite 204, Aurora, CO 80014.

Steel rusts. Even if it's painted, it can still rust and look lousy. Aluminum rusts, too. But just because these metals rust, doesn't mean you have to accept it. Fortunately, you can fight back and win the battle against corrosion.

To win, you need to be well prepared with the right tools, materials and information. As far as tools and materials are concerned, everything you need is at your local hardware store, paint store or home center. Just remember to bypass those products that promise a quick and permanent end to rust and to stick with the basics. The process is straightforward and, in some respects, remains the same as in the past. Remove as much of the rust as you can, then paint. Fortunately, today's corrosion-fighting products make this job easier than before.

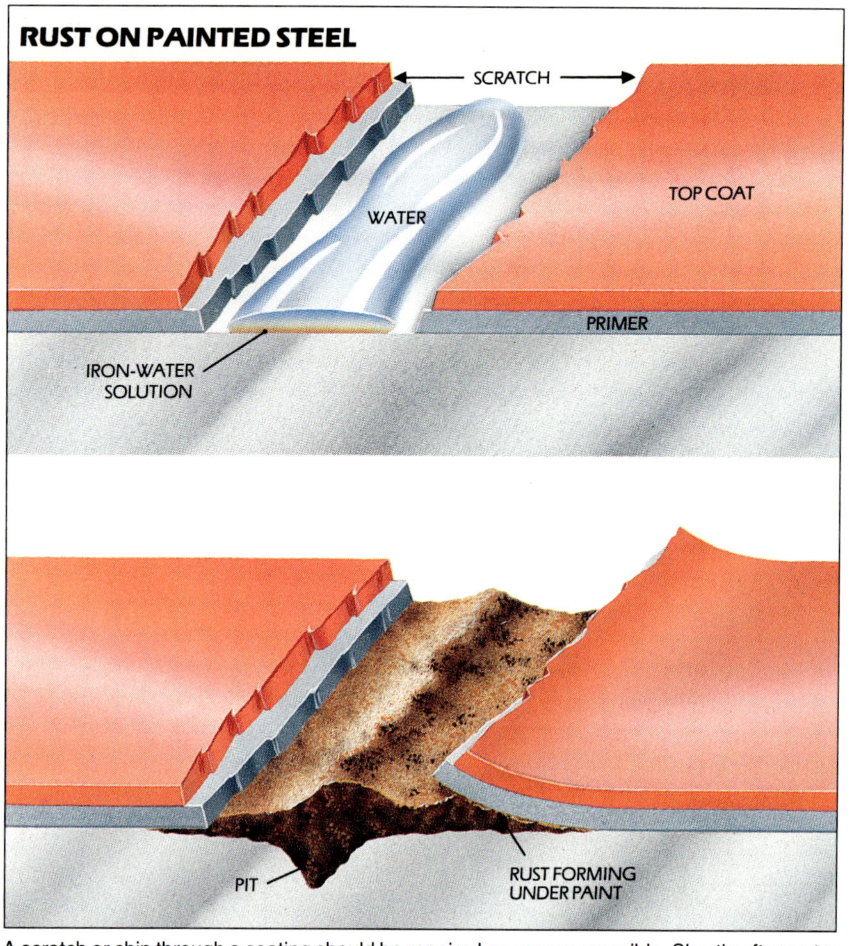

A scratch or chip through a coating should be repaired as soon as possible. Shortly after water collects on bare steel, the oxygen in the water combines with the iron in the steel and a small amount of iron is dissolved. An electrical imbalance between the solution and the surrounding steel causes a minute current flow. This results in rust and pitting. Rust has greater volume than steel, and this lifts the paint off the surface, which leads to more exposed steel and more rust. Moisture can also penetrate to the steel through pores in the paint film. Multiple coats of paint, with pores misaligned, prevent this.

Know the Enemy

Corrosion is not necessarily synonymous with rust. Rust is just one form of corrosion, namely the brown stuff that forms because of corrosion on steel. This article will deal with all the simple forms of corrosion found around the house: rusting steel, galvanic corrosion and corrosion on uncoated aluminum.

Here's a simplified version of the complex electrochemical process that causes rust to form on painted steel: First, moisture penetrates through pores in the paint film or through a scratch (see illustration). Then the oxygen in the water combines with the iron in the steel, and a minute amount of iron is dissolved, forming a solution. Because there is an imbalance of electrons between the solution and the surrounding steel, a flow of electrons, or current, begins. As long as the current flows, the steel will deteriorate (corrode) and rust will form.

Because the rust has more volume than the steel, it expands and helps form a blister under the paint. The blister will cause the paint to fail, exposing the steel to more moisture and accelerating the corrosion process.

The same situation can occur in reverse. If you paint over damp steel, you've trapped the moisture against the metal. Sun beating down on the metal will convert the moisture to vapor. The vapor will expand upward, lifting the paint in the process and forming a blister. Steel, like wood, should be dry when you paint it.

Four Rules of Success

Like everything else around us, steel obeys the laws of thermodynamics and always will return to a state of low energy. In other words, corrosion is the inevitable means by which steel returns to iron oxide, its most relaxed, low-energy form.

By expending a little energy of your own, you can greatly slow the decay of steel.

Here are four easy corrosion-fighting steps. Note that the steps are interrelated and that paint can play a role in each step.

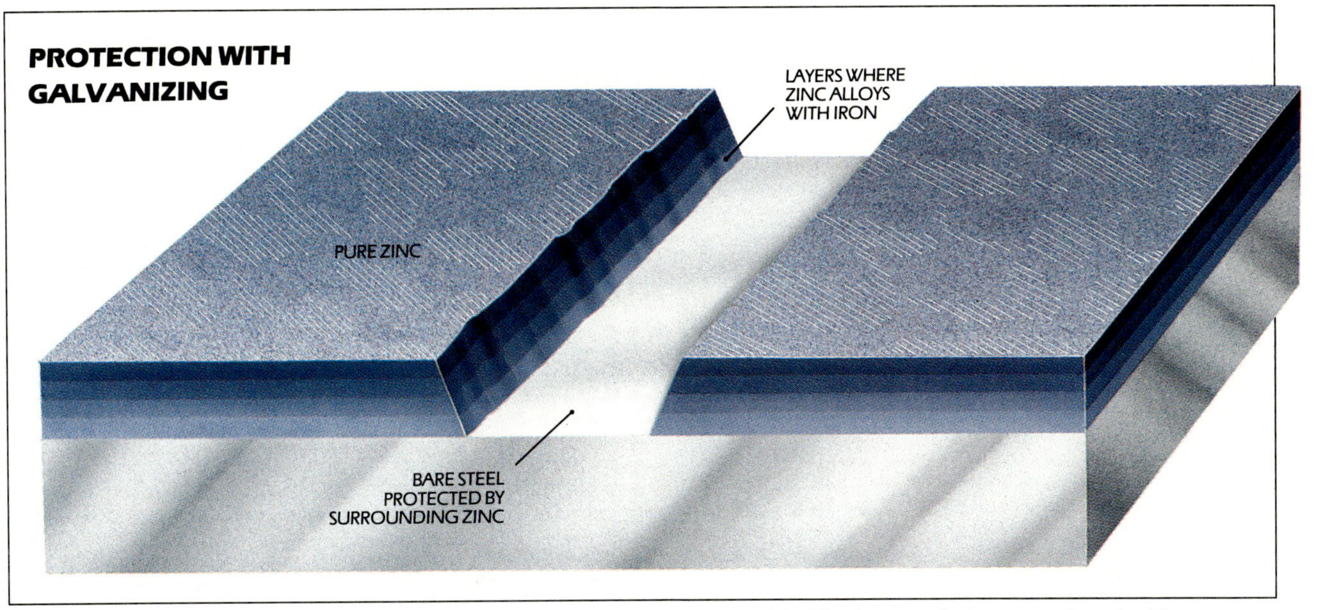

Zinc galvanizing has unique properties that make it valuable as a corrosion-fighting tool. The zinc will corrode before the steel does, sacrificing itself but saving the steel in the process. Even if scratched away, the zinc will protect nearby steel. Also, galvanizing bonds tenaciously to the steel because a metallurgical bond is formed between the two materials. The layers of zinc near the steel form an iron-rich alloy. The alloy layers have progressively less iron as you near the surface of the zinc. The top layer is pure zinc. Although painting will protect a galvanized surface, galvanized steel can be left unpainted. The weathered zinc on the surface forms a protective coating in its own right.

Step 1—Keep it clean. Dirt holds moisture, and we've seen the effect of moisture on steel.

Step 2—Keep it dry. No moisture, no rust. This puts a premium on repairing blistered paint and using the right paint for the job.

Step 3—Insulate it. Not only does paint keep the metal dry, almost all paints act as insulators. By stopping current flow, paint prevents corrosion. Also, a variety of substances—from salts to alkaline materials—accelerate the corrosion process. Paint protects the metal against these damaging substances.

Step 4—Galvanize it. Galvanized steel is coated with zinc. The steel is dipped in molten zinc (known as hot dipped), or it is plated by being immersed in an electrochemical bath (see illustration above). Homeowners can't be galvanizers, of course, but they can use galvanized hardware. They also can use a high zinc content primer.

Zinc is a special material, as far as steel is concerned. In corrosive conditions, it loses electrons at a faster rate than steel does. If you cover the steel with zinc, the zinc will corrode away, but the steel remains unscathed until the zinc is gone.

A related means of protection is to position a zinc bar—called an *anode*—near the steel. This is the method used to protect steel swimming pools. Likewise, magnesium anodes are used to protect hot-water tanks.

You might wonder why hot-water tanks don't use zinc anodes. The answer: At 120° F and above, zinc loses its effectiveness as an anode. In fact, it completely reverses its effectiveness, causing the steel to become the anode. Early galvanized hot-water tanks, for instance, rotted away quickly. Once manufacturers discovered the problem, they switched to magnesium anodes.

Look at the chart on page 159. This is known as the *Galvanic Series*. The farther apart metals are on the chart, the greater the corrosion when they come in contact. The separation between zinc and steel indicates how effective zinc is as a protectant when joined with steel.

Flashing

Suppose a piece of flashing works its way loose from your chimney (see illustration on page 158). Ignoring the fact that the flashing was improperly installed, your first idea is to refasten the loose flashing quickly by driving a couple of steel masonry nails into the mortar joints, and then caulking over the nailheads.

Don't do it. Looking at the Galvanic Series, you see that steel and stainless steel are far apart. Galvanic corrosion will result, especially when the caulk breaks down. The steel nailheads that are in contact with the stainless steel will corrode quickly, and the flashing will become loose and fall off. The nails will rust, expand and break apart more mortar, damaging the chimney. Instead, tuck point the joints with mortar where the flashing is loose.

Household galvanic corrosion occurs most frequently from quick and dirty repairs, such as when steel and copper pipe are connected. But the problem can be more subtle than that, and can occur even where steel meets stainless steel—where loose stainless-steel flashing has been tacked down with a steel nail, for instance. The steel nail will corrode badly. To determine which metal will corrode in a galvanic coupling, see the chart on page 159.

Gutters

If you have steel gutters on your house, clean them well. Tanic acid leaches out of leaves as they lay in your gutters. This acid is corrosive to steel gutters and stains aluminum, so keep the gutters clean.

Don't hold up sagging aluminum gutters with steel nails. Caulking over the nailheads only buys you a little time. Instead, use aluminum gutter spikes.

Railings

The posts that hold up the handrail will rust from exposure to rock salt, especially where the paint gets chipped by snow shovels. Build up a small mound of mortar or anchoring cement at the base of the posts to ensure that water runs away from the post.

Remember to seal at the base of the post with a good grade of exterior caulk. In case a gap opens up between the masonry and the post, you will need a flexible material to bridge the gap. Silicone and other exterior caulks fill the bill nicely here.

Outdoor Woodwork

Galvanized nails are better than noncoated nails, known as bright finish. Countersink nail holes where possible and putty the holes. Screws are also available with weatherproof coatings. If you live in a humid area, or near saltwater, a marine supply store may be able to furnish stainless-steel fasteners. Galvanized hinges, hasps and bolts are likewise preferable to nongalvanized ones.

Plumbing

Avoid connecting copper to steel pipe. Galvanic corrosion of the steel threads will cause plumbing leaks. If you must join the two materials, separate the metals with a nylon insulation union available at plumbing supply stores. Remember, Teflon tape is not enough to isolate the two metals. Threaded connectors will often pierce the Teflon. Use plastic pipe when you have a choice, especially with in-ground plumbing, such as sprinkler systems.

Hard water conducts electricity better than soft water. Both copper and steel plumbing will last longer if you install a water softener to deal with hard water. The steel-copper plumbing connections mentioned above corrode more quickly in hard water than in soft water.

Electrical Service

Between 1965 and 1973, about 1.5 million homes had aluminum wiring installed. In some early installations, galvanic corrosion occurred at electrical connections where copper met aluminum and moisture was present. This increased electrical resistance and caused arcing. In some cases, it caused electrical fires. Inspecting or repairing aluminum wiring is not a do-it-yourself job. Contact a licensed electrician.

Fuel Oil Storage Tanks

Most homeowners are reluctant to fill the oil tank at the end of the season. But condensation forms in an empty tank—even one that stores fuel oil. Condensation collects on the tank bottom under the oil and attacks the tank from the inside.

In-ground oil tanks are notorious for leaks. If the tank is more than 15 years old, you might start budgeting to replace it. Or at least contact your oil dealer and have a zinc or magnesium anode installed next to the tank to extend its life.

Storm Doors and Windows

Aluminum is not corrosion proof. Brushed-aluminum storm windows and storm doors form "white rust" or oxidation, especially in areas near saltwater. In case you're wondering why the storm windows look better on one side of the house than on the other, oxidation is worse on the side facing the prevailing wind.

There isn't too much you can do here, since it's difficult to paint aluminum. Hardware stores carry an aluminum cleaner that is quite effective at removing the oxidation, though it involves a lot of work. You also can wax and even apply varnish to brushed aluminum to forestall corrosion. If, however you're considering replacing storm doors or windows, choose those that are anodized aluminum or factory coated (typically white) because they hold up much better than the older brushed-aluminum models.

Paint: A Corrosion Tool

It's hard to say too much about paint when discussing corrosion prevention. When painting steel, use a primer and topcoat from one manufacturer. Don't mix brands on a painting project. To be effective, zinc primers must have at least 84% zinc by weight. Look at the label to determine this or call the paint company's technical service department.

Next, stick with major manufacturers. If you have questions, talk to the store's service people. Remember, most major paint stores have a commercial sales department that can be very informative.

Homeowners can't be paint chemists, but they can rely on trade organizations for good information. For instance, it may be listed on the container if the paint meets Steel Structures Painting Council (SSPC) specifications. You can always call the manufacturer and ask if the paint meets SSPC specs.

Military specifications are not easy to meet. The paint container may note that the product within meets certain military specifications. This, too, indicates a high-quality product.

Of course, no matter how good the paint, its success or failure is directly dependent on surface preparation.

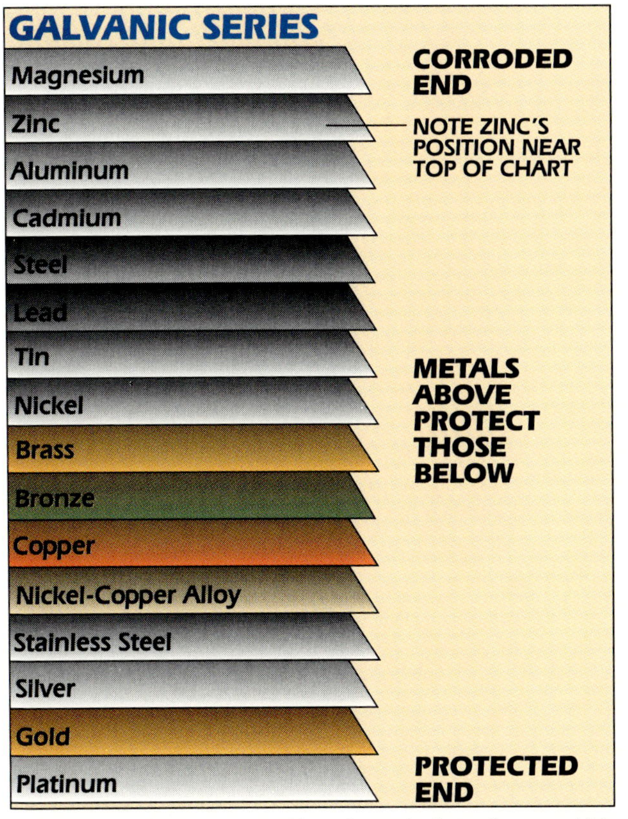

The Galvanic Series is a ranking of metals that tells you which corrode more readily than others. The metals at the top of the chart corrode before those below. That is, the metals above act as sacrificial anodes to the metals below. The farther apart metals are on the chart, the more drastic the corrosion between them when they come into contact. Notice the large distance between steel and copper or steel and stainless steel.

Index

METRIC CONVERSION

Conversion factors can be carried so far they become impractical. In cases below where an entry is exact it is followed by an asterisk (*). Where considerable rounding off has taken place, the entry is followed by a + or a - sign.

CUSTOMARY TO METRIC

Linear Measure

inches	millimeters
1/16	1.5875*
1/8	3.2
3/16	4.8
1/4	6.35*
5/16	7.9
3/8	9.5
7/16	11.1
1/2	12.7*
9/16	14.3
5/8	15.9
11/16	17.5
3/4	19.05*
13/16	20.6
7/8	22.2
15/16	23.8
1	25.4*

inches	centimeters
1	2.54*
2	5.1
3	7.6
4	10.2
5	12.7*
6	15.2
7	17.8
8	20.3
9	22.9
10	25.4*
11	27.9
12	30.5

feet	centimeters	meters
1	30.48*	.3048*
2	61	.61
3	91	.91
4	122	1.22
5	152	1.52
6	183	1.83
7	213	2.13
8	244	2.44
9	274	2.74
10	305	3.05
50	1524*	15.24*
100	3048*	30.48*

1 yard = .9144* meters

1 rod = 5.0292* meters

1 mile = 1.6 kilometers

1 nautical mile = 1.852* kilometers

Fluid Measure

(Milliliters [ml] and cubic centimeters [cc or cu cm] are equivalent, but it is customary to use milliliters for liquids.)

1 cu in = 16.39 ml
1 fl oz = 29.6 ml
1 cup = 237 ml
1 pint = 473 ml
1 quart = 946 ml
= .946 liters
1 gallon = 3785 ml
= 3.785 liters

Formula (exact):
fluid ounces × 29.573 529 562 5* = milliliters

Weights

ounces	grams
1	28.3
2	56.7
3	85
4	113
5	142
6	170
7	198
8	227
9	255
10	283
11	312
12	340
13	369
14	397
15	425
16	454

Formula (exact):
ounces × 28.349 523 125* = grams

pounds	kilograms
1	.45
2	.9
3	1.4
4	1.8
5	2.3
6	2.7
7	3.2
8	3.6
9	4.1
10	4.5

1 short ton (2000 lbs) = 907 kilograms (kg)

Formula (exact):
pounds × .453 592 37* = kilograms

Volume

1 cu in = 16.39 cubic centimeters (cc)
1 cu ft = 28 316.7 cc
1 bushel = 35 239.1 cc
1 peck = 8 809.8 cc

Area

1 sq in = 6.45 sq cm
1 sq ft = 929 sq cm
= .093 sq meters
1 sq yd = .84 sq meters
1 acre = 4 046.9 sq meters
= .404 7 hectares
1 sq mile = 2 589 988 sq meters
= 259 hectares
= 2.589 9 sq kilometers

Kitchen Measure

1 teaspoon = 4.93 milliliters (ml)
1 Tablespoon = 14.79 milliliters (ml)

Miscellaneous

1 British thermal unit (Btu) (mean) = 1 055.9 joules
1 calorie (mean) = 4.19 joules
1 horsepower = 745.7 watts
= .75 kilowatts
caliber (diameter of a firearm's bore in hundredths of an inch) = .254 millimeters (mm)
1 atmosphere pressure = 101 325* pascals (newtons per sq meter)
1 pound per square inch (psi) = 6 895 pascals
1 pound per square foot = 47.9 pascals
1 knot = 1.85 kilometers per hour
25 miles per hour = 40.2 kilometers per hour
50 miles per hour = 80.5 kilometers per hour
75 miles per hour = 120.7 kilometers per hour